# Music and Probability

# Music and Probability

David Temperley

The MIT Press
Cambridge, Massachusetts
London, England

MIT Press books may be purchased at special quantity discounts for business or sales promotional use. For information, please email special_sales@mitpress.mit .edu or write to Special Sales Department, The MIT Press, 55 Hayward Street, Cambridge, MA 02142.

This book was set in Sabon on 3B2 by Asco Typesetters, Hong Kong, and was printed and bound in the United States of America.

Library of Congress Cataloging-in-Publication Data

Temperley, David.
Music and probability / David Temperley.
    p.   cm.
Includes bibliographical references and index.
Contents: Probabilistic foundations and background—Melody I : the rhythm model—Melody II : the pitch model—Key-finding in polyphonic music— Applications of the polyphonic key-finding model—Bayesian models of other aspects of music—Style and composition—Communicative pressure.
ISBN-13: 978-0-262-20166-7 (hc : alk. paper)
ISBN-10: 0-262-20166-6 (hc : alk. paper)
1. Musical perception—Mathematical models. 2. Music and probability.
I. Title.

ML3838.T46   2007
781.2—dc22                                              2006046159

10   9   8   7   6   5   4   3   2   1

For my parents

# Contents

# Preface

The story of this book really begins in early 2001, when I was finishing up my first book, *The Cognition of Basic Musical Structures* (CBMS), and looking around for something new to work on. While satisfied with CBMS in many ways, I had certain nagging doubts about the project. CBMS a computational study of basic aspects of music perception— employed the approach of *preference rules*, in which many possible analyses are considered and evaluated using a set of criteria. Although it has many virtues, the preference rule approach seemed to have few adherents beyond myself and a few others in music theory and linguistics. This troubled me; if so many aspects of music cognition (meter, harmony, and the like) reflected "preference-rule-like" mechanisms, why were such mechanisms not widely found in other domains of cognition, such as language and vision? I was also troubled by the seemingly ad hoc and arbitrary nature of the preference-rule approach. One could develop a model by adding rules and tweaking their parameters in a trial-and-error fashion, but there didn't seem to be any principled basis for making these decisions.

At the same time—2001 or so—I was becoming increasingly interested in work in computational linguistics. In particular, I was intrigued by the progress that had been made on the basic linguistic problem of syntactic parsing. Computational models were now being developed that could take real-world text and derive syntactic structure from it with high rates of accuracy—an achievement that had hitherto been completely out of reach. These new computational models all involved probabilistic, and in particular Bayesian, methods. Having worked on the syntactic parsing problem from a *non*probabilistic perspective, I was aware of its formidable complexities and deeply impressed by the power of probabilistic models to overcome them.

At some point in 2001 (it was, I think, not an instantaneous "eureka" but a gradual realization over several months), everything came together: I realized that Bayesian models provided the answer to my problems with preference rule models. In fact, preference rule models were very similar to Bayesian models: I realized that many aspects of the *CBMS* models were already interpretable in Bayesian terms. (I would, incidentally, give great credit to Fred Lerdahl and Ray Jackendoff—the inventors of the preference rule approach—for anticipating probabilistic modeling in many ways, even though they did not frame their ideas in probabilistic terms.) But moving to a Bayesian framework was not merely putting "old wine in new bottles": it accomplished two crucial things. It connected musical preference rule models with a well-established field of research in cognitive science, encompassing not only work in computational linguistics but also in vision, knowledge representation, and other areas. And it also provided a rational foundation: It showed how, under certain assumptions about how musical surfaces are generated from structures, one can make logical inferences about structures given surfaces. The Bayesian approach also offered a way of thinking systematically and logically about musical information-processing models—which rules made sense, which ones didn't, what other rules might be included—and suggested a principled basis for setting their parameters.

I soon realized that I was not the first to have the idea of applying Bayesian methods to musical modeling. Several other researchers had also been working in this direction, both in Europe and in the United States. As my work proceeded, I decided that what was needed was a general study of probabilistic modeling of music, which would present my own ideas in this area and also survey work by others. The result is *Music and Probability*.

The book is intended to be accessible to a broad audience in music and cognitive science. I assume only a basic level of mathematical background; no prior knowledge of probability is required. With regard to music, also, only a basic knowledge of music fundamentals is needed—though an ability to sing, play, or imagine the musical examples will be helpful.

This project could not have been completed without a great deal of help, advice, and support from others. At the Eastman/University of

Rochester/Cornell music cognition symposium, where I presented research from the book on several occasions, a number of people—Betsy Marvin, Carol Krumhansl, Elissa Newport, Dick Aslin, and Panos Mavromatis, among others—provided valuable feedback. Collaborative work with Dave Headlam and Mark Bocko got me thinking about probabilistic approaches to the transcription problem. Paul von Hippel, Dirk-Jan Povel, Eric Loeb, Fred Lerdahl, and Nicholas Temperley read portions of the book (in earlier incarnations) and offered thoughtful and helpful comments. Craig Sapp assisted me in accessing and using the Essen folksong database. Several editors at journals (and anonymous reviewers at those journals) helped me to refine and shape material from the book that appeared earlier in articles: Irene Deliege at *Musicae Scientiae*, Diana Deutsch at *Music Perception*, and Doug Keislar at *Computer Music Journal*. In the later stages of the project, both Ian Quinn and Taylan Cemgil read an entire draft of the book; their feedback helped to sharpen my treatment and presentation of a number of issues.

Two people deserve special mention. The first is Daniel Sleator. Danny was not directly involved in this project; however, it was from him that I learned, not only how to program, but also how to think about computational problems. Many of the ideas in the book have their origins in my collaborative work with Danny in the 1990s, and some of the most important ideas—such as the use of dynamic programming—are due to him. Directly or indirectly, Danny's influence is present throughout the book.

To my wife, Maya, I am grateful for many things: for helping with the reference list, reading and critiquing parts of the book, and being the audience for practice run-throughs of numerous talks; for giving me the space and the time to write the book; and for providing unwavering support and encouragement throughout.

The website www.theory.esm.rochester.edu/temperley/music-prob contains a variety of materials related to the book: source code for the programs, testing materials, and MIDI files of the musical examples.

# 1
# Introduction

Almost fifty years ago, Leonard B. Meyer remarked on the fundamental link between musical style, perception, and probability:

Once a musical style has become part of the habit responses of composers, performers, and practiced listeners it may be regarded as a complex system of probabilities.... Out of such internalized probability systems arise the expectations—the tendencies—upon which musical meaning is built.... [T]he probability relationships embodied in a particular musical style together with the various modes of mental behavior involved in the perception and understanding of the materials of the style constitute the *norms* of the style. (1957/1967: 8–9)

To me (and I believe to many others who have read them), these words ring profoundly true; they seem to capture something essential about the nature of musical communication. The pursuit of Meyer's vision—toward an understanding of how probabilities shape music perception, and indeed music itself—is the underlying mission of this book.

In the four decades after Meyer's essay, the application of probabilistic ideas to music was pursued only sporadically, and without much success. In recent years, however, the conditions for this undertaking have become much more felicitous. Great progress has been made in the application of probability theory to other domains of cognitive modeling, introducing new techniques and demonstrating the enormous power of this approach. The last thirty years have also seen tremendous activity in the field of music perception and cognition, yielding much new evidence and theoretical insight about the workings of the musical mind. The time is ripe, then, for a reconsideration of music and probability.

If music perception is largely probabilistic in nature (and I will argue that it is), this should not surprise us. Probability pervades almost every aspect of mental life—the environment that surrounds us, and the way we perceive, analyze, and manipulate that environment. Sitting in my living room, I hear my wife call "mail's here!" from the next room, and within a few seconds I am heading toward the front door to retrieve the day's offerings from the mailbox. But what just happened? A pattern of sound energy impacted my ears, which I decoded as the words "mail's here" spoken by my wife. I infer that there is mail waiting for me, that I am being given an oblique instruction to pick it up, and that there is indeed something worth picking up. But none of these inferential leaps are infallible. It is possible that the words spoken were not "mail's here," but "Mel's here"—an unexpected visit from our neighbor Mel. It is possible also that, although something did indeed come through our mail slot, it was not the U.S. mail but a flyer from a local restaurant; or that the mail has been delivered, but is nothing but junk (the most likely possibility); or that my wife simply said "mail's here" as an informational update, and has already gone to pick up the mail herself. My pondering of the situation reflects all of these uncertainties, and the complex interactions between them. (If I don't actually have a neighbor named Mel, for example, then the probability that my wife said "Mel's here" is decreased.) But a moment later, these dilemmas are largely resolved. I hear a louder, clearer, more insistent *The mail is here!* from my wife, which clarifies both the words that were spoken and the intent behind them—she *does* expect me to get the mail. (Whether the mail contains anything worth getting remains to be discovered.)

This everyday situation captures several important things about the probabilistic nature of thought and perception. First, perception is a multi-leveled inferential process: I hear sounds, infer words from them, infer my wife's intended message from the words (and from the way she said them), and make further inferences about the state of the world. Each of these levels of knowledge contains some uncertainty, which may endure in my mind: even heading for the door, I may be uncertain as to what my wife said. As such, they lend themselves very naturally to a probabilistic treatment, where propositions are represented not in true-or-false terms but in levels of probability. Secondly, these probabilistic judgments are shaped by our past experience—by our observation of events in the world. In judging the likelihood that my wife wants me to get the mail, or that the mail (not Mel) is at the door, or that it contains something besides junk, I am influenced by the frequency of these various events happening in the past. Thirdly, producers of communication are sensitive to its probabilistic and fallible nature, and may adjust their behavior accordingly. My wife knew that I had not fully gotten her message the first time, and thus re-conveyed both the words and the intention in an amplified form.

Each of these three principles, I will argue, applies in profound and illuminating ways to music and music perception. Let us reconsider them, focusing on their musical implications:

1. *Perception is an inferential, multileveled, uncertain process.* In listening to a piece of music, we hear a pattern of notes and we draw conclusions about the underlying structures that gave rise to those notes: structures of tonality, meter, and other things. These judgments are often somewhat uncertain; and this uncertainty applies not just at the moment that the judgment is made, but to the way it is represented in memory. In the development section of a sonata movement, for example, we may be uncertain as to what key we are really in—and this ambiguity is an important part of musical experience. The probabilistic nature of music perception applies not only to these underlying structures, but to the note pattern itself. Certain note patterns are probable, others are not; and our mental representation of these probabilities accounts for important musical phenomena such as surprise, tension, expectation, error detection, and pitch identification.

2. *Our knowledge of probabilities comes, in large part, from regularities in the environment.* In listening to music, the probabilities we assign to note patterns and to the structures underlying them (key, meter, and the like) are shaped by our musical experience. Proof of this is seen in the fact that people with different musical backgrounds have different musical expectations, perceptions, and modes of processing and understanding music. This is not to say that our musical knowledge is *entirely* the result of environmental influence, or that it can be shaped without limit by that environment. But I think everyone would agree that that our experience plays a significant role in shaping our perceptions.

3. *Producers of communication are sensitive to, and affected by, its probabilistic nature.* In many cases, music production (in all its forms —composition, improvisation, and performance) is affected by perception, adjusting and evolving to facilitate the perceptual process. This is reflected in spontaneous individual choices—for example, with regard to performance expression; it is reflected, also, in the long-term evolution of musical styles and conventions.

These three principles are the underlying themes of the current study, and we will return to them many times throughout the book.

In the chapters that follow, I invoke a number of concepts from probability theory and probabilistic modeling. I rely most heavily on an axiom of probability known as *Bayes' rule*. In music perception, we are often confronted with some kind of surface pattern (such as a pattern of notes) and we wish to know the underlying structure that gave rise to it (for example, a key or a metrical structure). Bayes' rule allows us to identify that underlying structure, from knowledge of the probabilities of possible structures, and knowledge of the probability of the surface given those structures. We will also make use of concepts from information theory—in particular, the idea of *cross-entropy*. In plain terms, cross-entropy tells us, in a quantitative way, how well a model predicts a body of data; this can be a very useful way of objectively evaluating and comparing models. In chapter 2, I survey all the probability theory needed for the following chapters, present some simple examples, and briefly discuss applications in other domains.

While I believe that many aspects of music and music perception would lend themselves well to probabilistic treatment, my focus will be on two aspects in particular: meter and tonality. In chapter 3, I address a basic problem of music perception, the identification of meter, and propose a probabilistic model of this process. In chapters 4 and 6, I examine the problem of key perception from a probabilistic viewpoint. I first propose a model of key perception in monophonic music (melodies); I then expand this model to accommodate polyphonic music. With regard to both meter and key, the models I propose are not merely models of information retrieval, but also shed light on other aspects of perception. In particular, they lead very naturally to ways of identifying the probability of actual note patterns. This in turn provides a way of modeling cognitive processes such as error detection, expectation, and pitch identification, as well as more subtle musical phenomena such as musical ambiguity, tension, and "tonalness." These issues are explored in chapter 5 (with regard to monophonic music) and chapter 7 (with regard to polyphonic music).

In the final three chapters of the book, I explore a range of further issues in music and probability. Chapter 8 surveys some recent work by other authors, in which probabilistic methods are applied to a variety of problems in music perception and cognition: transcription, phrase perception, pattern perception, harmony, and improvisation. In chapter 9, I consider the idea of construing probabilistic models as descriptions of musical styles, and—hence—as hypotheses about the cognitive processes involved in composition. I use the key-finding and meter-finding models of chapters 3 and 4 as simple examples, showing how they can be seen to "reduce the uncertainty" of tonal music. I then consider the possibility of using this approach to evaluate Schenkerian theory, a highly influential theory of tonal structure.

For the most part, I will be concerned in this book with music of the pre-twentieth-century European tradition. (I will focus largely on "art music" of the eighteenth and nineteenth centuries, but will also consider folk music, as represented in a large corpus of computationally encoded European folk songs.) I do, however, give some attention to other musical idioms. In chapter 9, I explore the possibility of using probabilistic models to characterize differences between musical styles: for example, using the rhythm model of chapter 3 to quantify stylistic differences with regard to rubato and syncopation. In chapter 10, I pursue this idea further, suggesting that a probabilistic view may also help us to *explain* these cross-stylistic differences: music functions, in part, to convey certain kinds of information from the producer(s) to the perceiver, and some styles may be inherently better suited than others to these communicative goals. I will argue that this principle, which I call *communicative pressure*, has been an important factor in the evolution of musical styles.

Like much work in music cognition (the larger field to which this study belongs), the work I present here is interdisciplinary in nature. The underlying aim is to uncover the mental processes and representations involved in musical behaviors—listening, performing, and composing. My assumption is that we can best achieve this goal by bringing together methodologies from different disciplines. Many of the musical ideas and concepts in the book—the ideas on which my models are built—are well-established principles of music theory; in turn, the research I present here serves in part as a way of empirically testing some of those principles, at least with regard to their validity for music perception and cognition. At many points in the book, also, I will cite experimental psychological work, as such work has provided insight into many of the issues I discuss. But the primary methodology of this study is computational. My assumption is that, by trying to model aspects of cognition such as key-finding, error detection, and the like, we can gain insight into how these processes work in the human mind. Creating a computational model that performs such a process well does not prove that humans perform it in the same way; but it satisfies *one* important requirement for such a model, providing a computationally adequate hypothesis which can then perhaps be tested in more direct ways (for example, through experimental work).

Any attempt to model musical behavior or perception in a general way is fraught with difficulties. With regard to models of perception, the question arises of whose perception we are trying to model—even if we confine ourselves to a particular culture and historical milieu. Surely the perception of music varies greatly between listeners of different levels of training; indeed, a large part of music education is devoted to developing and enriching (and therefore presumably changing) these listening processes. While this may be true, I am concerned here with fairly basic aspects of perception—particularly meter and key—which I believe are relatively consistent across listeners. Anecdotal evidence suggests, for example, that most people are able to "find the beat" in a typical folk song or classical piece. (Experimental evidence supports this view as well, as I will discuss in chapters 3 and 4.) This is not to say that there is complete uniformity in this regard—there may be occasional disagreements, even among experts, as to how we hear the tonality or meter of a piece. But I believe the commonalities between us far outweigh the differences.

If the idea of discovering general principles of music perception through computational modeling seems problematic, applying this approach to *composition* may seem even more so. For one thing, the composers of European folk songs and classical music are no longer with us; any claims about their cognitive processes can never really be tested experimentally, and may therefore seem futile. I will argue, however, that musical objects themselves—scores and transcriptions—provide a kind of data about compositional processes, and we can evaluate different models as to how well they "fit" this data; the probabilistic approach provides rigorous, quantitative ways of achieving this. I should emphasize, also, that my goal is not to "explain" compositional processes in all their complexity, but rather to posit some rather basic constraints that may have guided or shaped these processes. In some cases, this approach may simply confirm the validity of musical principles whose role in composition was already assumed. In other cases, however, it may provide a new means of testing theories of compositional practice whose validity is uncertain, or even lead us to new ideas and avenues for exploration. In this way, I will argue, the probabilistic perspective opens the door to a new and powerful approach to the study of musical creation.

# 2
# Probabilistic Foundations and Background

In this chapter I present an introduction to some basic concepts from probability theory. I begin at the very beginning, not assuming any prior knowledge of probability. My exposition will be a somewhat simplified version of that usually found in probability texts. My coverage is also far from comprehensive; I present only the specific concepts needed for understanding the material of later chapters.[1] At the end of the chapter, I will survey some early work in the area of music and probability.

**2.1**
**Elementary**
**Probability**

The central concept of probability theory is the *probability function*. A probability function takes as input a variable with some value, and outputs the probability of the variable having that value.[2] For the probability function to be well-defined, every probability must be between 0 and 1, and the probabilities of all the values of the variable must sum to exactly 1. Suppose the variable $x$ has two values, 1 and 2; the probability that $x = 1$ is .6, and the probability that $x = 2$ is .4. Then we could write:

$$P(x = 1) = .6 \tag{2.1}$$

$$P(x = 2) = .4 \tag{2.2}$$

In many cases, the variable under consideration is implicit, and does not need to be named; only the value is given. If it was known that we were talking about variable $x$, we could simply write $P(1) = .6$ and $P(2) = .4$.

The set of probabilities that a function assigns to all the values of a variable is called a *distribution*.

Very often, the variables associated with probability functions represent events or states of the world. For example, a coin being flipped can be considered a variable that has two values (or "outcomes"), heads and tails: normally the probability function will be $P(\text{heads}) = 0.5$, $P(\text{tails}) = 0.5$. If we have a die with six possible outcomes, the probability of each outcome will normally be 1/6; if the die was weighted, this might not be the case, but in any case the probabilities of the six outcomes must all add up to 1.

Matters get more complex when we have more than one variable. For example, we might have two coins, C1 and C2. Suppose we want to know the probability of C1 coming up heads and C2 coming up tails. This is known as a *joint probability*, and can be written as $P(\text{C1} = \text{heads} \cap \text{C2} = \text{tails})$. An important question to ask here is whether the two variables are *independent*. In plain terms, if the variables are independent, that means they have no effect on one another (nor are they both affected by any third variable). In mathematical terms, if the variables are independent, the joint probability of two outcomes of the variables is just the product of their individual probabilities:

$$P(\text{C1} = \text{heads} \cap \text{C2} = \text{tails}) = P(\text{C1} = \text{heads})P(\text{C2} = \text{tails}) \qquad (2.3)$$

A more complex situation is where the variables are *not* independent. This brings us to the topic of conditional probability and Bayes' rule.

## 2.2 Conditional Probability and Bayes' Rule

Suppose you pass a little corner store every day. The store is open 50% of the time, at random times during the 24-hour day (whenever the owner feels like opening it). Suppose, further, that there is a light in the window of the store. Generally, when the store is open, the light is on—but not always. Sometimes the owner forgets to turn the light off when he closes the store, or perhaps there is a bad electric connection so that the light is sometimes off when the store is actually open. We have two variables, the state of the store (open or closed) and the state of the light (off or on), that are not independent of one another, and we want to look at the relationship between them. Here we employ the concept of *conditional probabilities*. We might ask, first of all, what is the probability that the light is on when the store is open? Suppose, somehow, we simply know this: when the store is open, there is a probability of .7 that the light will be on. We write this conditional probability as

Chapter 2

$$P(L = \text{on} \mid S = \text{open}) = .7 \tag{2.4}$$

The vertical bar indicates that we are expressing the probability of one event (or state) *given* another. We are now defining a conditional probability function, describing the state of the light given that the store is open. Such functions follow the same logic as ordinary probability functions—the probabilities of all outcomes must sum to 1. Thus, assuming the light can only be on or off, it must be that $P(L = \text{off} \mid S = \text{open}) = .3$. Suppose we know, also, that when the store is closed, $P(L = \text{on} \mid S = \text{closed}) = .2$; then it must be that $P(L = \text{off} \mid S = \text{closed}) = .8$.

Let us consider two other things we might want to know. (*Why* we might want to know them will become clear shortly.) First of all, what is the probability that the light is on *and* the store is open, or $P(L = \text{on} \cap S = \text{open})$? In this case, the two variables are not independent, so we cannot simply multiply their individual probabilities as in equation 2.3. Remember that the store is open at random times, but overall, it is open 50% of the time, so the probability that the store is open is .5. It is a basic fact of probability that for any events $A$ and $B$ (whether independent or not):

$$P(A \cap B) = P(A \mid B)P(B) \tag{2.5}$$

Therefore,

$$P(L = \text{on} \cap S = \text{open}) = P(L = \text{on} \mid S = \text{open})P(S = \text{open})$$
$$= .7 \times .5 = .35 \tag{2.6}$$

So, .35 (35%) of the time, the store is open and the light is on. We can also calculate $P(L = \text{on} \cap S = \text{closed}) = .2 \times .5 = .1$.

A further question: what is the *overall* probability that the light is on? (In other words, what proportion of the time is the light on?) The store is either open or closed at all times; so the probability that the light is on is equal to the proportion of time that the light is on and the store is open, plus the proportion of time the light is on and the store is closed. More formally,

$$P(L = \text{on}) = P(L = \text{on} \cap S = \text{open}) + P(L = \text{on} \cap S = \text{closed}) = .45 \tag{2.7}$$

This, too, exemplifies an important general fact: the probability of an event $A$ can be expressed as the sum of the joint probabilities of $A$ with all of the outcomes of another variable ($B_i$):

Probabilistic Foundations and Background

$$P(A) = \sum_i P(A \cap B_i) = \sum_i P(A \mid B_i)P(B_i) \qquad (2.8)$$

At this point, finally, we can actually ask something that somebody might want to know: *What is the probability that the store is open, given that the light is on?* Notice that this is a question with real practical significance. We're driving by, we see the light on, we need a gallon of milk, and we want to know what the probability is that it is actually worth stopping at the store. This is where Bayes' rule comes in. Bayes' rule says:

$$P(A \mid B) = \frac{P(B \mid A)P(A)}{P(B)} \qquad (2.9)$$

In fact, this rule can be derived quite easily from what we have seen so far. From equation 2.5:

$$P(A \cap B) = P(A \mid B)P(B) \qquad (2.10)$$

$$P(B \cap A) = P(B \mid A)P(A) \qquad (2.11)$$

Since $P(A \cap B) = P(B \cap A)$,

$$P(A \mid B)P(B) = P(B \mid A)P(A) \qquad (2.12)$$

$$P(A \mid B) = \frac{P(B \mid A)P(A)}{P(B)} \qquad (2.13)$$

Plugging in the numbers from the store example:

$$P(S = \text{open} \mid L = \text{on}) = \frac{P(L = \text{on} \mid S = \text{open})P(S = \text{open})}{P(L = \text{on})}$$

$$= \frac{.7 \times .5}{.45} = .78 \qquad (2.14)$$

So we see that, if the light is on, there is quite a high probability, .78, that the store is open.

The moral of this hypothetical little story is as follows. There was an underlying reality, the store being open or closed, which gave rise to a surface manifestation, namely the light being on or off. Using our knowledge about this relationship, and using Bayes' rule, we were able to make an inference about the state of the underlying reality given the state of the surface manifestation. Bayes' rule is useful in exactly that situation: it allows us to draw conclusions about a hidden variable based on knowledge of an observed one. To express this more formally, let us call the hidden variable the *structure*; the observed variable will be called the *surface*. Suppose we know, for every possible surface and every possible structure, $P(\text{surface} \mid \text{structure})$; and suppose we also know the overall probabilities of the surfaces and the structures. Then, using Bayes' rule, we can determine $P(\text{structure} \mid \text{surface})$:

$$P(\text{structure} \mid \text{surface}) = \frac{P(\text{surface} \mid \text{structure})P(\text{structure})}{P(\text{surface})} \quad (2.15)$$

In Bayesian terminology, $P(\text{structure})$ is known as the "prior probability" of the structure; $P(\text{structure} \mid \text{surface})$ is known as the "posterior probability" of the structure.

There is a useful short-cut we can take here. Suppose there are many possible structures, and all we want to know is the most likely one given the surface. The quantity $P(\text{surface})$ is the same for all structures; in that case, it can just be disregarded. (In the corner store example: $P(L = \text{on})$, the *overall* probability of the light being on, is the same, whether we are considering $P(S = \text{open})$ or $P(S = \text{closed})$.) Thus

$$P(\text{structure} \mid \text{surface}) \propto P(\text{surface} \mid \text{structure})P(\text{structure}) \quad (2.16)$$

(where "$\propto$" means "is proportional to"). To find the structure that maximizes the left side of this expression, we just need to find the structure that maximizes the right side. This means we need only know, for each structure, the probability of the structure, and the probability of the surface given the structure. In the case of the store example, suppose we only want to know the most likely state of the store (open or closed), given that the light is on. We can use equation 2.14 above, but disregarding $P(L = \text{on})$:

$$P(S = \text{open} \mid L = \text{on}) \propto P(L = \text{on} \mid S = \text{open})P(S = \text{open}) = .35 \quad (2.17)$$

$$P(S = \text{closed} \mid L = \text{on}) \propto P(L = \text{on} \mid S = \text{closed})P(S = \text{closed}) = .1 \quad (2.18)$$

We need only calculate the right-hand side of these two expressions; the one yielding the highest value indicates the most probable state of the store, open or closed. Thus we find that, given that the light is on, the store is much more likely to be open than closed. We will often make use of this simplifying step in following chapters.

One further expression will also be useful. Putting together equations 2.5 and 2.16, we can see that

$$P(\text{structure} \mid \text{surface}) \propto P(\text{surface} \cap \text{structure}) \quad (2.19)$$

Probabilistic Foundations and Background

Thus the most probable structure given a surface is the one that yields the highest joint probability with the surface. This slight reformulation of equation 2.16 is more convenient in some cases.

The Bayesian approach has proven to be extremely useful in a variety of areas of cognitive modeling and information processing; in recent years it has been widely applied in fields such as speech recognition (Jurafsky and Martin 2000), natural language parsing (Manning and Schütze 2000), vision (Kersten 1999), decision making (Osherson 1990), and concept-learning (Tenenbaum 1999). Just two examples will be given here, to give a flavor of how the Bayesian approach has been used. The first concerns the problem of speech recognition. In listening to speech, we are given a sequence of phonetic units—phones—and we need to determine the sequence of words that the speaker intended. In this case, then, the sequence of phones is the surface and the sequence of words is the structure. The problem is that a single sequence of phones could result from many different words. Consider the phone sequence [ni], as in "the knights who say 'ni'," from *Monty Python and the Holy Grail* (this example is taken wholesale from Jurafsky and Martin 2000). Various words can be pronounced [ni], under certain circumstances: "new," "neat," "need," and "knee." However, not all of these words are equally likely to be pronounced [ni]. The probability of the pronunciation [ni] given each word (according to Jurafsky and Martin, based on analysis of a large corpus of spoken text) is as follows:

new    .36
neat   .52
need   .11
knee   1.00

This, then, is $P(\text{surface} \mid \text{structure})$ for each of the four words. (For all other words, $P(\text{surface} \mid \text{structure}) = 0$.) In addition, however, some of the words are more probable than others—the prior probability of each word, $P(\text{structure})$, is as follows:

new    .001
neat   .00031
need   .00056
knee   .000024

We then calculate $P(\text{surface} \mid \text{structure})P(\text{structure})$ for each word:

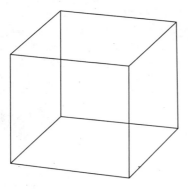

**Figure 2.1**
This pattern of lines could be produced by many different three-dimensional shapes, but it is always perceived as a cube.

| | |
|---|---|
| new | .00036 |
| neat | .000068 |
| need | .000062 |
| knee | .000024 |

From equation 2.16, we know that this is proportional to $P(\text{structure} \mid \text{surface})$. The structure maximizing this quantity is "new"; thus this is the most probable word given the phone string [ni]. This probabilistic method has played an important role in recent models of speech recognition.

Bayesian modeling is also an approach of increasing importance in the study of vision. In vision, the perceptual problem is to recover information about the world—or "scene" ($S$)—from a noisy and ambiguous visual image ($I$); we wish to know the most probable scene given the image, that is, the $S$ maximizing $P(S \mid I)$. Using Bayesian logic, we know that $P(S \mid I) \propto P(I \mid S)P(S)$. What this expression tells us is that vision depends not only on knowledge about how visual scenes cause images, $P(I \mid S)$, but also on the prior probability of different scenes, $P(S)$—that is, the probability of different events or objects in the world. A pattern of lines like that in figure 2.1 could be produced by many three-dimensional shapes, but we see it as a cube, because cubes are much more likely to occur in the world than other possible forms (Knill, Kersten, and Yuille 1996). In figure 2.2, an animation shifting from A to B—in which the shadow moves while the square remains stationary—creates the illusion that the square is moving away from the background;

A                                        B

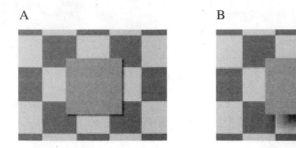

**Figure 2.2**
An animation moving from A to B creates the illusion that the square is moving away from the background. From D. Kersten, "High-level vision as statistical inference," in M. S. Gazzaniga (ed.), *The New Cognitive Neurosciences* (MIT Press, 1999). Used by permission.

it could just as easily be due to movement in the light source, but we know that objects are more likely to move than light sources (Kersten 1999). (The percept of a moving square is more common when the shadow is *below* the square than when it is above, because a light source is more likely to come from above than below.) While the idea that vision requires "knowledge about the world" is not new, Bayesian logic provides a powerful and natural way of integrating such information with other kinds of visual knowledge.

**2.3
Other Probabilistic
Concepts**

Bayesian reasoning is the foundation for much of the research presented in the following chapters. However, several further concepts from probability theory are also important. Among them are the ideas of *entropy* and *cross-entropy*.

Suppose that scientists studying outer space suddenly begin to receive strange electrical signals from a distant galaxy. The signals consist of two symbols; their exact nature is not important, but let us call them A and B. The scientists first receive the following signal—10 symbols, including 6 As and 4 Bs:

A A B A A B B A B A

The scientists study this signal and try to understand its source. They agree that it was probably produced by some kind of machine generating a random sequence of As and Bs. Beyond this, however, the scientists cannot agree. One group, on the basis of simplicity, hypothesizes that the generating source had probabilities of $P(A) = .5$ and $P(B) = .5$. Of course, the data does not exactly fit these proportions, but a source with these probabilities might well produce such data—just as, if you were flipping a completely fair coin 10 times, it might well come up with 6 heads and 4 tails. The second group maintains that there is nothing to particularly argue for this "50/50" model. Instead, they argue, it is best to assume that the source's probabilities exactly fit the data, $P(A) = .6$ and $P(B) = .4$; we will call this the "60/40" model.

The scientists then learn that a large new body of data has become available from the source—a stream of 1000 more symbols. They agree that they will test their two theories, the 50/50 model and the 60/40 model, in the following way. Each model assigns a certain probability to the new data occurring (whatever it turns out to be); whichever model assigns the higher probability to the data is the better model.

The data is studied, and it proves to consist of 599 As and 401 Bs. All the scientists agree, from studying the data, that the symbols are independent from each other; each symbol is a separate event generated from the source. Thus each model can assign a probability to the data by evaluating each event one by one; for example, the 60/40 model assigns a probability of .6 to each A and .4 to each B. The probability of the entire symbol stream is the product of all these probabilities. Let us put all the As together, and all the Bs. Then the 60/40 model assigns the following probability to the stream:

$$
\begin{array}{cc}
(599 \text{ As}) & (401 \text{ Bs}) \\
\overbrace{\text{A A A A} \ldots\text{A}} & \overbrace{\text{B B B B} \ldots\text{B}} \\
.6 \times .6 \times .6 \times .6 \ldots \times .6 & \times .4 \times .4 \times .4 \times .4 \ldots \times .4 \\
\end{array}
$$

$$= .6^{599} \times .4^{401} \tag{2.19}$$

The 50/50 model assigns the stream a probability of $.5^{599} \times .5^{401}$.

Numbers like $.6^{599} \times .4^{401}$ are extremely small, as probabilities often are, and thus somewhat unwieldy. When comparing probabilities, a common step is to take their natural logarithms. The function $\log x$ is monotonically increasing, meaning that if $\log x$ is greater than $\log y$, then $x$ is greater than $y$. So if all we want to know is which among a set of probabilities is greatest, comparing their logarithms works just as well. Taking the logarithms of the expressions above, and using standard techniques for manipulating logarithms:

$$\log(.6^{599} \times .4^{401}) = \log(.6^{599}) + \log(.4^{401})$$

$$= 599 \log(.6) + 401 \log(.4) \qquad (2.20)$$

$$\log(.5^{599} \times .5^{401}) = \log(.5^{599}) + \log(.5^{401})$$

$$= 599 \log(.5) + 401 \log(.5) \qquad (2.21)$$

We could calculate these numbers quite easily and get our answer. This would give us a kind of "score" for each model, indicating how well it fits the data. But notice that these scores are affected by the length of the signal (1000 symbols), which is really irrelevant. What we are really interested in is more like the predictive power of the models *per symbol*. To put it another way, the important thing about the data is that it contains 59.9% As and 40.1% Bs; it doesn't matter whether it contains 1000 symbols or 1,000,000.[3] So let us replace the "event counts" above with proportions of 1. This gives us the following scores for the 60/40 model (equation 2.22) and the 50/50 model (equation 2.23):

$$.599 \log(.6) + .401 \log(.4) = -.673 \qquad (2.22)$$

$$.599 \log(.5) + .401 \log(.5) = -.693 \qquad (2.23)$$

The 60/40 model yields the higher score, and thus assigns a higher probability to the data than the 50/50 model. By the agreement of the scientists, then, the 60/40 model fits the data better and thus is the better model—the model that they will announce to the world.

What we have just derived is a measure called *cross-entropy*. Basically, cross-entropy allows us to measure how well a model fits or predicts a body of data. More generally, given a variable with a set of possible outcomes $(x)$, a model which assigns a probability $P_m(x)$ to each outcome, and an observed proportion of events $P(x)$ for each outcome, the cross-entropy $H(P, P_m)$ is defined as

$$H(P, P_m) = -\sum_x P(x) \log P_m(x) \qquad (2.24)$$

This is the same as what we calculated in equations 2.22 and 2.23, except with a negative sign in front of it; this means that a model with higher cross-entropy predicts the data *less* well.[4]

Cross-entropy is an extremely powerful idea; it provides a way of systematically comparing the predictive power of different models. Another way of thinking about cross-entropy is also useful. Suppose we have a stream of data, $D$, consisting of $n$ symbols or events. The formula for cross-entropy groups equivalent events into categories $(x)$; the probability assigned to each category by the model, $\log P_m(x)$, is weighted according to its count in the data, $P(x)$. But we might also have a model which simply assigned a single probability to the entire data stream. In that case, the cross-entropy would simply be

$$H(D, P_m) = -(1/n) \log P_m(D) \tag{2.25}$$

This alternative definition is often more intuitive, and we will sometimes use it in later chapters.

One could also measure the cross-entropy of a distribution with itself. (In effect, this is treating the distribution as a "model" which is then tested against itself.) This is known simply as the *entropy* of the distribution. For any probability function $P(x)$, the entropy $(H)$ is defined as

$$H = -\sum_x P(x) \log P(x) \tag{2.26}$$

Entropy is sometimes described as the amount of uncertainty, surprise, or information in a body of data.[5] A stream of symbols that are all the same (for example, a sequence of As) will have minimum entropy $(0)$; a stream consisting of many different symbols evenly distributed will have very high entropy. Cross-entropy, by contrast, is the amount of uncertainty in the data *given a model*; if the model is any good, it will help us predict the data and thus reduce its uncertainty. For our purposes, entropy is of less interest than cross-entropy, but it was used in some early probabilistic models of music, as will be discussed in section 2.4.

A few further lessons can be drawn from our outer-space story. Notice, first of all, that it was important for the scientists to test their models on data that they had not seen before. If they had seen the data, they simply could have defined a model which assigned a probability of 1 to the data, and 0 to everything else. In general, then, in testing a model, it is important *not* to test it on the same data on which the model was based. We should note, however, that there are also other criteria that could be involved in evaluating models, besides sheer "goodness of fit" to the data—for example, criteria of simplicity or elegance. By criteria such as these, a model like the one just suggested (assigning a probability of 1 to the data) might not do very well. Simplicity and elegance are not easy

Probabilistic Foundations and Background

things to define quantitatively, but ways of doing this have been proposed, as we will discuss in chapter 8.

The outer-space story presented above might also be formulated in Bayesian terms. The scientists were presented with a surface pattern, a sequence of symbols, and wanted to know the nature of the source giving rise to it. They had two models to choose from, and wanted to know which one was most probable, given the data. They used Bayesian reasoning (compare equation 2.16):

$$P(\text{source} \mid \text{data}) \propto P(\text{data} \mid \text{source}) P(\text{source}) \qquad (2.27)$$

In using cross-entropy, the scientists were essentially computing $P(\text{data} \mid \text{source})$ for each source model; the source model maximizing this term was then assumed to be the model maximizing $P(\text{source} \mid \text{data})$. Notice that they did not consider $P(\text{source})$, the prior probability of the different models. Rather, they implicitly assumed that there were just two possible sources (the 50/50 model and the 60/40 model), to which they assigned equal probabilities of .5; if that were the case, then factoring in P(source) would not change the results. We might also imagine a case where the prior probabilities were *not* equal. For example, suppose there were known to be two kinds of sources in the galaxy, a 50/50 type and a 60/40 type, but the 60/40 type was four times as common as the 50/50 type; then we might wish to assign prior probabilities of .8 for the 60/40 model and .2 for the 50/50 model.

As another complicating factor, suppose that the symbol stream had looked something like this:

A A A A A B B B A A B B B B B B B B A A A A A A A B B B ...

While there are roughly as many As as Bs in this sequence, it no longer seems very plausible that the symbols are independent. Rather, every A seems to have a high probability of being followed by another A, while most Bs are followed by another B. Such a situation is known as a *Markov chain*. The case just described, where each event is dependent only on the previous one event, is a first-order Markov chain; it might also be that, for example, each event was dependent on the previous two events, which would be a second-order Markov chain. More complex techniques for modeling sequences of symbols have also been developed, notably *finite-state models*; we will discuss these in chapter 8.

We could imagine a first-order Markov chain as the surface in a simple Bayesian model—so that each event was dependent on the previous event, but also on an underlying structure. That is essentially the situation with the monophonic pitch model presented in chapter 4, where melodic events are assumed to be dependent on the underlying key and range and also on the pitch interval to the previous event. Alternatively, we might suppose that the structure itself was a first-order Markov chain—a series of underlying events, each one dependent on the last, with each event giving rise to some kind of surface pattern. This is known as a *hidden Markov model*, and essentially describes the polyphonic key-finding model in chapter 6. It also describes the rhythmic model in chapter 3, at a very basic level, though the situation here is much more complex.

## 2.4 Early Work on Music and Probability

Until very recently, the application of probabilistic methods to music research was a relatively unexplored area. However, there have been occasional efforts in this direction, going back several decades. In this section, I present a brief review of earlier work on music and probability. My focus will be on work that is *not* Bayesian in character. Bayesian studies of music—all of which have appeared within the last eight years—will be surveyed in later chapters (models of rhythm in chapter 3, models of other aspects of music in chapter 8).

We begin with the work of Leonard Meyer, whose 1957 essay "Meaning in music and information theory" was quoted at the beginning of this book. Meyer was one of the first to suggest that musical communication could be viewed in probabilistic terms. In listening to music, he observed, we are constantly confronted with uncertainty as to what will occur next. We form expectations which may or may not be fulfilled—expectations based both on general knowledge of the style and on the particular "intra-opus norms" created by the piece. (Meyer noted that the dependence of musical events on previous events suggests a connection with Markov processes.) In Meyer's view, music only conveys meaning and expressive effect when expectations are violated in some way. Meyer also noted the possibility of using entropy or information content to quantitatively describe and compare musical styles. (He observed in particular that "modern" music—remember that he was writing in 1957—is often characterized by extremely high information.) However, he was skeptical about this possibility, given the current state of knowledge; success in this enterprise, he suggested, would require "a more precise and empirically validated account of mental behavior" and "a more precise and sensitive understanding of the nature of musical experience" (1957/1967: 20).

Meyer's essay reflects broader intellectual currents of the time. In 1957, the concept of entropy (in its probabilistic sense) had recently been introduced as part of the new field of *information theory* (Shannon 1948)—a field that was initially concerned with technical matters such as the communication of electrical signals across noisy phone lines, but which captured interest and attention across many disciplines. Influenced by this intellectual trend and perhaps by Meyer as well, a number of authors in this period pursued the idea of measuring entropy in music. For example, Youngblood (1958) set out to measure the entropy of pitch patterns in different musical styles. Given a sequence of pitches, Youngblood reasoned, we can measure its entropy simply by determining the distribution of scale-degrees (pitch-classes in relation to the key), defining this as a probability function, and applying the usual definition in equation 2.26. Youngblood examined three small corpora of pieces by Romantic composers—Schubert, Mendelssohn, and Schumann—as well as a corpus of Gregorian chant, and calculated the entropy in each one.[6] He concluded that Gregorian chant featured lower entropy than any of the Romantic composers. In a similar vein, Pinkerton (1956) measured the scale-degree entropy of nursery rhymes. Somewhat later, Knopoff and Hutchinson (1983) measured scale-degree entropy in larger corpora of pieces by Mozart, Schubert, and other composers, finding an overall increase in entropy from the seventeenth to the nineteenth century. (Snyder [1990] reanalyzed the same corpora, with certain modifications—for example, introducing enharmonic or "spelling" distinctions so that, e.g., $\flat\hat{5}$ and $\sharp\hat{4}$ are treated as different scale-degrees.) Brawley (1959) undertook a similar study in the rhythmic domain, measuring the entropy of short rhythmic patterns in a variety of different pieces; Hiller and Fuller (1967) measured entropy in Webern's Symphony Op. 21, considering both rhythmic and pitch parameters.

A perceptive critique of this early probabilistic research was offered by Cohen (1962). (While Cohen's study predates some of the studies mentioned above, his criticisms largely apply to these later studies also.) Cohen noted that the purpose of this research was, at least in part, to measure the uncertainty or complexity of different kinds of music from the listener's point of view. However, he also identified some serious flaws in this approach. The entropy model assumes that a musical corpus is perceived using probabilities gathered from the corpus itself; but a listener hearing the corpus for the first time obviously does not have knowledge of these probabilities. In another important respect, Cohen argued, the listener has *more* knowledge than the model assumes. In hearing a piece by Schubert, our expectations are surely not based solely on knowledge of Schubert's music, but also on broader experience of Romantic music, tonal music, and perhaps even more general kinds of musical knowledge.[7] Thus, in measuring the perceived uncertainty or complexity of a musical corpus, there is no reason to assume that the probability distribution in the listener's mind is identical to the actual distribution in the corpus. Entropy indicates the complexity of a corpus as an isolated, self-contained system; but this is not of much relevance to perception, unless it can be argued that the corpus truly represents the musical experience of the listener.

From our point of view, however, there is another serious failing to this early probabilistic work. Listening to a piece involves more than just processing a pattern of surface events. Rather, it involves inferring *structures* from those events, structures which then guide our expectations and interpretation of future events. Our perception of a sequence of pitches, for example, is very much influenced by knowledge of the key; we infer the key of the piece from the pitches already heard, and this conditions our expectations for subsequent pitches. The key of the piece may then change, changing our pitch expectations accordingly. The identification of the underlying key structure and the interpretation of surface events form a complex, intertwined perceptual process. Youngblood and others tacitly acknowledge the importance of key, in that their models reflect scale-degrees rather than actual pitch-classes (thus assuming that the key has already been identified). But they give no account of how the key is determined, nor do they address the complex interactions between surface and structure. I will argue that this complex cognitive process, and other important aspects of music cognition, can be very effectively modeled using probabilistic means.

Finally, we should briefly consider a very different area of engagement between music and probability: composition. Since the 1950s, a number of composers and researchers have employed probabilistic techniques in the generation of music. In some cases, the aim has been to synthesize new music in an existing style. Such attempts are closely related to the "entropy" studies discussed earlier, as they usually involve the gathering of data (distributions of pitches, rhythms, intervals, and the like) from a musical corpus; these distributions are then used to generate random (or "stochastic") choices, producing music with the same statistical properties as the corpus. For example, Pinkerton (1956) used such a method to generate new nursery tunes; Brooks et al. (1957) used it to generate hymn tunes. More recently, Conklin and Witten (1995) present a generative model of Bach-style chorale melodies; they use a "multiple-viewpoint" approach, which abstracts a variety of kinds of information from the data (pitch, duration, position in measure, contour, and many other things) and combines these parameters in various ways to generate new music. Ponsford et al. (1999) use probabilistic methods to generate Baroque sarabandes, incorporating third-order and fourth-order Markov models. In other cases, a set of possibilities is generated by stochastic means; these are then filtered using explicit rules to choose the best one (this is known as a "generate-and-test" method). Hiller and Isaacson (1959) used this approach, filtering randomly generated music through contrapuntal rules to create music in the style of Palestrina. Still other composers, notably John Cage and Iannis Xenakis, have employed stochastic methods with a very different aim—not to simulate existing styles, but to develop new musical effects and languages.

Quite apart from the aesthetic value of stochastically generated music (which is not our concern here), it might also be of interest in music cognition research. For example, if it turned out that stochastically generated hymn tunes were indistinguishable from real ones by competent listeners of the style, this might shed interesting light on how musical styles are cognitively represented. However, the possibility of using stochastically generated music in experimental cognition research has not been much explored. We will not consider it further here, though it is certainly an intriguing possibility for the future.

# 3
# Melody I: The Rhythm Model

**3.1**
**Rhythm and Meter**

Our focus in this chapter is on what I will call the listener's *rhythmic understanding* of a melody. In hearing a melody, we do not simply perceive it as a series of continually varying long or short notes. Rather, we impose on it a rich and complex hierarchical structure. Our task here is to develop a computational model which can simulate this process—processing a melody and arriving at the same rhythmic analysis that a listener would. Before proceeding, we must examine more closely the nature of this rhythmic understanding.

Consider the rhythmic pattern in figure 3.1. The pattern is represented simply as a series of note-onsets in time (with timepoints indicated in milliseconds), as might be produced by a human performer. A set of possible rhythmic understandings of the pattern is shown underneath, in rhythmic notation. The notation in A represents the pattern in a 2/4 metrical framework; in B, it is in 3/4, so that the last note is on the "downbeat." In C, the pattern is in 6/8, so that the eighth-note is strong rather than weak. In D, the short note is not located on a beat at all—in musical terms such a note might be considered a grace note or "extrametrical" note. In E, the time signature is 2/4 and the pattern is represented with the same note values as in A; but now the notes are aligned with the barlines in a different way, so that the short note is metrically strong. In hearing a pattern of onsets, the listener must recover the correct rhythm—that is, the one intended by the performer and composer—out of all the possible ones: in this case, choosing analysis A (let us assume this is correct) rather than analyses B, C, D, or E, or indeed an infinite number of other possible analyses. Despite the complexity of this task,

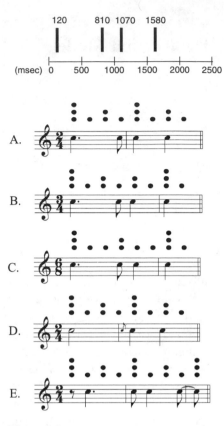

**Figure 3.1**
A pattern of onsets in time, with five possible rhythmic understandings.

listeners generally perform it with relative ease, and there is usually general agreement (though not always *complete* agreement) as to the correct rhythmic interpretation of a melody.[1]

As indicated by figure 3.1, rhythmic notation provides a convenient way of representing rhythmic understandings of a note pattern. There is another useful method for this as well, based on the concept of a *metrical grid*. A metrical grid is a framework of several levels of beats, corresponding to different rhythmic values—for example, a piece might have sixteenth-note, eighth-note, quarter-note, half-note, whole-note, and double-whole-note beat levels. Each of the rhythmic notations in figure 3.1 corresponds with a particular metrical grid aligned in a certain way with the notes (the metrical grid for each notated rhythm is shown above

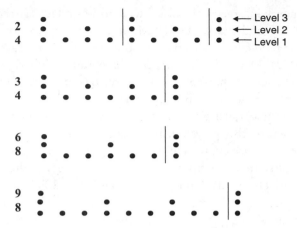

**Figure 3.2**
Metrical grids for four common time signatures.

the staff). Generally, in Western music, every second or third beat at one metrical level is a beat at the immediately higher level (if there is one). The duple or triple relationships between levels define different time signatures; in 3/4 time, for example, every third quarter-note level beat is a beat at the next level up (the dotted-half-note level, in this case). The grids for four common time signatures are shown in figure 3.2. Generally, one particular level of the grid is perceived as being especially salient, and is identified as "the beat" in colloquial terms—for example, the quarter-note level in 2/4 or the dotted-quarter in 6/8; this is called the "tactus" level. Beats within each level tend to be roughly equally spaced in time, but not exactly; human performers are unable to perform rhythms with perfect precision and usually do not even attempt to do so.

Under this view, understanding the rhythm of a melody consists, in large part, of inferring the correct metrical grid. (The metrical grid of a piece is also sometimes called its *metrical structure* or simply its *meter*.) Thus the perception of meter is an extremely important part of music cognition. Research in music psychology provides abundant support for this view; it has been shown that meter impacts musical experience and behavior in many important ways. Patterns that are similar in their metrical structure tend to be judged as similar (Gabrielsson 1973); the same melody heard in two different metrical contexts is often judged to be a completely different melody (Sloboda 1985; Povel and Essens 1985). Patterns that are ambiguous in metrical terms—or that conflict with an underlying metrical pulse—tend to be judged as rhythmically complex (Povel and Essens 1985). Meter affects expectation, in that it governs our predictions as to the temporal locations of future events (Jones et al. 2002). Meter also impacts the perception of other musical dimensions as well, such as harmony and phrase structure; we tend to hear changes of harmony at strong beats, and we tend to hear successive phrase boundaries at parallel points in the metrical grid (Temperley 2001a). Metrical structure also plays an important role in music performance. It affects performance expression, in that metrically strong notes tend to be played slightly more legato and louder than others (although these effects are relatively small) (Sloboda 1983; Drake and Palmer 1993). Even performance errors betray the influence of meter: when performers play a note in the wrong place, the played location tends to be a beat of similar metrical strength to the correct one (Palmer and Pfordresher 2003).

Altogether, it is difficult to overstate the importance of meter in the mental processing and representation of music. For this reason, the question of how listeners identify the meter of a piece is of considerable interest. The goal of the present chapter is to address this question from a computational perspective, using techniques of Bayesian probabilistic modeling. We will focus on the rhythmic idiom of traditional European music—represented, for example, by classical music and European folk music—and attempt to model the perception of listeners who are familiar with this style. We will further limit the problem to *monophonic* music: that is, music in which only a single note is present at a time. We begin by considering some other work that has been done on the perception of meter.

<table>
<tr><td>

**3.2**<br>**Previous Models of**<br>**Meter Perception**

</td><td>

Modeling meter perception has been an active area of research for over three decades, drawing important contributions from music theory, music psychology, and artificial intelligence. I have surveyed this work rather extensively elsewhere (Temperley 2001a) and will offer only a very brief overview here, focusing on computational approaches to the problem. Even computational models of meter are too numerous to list here; in a recent study I compiled a list of 25 such models (Temperley 2004a).

Computational models of meter perception may be categorized in several different ways. With regard to the input, we might distinguish beween models that assume a symbolic representation, in which notes have already been identified, and models which operate directly from

</td></tr>
</table>

audio input. While a large majority of models have been of the "symbolic" kind, several "audio" models have been proposed in recent years (Scheirer 1998; Goto 2001). Among symbolic-input models, some are restricted to "quantized" input, in which notes are represented as integer multiples of a short rhythmic unit—for example, the rhythm in figure 3.1A might be represented as 3–1–2–2. Others accept input generated from a human performance (on an electronic keyboard, for example), in which note times are represented at a much finer scale (e.g. milliseconds) and may not be perfectly regular; the onset pattern in figure 3.1 is an example of such input. Some models derive only a single level of beats for an input; others derive multiple levels. Most models confine themselves to monophonic input, but a few are designed to handle polyphonic input as well (Temperley and Sleator 1999; Dixon 2001).

In terms of approach, computational meter models have pursued a wide variety of strategies. Some models adopt the "rule-system" approach of classical artificial intelligence: note-onsets are examined one by one in a left-to-right fashion, and beat levels are gradually built up in an explicit rule-governed procedure (Longuet-Higgins and Steedman 1971; Lee 1991). Other models adopt a connectionist approach, in which rhythmic values are represented by nodes in a neural network (Desain and Honing 1992); or an oscillator-based approach, in which an oscillator (or set of oscillators) "entrains" to the phase and period of an input pattern (Large and Kolen 1994). Still others adopt a constraint-satisfaction or "preference-rule" approach, where many analyses of an entire input are considered and evaluated by various criteria; the preferred analysis is the one that best satisfies the criteria (Povel and Essens 1985; Temperley and Sleator 1999; Temperley 2001a). And other models combine these approaches in various ways. Of particular interest in the current context are several recent models of meter perception that employ probabilistic approaches; it is appropriate here to describe these models in greater depth.

Cemgil and colleagues have proposed Bayesian approaches to two different aspects of the meter-finding problem. The model of Cemgil et al. (2000a) converts a performed rhythmic pattern (a "performance") into a quantized rhythmic representation (a "score"), in which each note is given a fractional label representing its position in the measure: for example, a note occurring one quarter-note after the barline in a 3/4 measure would be represented as 1/3. The goal is to determine the score maximizing $P(\text{score} \mid \text{performance})$; using Bayesian reasoning, the authors note that this will also be the one maximizing $P(\text{performance} \mid \text{score})P(\text{score})$.

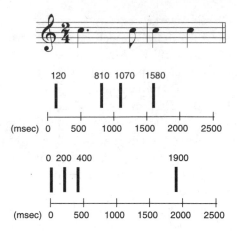

**Figure 3.3**
A rhythmic pattern, with a likely performance (above) and an unlikely one (below).

$P$(performance | score) captures the fidelity of the performance to the score. Consider a notated rhythm such as that in figure 3.3, and the two possible performances shown below. The first performance, though slightly irregular, seems fairly plausible (as noted above, we do not expect human performance to be perfectly accurate); the second performance seems much less likely. Cemgil et al. propose a procedure for estimating $P$(performance | score) based on experimental perception and production data. $P$(score) reflects the probability of a set of score-position labels. In Cemgil et al.'s model, this depends on the depth of rhythmic levels implied by the score positions; a score position of 5/16 implies a greater depth (hence lower probability) than 1/4. The model, at least in its fully specified version, is only capable of identifying score positions for very short (four-onset) rhythmic patterns.

In another study, Cemgil et al. (2000b) propose a "beat-tracking" system which derives a single level of tactus beats for a piece. Here, too, a Bayesian approach is used; the probability of a beat pattern or "tempo track" given an onset sequence depends on the prior probability of the tempo track and the probability of the onset sequence given the tempo track. $P$(tempo track) is estimated using a complex technique known as Kalman filtering; essentially, this favors a tempo track in which pulses are relatively evenly spaced. $P$(sequence | tempo track) is estimated by creating a "smoothed" representation of the pulses of the onset sequence, and multiplying this smoothed pulse train with the pulses of the tempo

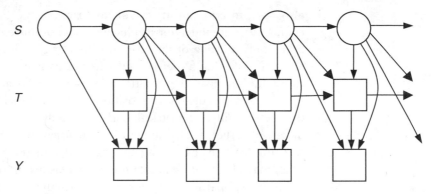

**Figure 3.4**
After Raphael 2002a. $S$ units represent score positions; $T$ units represent tempo values; $Y$ units represent positions of notes in time.

track; a more probable pulse sequence is one whose onsets are close to the pulses of the tempo track.

The model of Raphael (2002a) is similar to Cemgil et al.'s (2000a) model, in that it assigns score-positions (fractional positions within the measure) to a pattern of onsets. In this case the process is accomplished using a "graphical" probabilistic model (see figure 3.4). In such a model, the nodes represent events or states of the system, and the connections between nodes represent probabilistic dependencies between them.[2] The $S$ units in figure 3.4 represent score positions of notes; $T$ units represent tempo values (beats per minute); and $Y$ units are actual note locations in time (represented as time intervals from the previous note). The probability of a note $S_n$ occurring at a particular score position depends on the score position, and also on the position of the previous note ($S_{n-1}$). (The distribution of $S_n \mid S_{n-1}$ is gathered from actual musical data.) The probability of tempo unit $T_n$ having a certain tempo depends mainly on the tempo of the previous unit (though this distribution is also affected by the distance between $S_n$ and $S_{n-1}$). The exact time of the note $Y_n$ (in relation to the previous note) is then a function of $T_n$, the score position of the previous note $S_{n-1}$, and the score position of the current note $S_n$. In determining the meter of a pattern, the model is given the note locations, and must determine the hidden score positions and tempo values; this can be done, in Bayesian fashion, using knowledge of the graphical network.

The models of Cemgil et al. and Raphael are important contributions to the probabilistic modeling of meter perception. However, they are also open to criticism in several important ways. First, neither Cemgil et al.'s (2000a) model nor Raphael's model produces an explicit metrical grid—only a listing of the score position of each note in relation to the measure. Inferring a metrical grid from this may be nontrivial in some cases; for example, the notations in figures 3.1B and C would be the same in terms of their score-position representations (0–1/2–2/3–1), but they reflect different metrical grids. (Cemgil et al.'s [2000a] model, as discussed earlier, is also limited in that it can only analyze very simple rhythmic patterns.) Ignoring the metrical grid (in particular the tactus level) may also be undesirable for other reasons. It appears that the tactus level has particular importance in rhythmic timing, as the "time-keeper" level from which other levels are generated (Shaffer 1984). In Cemgil et al.'s (2000b) model, the tactus level *is* represented, but in this case there is no representation of lower or upper levels. In contrast to these models, the model presented below generates an explicit three-level metrical grid. Cemgil et al's (2000a) model and Raphael's model are also highly complex, involving a large number of parameters; I will try to show here that meter-finding can be done quite effectively with far fewer parameters. On the other hand, the current model itself leaves considerable room for improvement (as will be seen below). The best way of modeling rhythm perception probabilistically remains to be determined, and may well combine ideas from all of these models.

## 3.3 A Probabilistic Rhythm Model

In what follows, I propose a new probabilistic model of meter perception. The input to the model is a list of notes, representing the pitch (in integer notation, middle C = 60), and ontime and offtime (both in milliseconds) of each note. (The input is assumed to be monophonic.)

Our approach here follows the logic of Bayesian modeling, as presented in section 2.2. The task is to infer a structure from a surface; in this case, the surface is a pattern of note-onsets and the structure is a metrical grid. We saw earlier that the probability of a structure given a surface depends on the prior probability of the structure and the probability of the surface given the structure (see equation 2.16). In terms of the current framework:

$$P(\text{grid} \,|\, \text{onset pattern}) \propto P(\text{onset pattern} \,|\, \text{grid})P(\text{grid}) \qquad (3.1)$$

The grid that maximizes the expression on the right will be the most probable one given the onset pattern. In order to infer the most probable grid, then, we must have a *generative* model of rhythm—a model in-

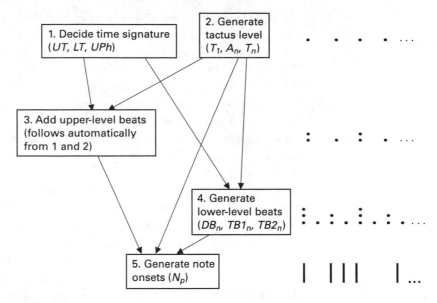

**Figure 3.5**
A schematic diagram of the generative process, showing variables set at each stage.

dicating the probabilities of different grids being generated, and the probabilities of different onset patterns arising given a grid.[3] (This generative model—like those presented in later chapters—is not intended as a model of the creative process, only as a model of how listeners might model that process for the purposes of meter perception.) In presenting the rhythm model, then, I begin by sketching the generative process that is assumed.

**3.4
The Generative Process**

The generative process creates a three-leveled metrical grid, with a tactus level (level 2), a higher level (level 3) and a lower level (level 1). It then uses this grid to generate a pattern of onsets. The process is shown schematically in figure 3.5. We assume a line of timepoints called "pips," occurring at 50-msec intervals; beats and note-onsets may only occur at pips.

The process begins with several basic decisions concerning the metrical structure. Like all decisions in the generative process, these decisions can be thought of as random variables controlled by distributions. (The way these distributions are set will be described shortly.) The first variable,

*UT*, dictates whether the upper level of the time signature (level 3) is duple (in which case every second level 2 beat is a level 3 beat) or triple (in which case every third level 2 beat is a level 3 beat). Another variable, *UPh*, controls the "phase" of level 3 in relation to level 2—that is, whether the first level 3 beat in the piece is the first, second, or third level 2 beat. (The third option is only possible when level 3 is triple.) The variable *LT* dictates whether level 2 is duple or triple in relation to level 1; that is, whether 1 or 2 level 1 beats elapse between each pair of level 2 beats. In this case, the phase is assumed to be 0, that is, the first level 1 beat is always a level 2 beat. (As shown in figure 3.2, these duple/triple decisions correspond to different musical time signatures: for example, a grid with a triple upper level and a duple lower level represents 3/4 time.) The tactus level (level 2) is then generated. (The generation of the tactus level is independent of the "time-signature" decisions described above; see figure 3.5.) First a beat is placed at time zero. The variable $T_1$ then dictates the length of the first "tactus interval" (the interval between adjacent tactus beats), and hence the location of the second beat. Subsequent tactus intervals are then assigned by variables $T_n$ using a distribution which dictates the probability of each tactus interval, given the previous interval $T_{n-1}$. At each tactus beat, the variable $A_n$ (for "another") dictates whether to generate another beat at all or to simply end the tactus level.

Once the tactus level is generated, level 3 beats are then defined (as a subset of the tactus beats); this follows automatically given the location of the tactus beats and the phase and period of the upper level. The determination of level 1 beats is more complex; every level 2 beat is also a level 1 beat, but additional level 1 beats must be located in between. If level 2 is duple, variables $DB_n$ represent the position of each lower-level beat in relation to the previous tactus beat. If level 2 is triple, there are two variables for each tactus beat, $TB1_n$ and $TB2_n$, representing the locations of the two lower-level beats.

The process of generating a metrical structure, as presented above, involves a number of probabilistic parameters: for example, the probability of the upper level being duple versus triple. How should these parameters be set? One of the premises of the current study, as described in chapter 1, is that listeners learn probabilities from regularities in their environment. Thus, in modeling a listener's rhythmic perception—for example, the probability they assign for a piece being in duple versus triple meter—we should assume that the probabilities roughly reflect the distribution of time signatures in music they have heard. Of course, it is not really possible to capture these probabilities precisely; the listener's experience involves many different kinds of music and varies greatly from one listener to another. Here we adopt a rather idealized approach to this problem: We derive the model's parameters from a corpus of European folk songs, The Essen Folksong Collection (Schaffrath 1995).[4] The corpus, containing 6,217 songs from different regions of Europe, is available in a computationally encoded format known as "Kern" format, showing notes with pitches and rhythmic values, time signatures, barlines, and other information (Huron 1999).

Using the Essen corpus, we can derive a number of the model's parameters empirically. For example, what is the probability of a song having a duple versus triple upper level? This was measured in the Essen corpus by counting the occurrences of different time signatures. The time signatures 4/4, 2/4, and 6/8 (along with several less common ones) imply a duple upper level, while 3/4 implies a triple upper level. It was found that .76 of songs have a duple upper level; thus, $P(UT = \text{upper}) = .76$. (It then follows automatically that $P(UT = \text{triple}) = 1 - .76 = .24$.) In a similar way, information was gathered regarding the lower level; time signatures 4/4, 2/4, and 3/4 all imply a duple tactus level, while 6/8 implies a triple tactus level. Data was also gathered about the phase of the upper level: How many tactus beats elapse before the first upper level beat. The resulting parameter values (along with others discussed below) are shown in table 3.1.

Other parameters of the model could not so easily be set using the Essen corpus. Recall that the model needs a distribution to dictate the length of the first tactus interval (we will call this the "$T_1$ distribution"), and another one to dictate the probabilities for each subsequent tactus interval, given the previous interval (the "$T_n \mid T_{n-1}$ distribution"). It also needs a distribution to dictate the placement of lower-level beats (the "lower-level distribution"). Here, we encounter issues of music performance. It is widely assumed (and has been shown in music psychology) that tactus intervals tend to be within a certain absolute range, centered around 700 msec or so (Lerdahl and Jackendoff 1983; Parncutt 1994); it is also well known that tactus intervals tend to remain roughly regular (varying only slightly and gradually) within a piece (Shaffer 1984; Large and Kolen 1994; Cemgil et al. 2000b). To capture these tendencies, we use the following function ($T_n$ and $T_{n-1}$ are measured in pips):

$$P(T_n \mid T_{n-1}) = 0.0 \qquad \text{for } T_n < 9 \text{ or } T_n > 22$$

$$= \exp(-(0.5 \times (T_n - T_{n-1}))^2) \quad \text{otherwise} \qquad (3.2)$$

**Table 3.1**
The parameters used by the meter-finding model.

| Variable | Probabilities |
|---|---|
| $UT$: Duple or triple upper level? | |
| $\quad P(UT = \text{duple})$ | .76 |
| $\quad P(UT = \text{triple})$ | .24 |
| $LT$: Duple or triple lower-level? | |
| $\quad P(LT = \text{duple})$ | .78 |
| $\quad P(LT = \text{triple})$ | .22 |
| $UPh$: Phase of upper level (if $UPh = n$, the $n$th level 2 beat is a level 3 beat) | |
| $\quad P(UPh = 1 \mid UT = \text{duple})$ | .65 |
| $\quad P(UPh = 2 \mid UT = \text{duple})$ | .35 |
| $\quad P(UPh = 1 \mid UT = \text{triple})$ | .33 |
| $\quad P(UPh = 2 \mid UT = \text{triple})$ | .667 |
| $\quad P(UPh = 3 \mid UT = \text{triple})$ | .003 |
| $A_n$: Generating another tactus beat? | |
| $\quad P(A_n = \text{yes})$ | .95 |
| $\quad P(A_n = \text{no})$ | .05 |
| $T_1$: Initial tactus interval (in pips) | |
| $\quad P(T_1 = i)$ for $i = \{9, 10, 11, 12, 13,$ $14, 15, 16, 17, 18, 19, 20, 21, 22\}$ | $\{.1, .2, .3, .23, .13, .03, .006, .002, .001,$ $.0006, .0002, .0001, .00005, .00005\}$ |
| $T_n$: Non-initial tactus intervals (in pips) | |
| $\quad P(T_n \mid T_{n-1})$ | |
| $\qquad$ for $T_n < 9$ or $T_n > 22$ | 0.0 |
| $\qquad$ otherwise | $\exp(-(0.5 \times ((T_n - T_{n-1}))^2)$ (These scores are normalized to sum to 1 for a given $T_{n-1}$) |

Location of lower-level beats (represented as intervals from the previous tactus beat. $T_n$ is the current tactus interval. All values are in pips. $T_n/2$, etc., are rounded down to the nearest integer)

$\quad DB_n$ (Duple lower-level beat): $P(DB_n) = F(|DB_n - (T_n/2)|)$
$\quad TB1_n$ (Triple lower-level, first lower-level beat): $P(TB1_n) = F(|TB1_n - (T_n/3)|)$
$\quad TB2_n$ (Triple lower-level, second lower-level beat): $P(TB2_n) = F(|TB2_n - ((2 \times T_n)/3)|)$

| | |
|---|---|
| $\quad F(0)$ | .32 |
| $\quad F(1)$ | .24 |
| $\quad F(2)$ | .08 |
| $\quad F(3)$ | .02 |
| $\quad F(i)$ for all $i > 3$ | .0 |
| | (These scores are normalized to sum to 1 for each variable) |

**Table 3.1**
(continued)

| Variable | Probabilities |
|---|---|
| $N_p$: Probabilities of note-onsets at pips, given the beat level of the pip, $BS_p$. $BS_p = 0$ indicates the pip is not a beat at all. | |
| $P(N_p = \text{yes} \mid BS_p = 3)$ | .95 |
| $P(N_p = \text{yes} \mid BS_p = 2)$ | .74 |
| $P(N_p = \text{yes} \mid BS_p = 1)$ | .38 |
| $P(N_p = \text{yes} \mid BS_p = 0)$ | .01 |
| $P(N_p = \text{yes} \mid \text{first tactus beat})$ | .6 |
| $P(N_p = \text{no}) = 1 - P(N_p = \text{yes})$ | |

These scores are then normalized so that they sum to 1 for a given $T_{n-1}$. This formula dictates that, given a tactus interval of length $l$, the probability for the following interval follows a bell-shaped or "normal" distribution centered around $l$. (The distribution for $T_n$ given a previous interval of 700 msec is shown in figure 3.6.) In this way, we capture the preference for regularity within the tactus. However, there is also a global constraint which prevents tactus intervals from ever becoming greater than 22 pips (1100 msec) or less than 9 pips (450 msec).[5]

Regarding the lower-level distribution, we define the most probable location for a duple lower-level beat to be roughly halfway between the tactus beats on either side, with deviations from this being increasingly improbable (again, a normal distribution is used). For triple lower-level beats, a similar approach is used, with an equal division of the tactus interval (into three parts) again being most probable.

With the metrical grid now complete, a series of note-onsets is generated. Like beats, note-onsets may only occur at pips. Each pip is governed by a variable, $N_p$, representing whether or not a note-onset occurs there. The probability of a note at a pip depends only on whether or not there is a beat at that pip, and if so, what its level or "strength" is. These parameters, too, were set using the Essen database, by looking at the proportion of beats at which note-onsets occur. It was found that upper-level beats have coinciding notes 95% of the time, tactus-level beats have notes 74% of the time, and lower-level beats have notes 38% of the time (see table 3.1). (In this case, a tactus-level beat was defined as a level 2 beat that is not also a level 3 beat; similarly with lower-level beats.) This data strongly reflects the conventional wisdom that stronger beats

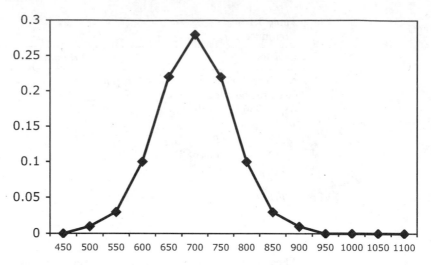

**Figure 3.6**
Probabilities for a tactus interval $T_n$ (in msec) given a previous interval $T_{n-1}$ of 700 msec.

are more likely to have note-onsets than lower-level beats (Lerdahl and Jackendoff 1983; Palmer and Krumhansl 1990). A special parameter was set for the first tactus beat; since the grid is always assumed to begin with a tactus beat, a song with no note on this beat in effect has a sub-tactus "upbeat." One further parameter is needed: the probability of a note occurring on a pip that is not a beat at all. This information could not be gathered empirically (since it is not known how many pips there will be in a song), so it was estimated using trial-and-error testing as .01.

**3.5
The Meter-Finding
Process**

Using the procedure just described, we can stochastically generate a metrical grid and a pattern of note-onsets based on that grid. Our ultimate aim, however, is not to generate grids and rhythms, but to incorporate this generative process into an *analytical* process which infers the metrical structure of a melody. We now turn to a description of this process. The meter-finding process has knowledge of the generative model presented in the previous section (along with the parameters), and uses this knowledge in a Bayesian fashion to determine the most likely metrical grid given a monophonic pattern of onsets.

As noted earlier, the grid maximizing $P(\text{grid} \mid \text{onset pattern})$ will be the one maximizing $P(\text{onset pattern} \mid \text{grid})P(\text{grid})$. To rigorously find the most probable grid for an onset pattern, this latter quantity must be calculated for all possible grids. For a given grid—specifying beats at particular pips—this could be done quite easily, using knowledge of the generative process. We can calculate the prior probability of a grid as the product of the probabilities for all the decisions that went into its generation. We can also easily calculate the probability of the onset pattern given the grid, as the product of the $P(N_p)$ values for all pips. Using the variables defined in the previous section, $P(\text{onset pattern} \mid \text{grid})P(\text{grid})$ can thus be expressed as follows:

$P(\text{onset pattern} \mid \text{grid})P(\text{grid})$

$$= P(UT) \times P(LT) \times P(UPh) \times P(T_1)$$

$$\times \prod_2^t P(A_n) \times \prod_2^{t-1} P(T_n \mid T_{n-1}) \times \prod_1^{t-1} P(DB_n) \times \prod_1^q P(N_p) \qquad (3.3)$$

where the symbol $\prod$ means "product"; $t =$ the number of tactus beats in the piece; $q =$ the number of pips in the piece; and other variables are as defined in the previous section. (In a piece with a triple lower level, $P(DB_n)$ would be replaced by $P(TB1_n) \times P(TB2_n)$, representing the two lower-level beats within each tactus interval.)

Unfortunately, performing this process for all possible metrical grids is neither computationally feasible nor psychologically plausible. There is a combinatorially huge number of different grids to choose from, with beats at different timepoints; we cannot simply consider them all one by one. The problem is tractable, however, due to certain independence assumptions in the generative process. What follows in the remainder of this section is a description of how this problem is solved. This procedure is rather complex, and is not essential for understanding what follows; the essential point is simply that the model determines, for a given onset pattern, the grid maximizing $P(\text{onset pattern} \mid \text{grid})P(\text{grid})$.

We can best approach the problem by first forgetting about notes, and simply considering metrical grids in isolation. First, how can we identify the most probable tactus level over a given span of time? Here we can use an approach known as dynamic programming (see figure 3.7). We proceed left to right; at each pip $i$, we consider each pip $j$ as a possible previous tactus beat (within the allowable range for tactus intervals), and we determine the best (most probable) tactus level ending with a tactus interval at $(j, i)$.[6] The probability of a tactus interval $(j, i)$ depends on

Melody I: The Rhythm Model

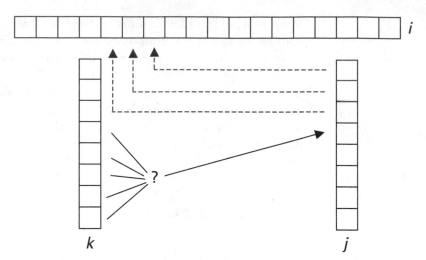

**Figure 3.7**
The dynamic programming table used to compute the tactus level. Columns correspond to pips; cells within each column correspond to previous pips (as indicated by the dotted arrows); thus each cell represents a possible tactus interval $(j, i)$. We proceed through the pips left-to-right. To fill in a cell of the table, we must compute the best analysis ending with beats at $j$ and $i$, $TA_{j,i}$. To do this, we must consider adding a beat at $i$ on to each possible $TA_{k,j}$, also factoring in $P(T_n = i - j \mid T_{n-1} = j - k)$. After choosing the best analysis, we record the score for that analysis and the $k$ that it entails. At the end of the piece, we choose the best analysis in the final column, and trace that inductively back through the piece.

the previous tactus interval (as defined in equation 3.2), so for each possible previous tactus beat $k$, we must consider the best analysis ending with the tactus interval $(k, j)$ (already calculated), factoring in the probability of a further beat at $i$. We choose the $k$ that yields the best score, remembering this $k$; this is now our best analysis ending in $(j, i)$. When we get to the end of the piece (the offset of the last note is assumed to be the last tactus beat location), some $(j, i)$ has the highest-scoring analysis overall, and this can be traced back inductively to yield the best tactus analysis.

This process must now be expanded to incorporate the notes, as well as the lower-level beats. Consider a single (conjectural) tactus interval, $(j, i)$. We know that note-onsets occur at certain pips within the interval, possibly including a note at pip $i$; call this the "note pattern" for the tactus interval. (We disregard the possibility of a note at pip $j$; this is considered part of the previous tactus interval.) The probability of notes being generated within this interval depends only on the beat structure: the location of the tactus beats (which we know), their strength (assume they are level 2 beats, though they might also be level 3, as discussed below), and the location of possible level 1 beats in between. If we assume that level 2 is duple, we can consider all possible locations for the intervening level 1 beat; for each possible location, we calculate the probability of a level 1 beat being generated there, along with the probability of the note pattern given level 2 and level 1 beats at the assumed locations. The level 1 beat location yielding the highest score is then the "best duple analysis" for the interval $(j, i)$. Now this score can simply be factored into the score for $(j, i)$ in the dynamic-programming process described above (assuming that level 2 is duple). Since the best duple analysis of $(j, i)$ does not depend in any way on beats or notes outside of this interval, it only needs to be calculated once; this is done for each possible tactus interval before the dynamic-programming process begins. Triple analyses are similarly calculated, and the whole search process is then run twice, once for a duple tactus level and once for a triple tactus level.

The search process just described yields the best analysis for levels 1 and 2, given the note pattern. We have not yet considered level 3 beats. The strength of a tactus beat (whether it is level 2 or 3) affects the probability of a note being generated at that point; so we must generate tactus-interval analyses for both of these possibilities. Then, in doing the dynamic-programming search, we must consider the possibility of each $(j, i)$ interval being at each possible position in the grid—for example, a 3/4 analysis with a level 3 beat at $i$—adding it on to the appropriate $(k, j)$ analyses and factoring in the appropriate tactus-interval analysis. At the end of the process, we have the best possible analysis for each upper-level period and phase, and we can compare them and choose the best one.

We should note, in passing, that this search procedure essentially operates in a "left-to-right" manner—analyzing the piece as it unfolds in time. (The process does involve the preliminary step of calculating lower-level analyses for each tactus interval, but this could quite easily be incorporated into the left-to-right process as well.) In this way, the model could be considered as a model of metrical analysis as it actually occurs during listening. I will not explore this possibility here, but leave it as a topic for further investigation.

An example of the model's output is shown in figure 3.8, for one of the songs in the Essen corpus. The correct notation is shown at the top; the model's output is shown below. The output shows each pip, represented

```
                             x                               x
         x                   x                x              x
         x         x         x         x      x       x      x       x
  0 | G o o o o o o o o o | o C o o o o o o o o | o o B o o o o A o o | o o G o o o o o G o
                             x                                                          x
         x                   x                x              x              x           x
         x         x         x         x      x       x      x       x      x           x
 40 | o o o o C o o o o o | o o o o G o o o o o | E o o o o F o o o o | o G o o o o o o E o o
                             x                         x                    x
         x                   x                x        x                    x
         x         x         x         x      x        x         x          x         x
 80 | o o o o o o o o F o | o o o o D o o o o E | o o o o o o o o o o | F o o o o D o o o o
         x                                     x              x             x
         x                   x                 x             x              x
         x         x         x         x       x             x       x      x            x
120 | o E o o o o o o o o | o o o D o o o o o o | o o o C o o o o o o | o o o o o o o o o o
         x                            x               x              x            x
         x                   x        x       x       x       x      x            x
         x         x         x        x       x       x       x      x            x
160 | o o o o o o o o o o | o o o o o o o C o o | o o o C o o o o B o | o o o D o o o o o C
                             x                        x              x
         x                   x                x       x              x            x
         x         x         x        x       x       x       x      x            x
200 | o o o o A o o o o o | B o o o o o o o o o | o A o o o o o o o o | o o o o G o o o o o
                             x                        x
         x                   x                x       x
         x         x         x        x       x       x
240 | o o o o o o o o o o | o o o o o o o
```

**Figure 3.8**
"Deut1334," from the Essen Folksong Collection, showing the model's metrical analysis.

either with a note-name (if a note occurs there) or with "o" (if no note occurs); the metrical grid is indicated above that, showing the three metrical levels with x's. Vertical bars mark every tenth pip, indicating 500-msec intervals.

One remaining problem is to determine the overall probability of an onset pattern. From equation 2.8, we can see that for any surface,

$$P(\text{surface}) = \sum_{\text{structure}} P(\text{surface} \mid \text{structure}) P(\text{structure}) \tag{3.4}$$

In terms of the current model:

$$P(\text{onset pattern}) = \sum_{\text{grid}} P(\text{onset pattern} \mid \text{grid}) P(\text{grid}) \tag{3.5}$$

We formulated an expression for $P(\text{onset pattern} \mid \text{grid})P(\text{grid})$ in equation 3.3 above. In theory, we could compute this quantity for all grids and sum them together; this cannot be done in practice, due to the enormous number of possible grids. Here again, we can use a dynamic-programming strategy. Briefly, at each tactus interval $(j, i)$, we now compute the total probability of *all* analyses up to that point ending in $(j, i)$. For each tactus interval, we must also compute the total probability of all duple analyses and all triple analyses of that interval given the note pattern. The dynamic-programming process then yields the total probability of all metrical grids arising in combination with the note pattern. Probabilities for different time signatures and phases simply sum together.[7] The significance of $P(\text{onset pattern})$ will be considered in chapter 5.

**3.6**
**Testing the Model**
**on Meter-Finding**

Now that we have a meter-finding model, the next step is to test it. The test presented below uses a 65-song subset of the Essen Folksong Collection— the same corpus used for setting the model's parameters.[8] (This test set was *not* included in the corpus used for parameter-setting.) The Essen corpus represents rhythms in a symbolic fashion, similar to rhythmic notation. Given such data, one could generate performances of the melodies straight from the data, with perfectly regular timing. However, it seemed preferable to use input which reflected the irregular and complex timing of human performance. Thus the 65 melodies were performed by a semi-professional pianist (myself) on a MIDI keyboard; files for each melody showing the pitch, ontime, and offtime of each note were then generated from these performances.

In testing a meter-finding model, we encounter the difficult problem of how to judge the correctness of a metrical grid. This presumably involves measuring its similarity to the correct metrical grid, but it is not clear exactly how that should be done. One may judge a grid simply on whether its "time signature" is correct (the duple/triple relationships between levels), but ideally one would also judge it in terms of the exact placement of beats in relation to the notes. (Two analyses could have the same grids, but aligned in different ways with the music; compare figures 3.1A, D, and E, for example.)

One solution to this problem is an evaluation system that I have proposed elsewhere (Temperley 2004a), the "note-address" system. Under this scheme, each note is assigned an address representing its position in the correct metrical grid. A note address is an $(N + 1)$-digit number, where $N$ is the number of levels in the grid. Each digit represents the

Melody I: The Rhythm Model

| Ontime | Offtime | Pitch | Note Address |
|--------|---------|-------|--------------|
| 0 | 502 | 57 | 10000 |
| 475 | 942 | 54 | 11000 |
| 936 | 1317 | 57 | 12000 |
| 1405 | 1864 | 57 | 20000 |
| 1868 | 2073 | 55 | 21000 |
| 2080 | 2343 | 54 | 21100 |
| 2339 | 2631 | 55 | 22000 |
| 2826 | 3297 | 55 | 30000 |
| 3285 | 3768 | 52 | 31000 |
| 3755 | 4253 | 55 | 32000 |
| 4228 | 4474 | 54 | 40000 |
| 4476 | 4722 | 52 | 40100 |
| 4703 | 4954 | 54 | 41000 |
| 4946 | 5163 | 55 | 41100 |
| 5181 | 5514 | 57 | 42000 |

**Figure 3.9**
"Deut0214," from the Essen corpus, mm. 1–4, showing note-addresses for the correct metrical analysis. Ontimes and offtimes (in milliseconds) represent the performance used for testing.

number of beats at the corresponding level (call it level $L_n$) that have elapsed at that timepoint (the timepoint of the note's onset) since the last beat at level $L_{n+1}$: if the most recent $L_n$ beat is a $L_{n+1}$ beat, the digit is 0; if it is the first $L_n$ beat after an $L_{n+1}$ beat, the number is 1; if it is the second, the number is 2. The leftmost digit corresponds to the highest metrical level and simply counts beats at that level (this number may grow to two or more digits as the piece progresses); the rightmost digit indicates whether the note corresponds with a beat at all. Figure 3.9 shows an example. To evaluate a metrical model's analysis of a piece, we can convert its analysis to note-addresses and compare these with the correct ones. One could simply evaluate the model in terms of the proportion of notes that are assigned the correct address; alternatively, and more revealingly, separate scores can be assigned for each digit, indicating the proportion of notes correctly labeled at level 1, level 2, and so on. In comparing two note-address lists, the highest level of the addresses is redundant, since any difference at this level will result in differences at the next lower level; thus the highest level is ignored in the evaluation process.

The rhythm model was evaluated using the Essen test set described earlier. The model's analyses of the songs were converted to note-address

**Table 3.2**
Tests of the Bayesian meter-finding model and the Melisma model on the Essen folksong test set, using the note-address evaluation system.

| Model | Level 2 | Level 1 | Level 0 | Overall score |
|---|---|---|---|---|
| Bayesian model | 0.701 | 0.709 | 0.967 | 0.793 |
| Melisma model | 0.736 | 0.885 | 0.975 | 0.865 |

lists, and these were compared with correct note-address lists. Since the model only generates three metrical levels, the addresses have four digits; the rightmost one is the "extrametrical" digit, indicating whether the note coincides with any beat at all. The correct addresses reflect levels for however many levels are specified in the notation; however, we only consider the levels of the correct addresses that correspond to levels in the model's addresses. (One problem here is that the rightmost—"extrametrical"—digit in the model's addresses might correspond to the "sixteenth-note" digit in the correct addresses. For present purposes, we simply assume that the extrametrical digit in the model's addresses really represents sixteenth-notes; that is, every note that the model does not place on an eighth-note beat is assumed to be placed on a sixteenth-note beat.)

Table 3.2 shows the results. One slightly counterintuitive thing about the note-address system is that the addresses at one level really indicate the placement of beats at the corresponding metrical level and the level immediately above. Thus the level 0 score reflects the placement of the level 1 beats, the level 1 score reflects levels 1 and 2, and the level 2 score reflects levels 2 and 3. Roughly speaking, the results suggest that the placement of level 1 beats is highly accurate; the placement of level 2 and level 3 beats is somewhat less so. The overall score simply reflects the average of the scores for all three levels.

**3.7**
**Problems and**
**Possible**
**Improvements**

It is difficult to assess the rhythm model's level of performance on this test. While a large number of metrical models have been proposed, only a few have been tested in any systematic way, and none have been tested on a corpus of performed melodies similar to the one used here.[9] By way of comparison, the corpus was also given to the Melisma metrical model of Temperley and Sleator (1999; see also Temperley 2001a); the Melisma model obtained somewhat better results (see table 3.2). The Melisma model will not be described in detail here; like the current probabilistic

Melody I: The Rhythm Model

**Figure 3.10**
An excerpt from "Oestr102" from the Essen corpus. (A) The correct analysis; (B) the model's analysis.

model, it operates by considering many analyses of the entire piece and evaluating them numerically, using mostly the same criteria as the current model, and using a very similar dynamic-programming search strategy. However, it is much more ad hoc, and is not constrained—as the current model is—by the need to make everything interpretable in probabilistic terms. One important difference between the Melisma model and the current model is that the former also considers the length of notes in evaluating them as possible beat locations; this will be discussed further below.[10]

We can also evaluate the probabilistic model, and get a sense of some of the problems that arise, by examining its individual analyses. On many of the songs, the model's output is essentially perfect. Figure 3.8 gives one example; the model finds the correct time signature (duple upper level and duple tactus) and the correct upper-level phase (the first level 3 beat occurs on the second level 2 beat), and places all tactus and lower-level beats in the correct positions. In other cases, however, the model made significant errors—choosing the wrong meter altogether, or getting the right meter but with the beats in the wrong places. In some of these cases, it seemed clear that other kinds of musical information would be needed in order to achieve the right analysis. One important factor in meter perception is repeated patterns (a factor sometimes known as "parallelism"); there is a strong preference to align the meter with patterns so that strong beats occur at the same location in each instance of the pattern (Temperley and Bartlette 2002). In the melody shown in figure 3.10, the model identified a "quarter-note" tactus (with beats on every second note), but a human listener would probably have detected the repeated three-note pattern and thus identified the correct "dotted-quarter-note" tactus. Harmony is sometimes a factor in meter as well, in that there is a preference to locate strong beats on clear

**Figure 3.11**
The opening of "Ukrain11," from the Essen corpus. (A) The correct analysis; (B) the model's analysis.

changes in harmony (Lerdahl and Jackendoff 1983; Temperley 2001a). In a few cases, it appears that consideration of harmony would have avoided errors made by the model.

A number of other factors have been shown to affect the perception of meter. In general, anything that gives accentuation or emphasis to an event can make it a preferred beat location. Harmonic change is one example; loudness is another (we tend to locate strong beats on louder notes, other things being equal); linguistic stress is another (in music that is sung with text). Such sources of accentuation are sometimes known as "phenomenal accents" (Lerdahl and Jackendoff 1983). Considering loudness and linguistic stress would not help with the current input materials, of course, since this information is not represented.

One kind of phenomenal accent that *is* relevant in the current context is note length. It is a well-established principle of rhythm perception that there is a tendency to infer stronger beats on longer notes (Lerdahl and Jackendoff 1983; Lee 1991). (In work on meter perception, the length of a note is generally defined as its "inter-onset interval"—the distance from its onset to the onset of the next note.) In the melody in figure 3.11, for example, the model placed a strong (level 3) beat on the first note, but a human listener would probably have favored the second note as a strong-beat location due to its greater length. As noted earlier, the Melisma meter-finding model does consider note length, and this may account in part for its superior performance. How could one incorporate this factor into a probabilistic meter-finding model? One way to do this was proposed by Raphael (2002a). In Raphael's meter-finding model (discussed earlier), the generative process involves a sequence of score-time decisions; at each point, the model is deciding whether the next note should be at 1/4, 1/3, 3/8, and so on. This decision is affected

Melody I: The Rhythm Model

by the score-times themselves (some may be more probable event locations than others), but also by the score-time of the *previous* note; and this allows the length factor to be incorporated. For example, if the previous note is at 3/8, it might be highly probable to have a note at 1/2 (making the note at 3/8 a short note); by contrast, if the previous note is at 1/2, then the probability of the next note being one eighth-note later may be much lower. As discussed earlier, Raphael's model was based on statistical data gathered from a corpus, recording the frequency of each "$S_n | S_{n-1}$" transition—the number of times an event at 3/8 was followed by one at 1/2, and so on. While the sensitivity of Raphael's model to note length is certainly a virtue, one wonders if this factor could be incorporated in a more general way rather than simply as an emergent feature of a large number of different cases.

The current model operates by a fundamentally different principle than Raphael's: rather than choosing score-times for a series of notes, our generative process makes note decisions (onset or no onset) for a series of timepoints. In this framework, it is not so easy to incorporate the note-length factor. One could incorporate length into the note decisions, choosing the length of each note as it is generated and assigning a higher probability of long notes on stronger beats. But if the length of a note is defined in terms of inter-onset interval, then the note decisions made at different pips are no longer independent of one another; if a note of 10 pips in length occurs at one pip, then no note can occur at the following 9 pips.[11] What we need to do is relax the independence of note decisions in a controlled way. One way to address this problem would be to make the note status of lower-level beats dependent on that of higher-level beats. For example, we could give high probability to a note on a level 1 beat only if a note occurred on the following level 2 beat; this would then indirectly give low probability to "long" notes on level 1 beats. This would involve a fundamental reworking of the model, since notes would have to be generated in a hierarchical fashion, with higher-level notes generated first. This solution is currently under investigation but will not be pursued further here.

Clearly, the model leaves considerable room for improvement. Its level of performance, while respectable, is significantly below that of the Melisma model (Temperley and Sleator 1999). However, I believe it is still of interest, for several reasons. The probabilistic basis of the model gives it a rational foundation which the much more ad hoc Melisma model did not have. The fact that this probabilistic approach—which has yielded successful models of speech recognition, syntactic parsing, and visual processes—can also be applied successfully to the meter-finding problem gives it further plausibility as a general hypothesis about the workings of the human mind. The probabilistic approach also sheds light on other issues relating to rhythm and meter. In particular, as noted above, the model offers a very natural way of calculating the probability of a rhythmic *surface* (a pattern of onsets); the implications of this will be explored in chapter 5.

Two further issues require brief comment. First, since most of the music we hear is polyphonic, not monophonic, it is important to consider how well the current probabilistic approach might apply to polyphonic music. It seems clear that the same basic principles assumed here also apply in polyphonic situations: beats are roughly evenly spaced, and event-onsets are more likely to occur on stronger beats. The main difference is that multiple onsets must be allowed at a given point; the generative process would need to be modified to allow this possibility. (As in the monophonic case, the function for generating onsets at a timepoint seems to depend on the beat strength; a strong beat is surely more likely to have multiple onsets than a weaker beat.) Once this factor is incorporated, it appears that the current approach might apply quite well to polyphonic music; I hope to explore this possibility in the future.

The second issue concerns the musical domain to which the model applies. I stated earlier that the model is intended to capture "the rhythmic idiom of traditional European music." I would include in this category not only European folk music (the genre on which the model was actually tested), but classical music, hymns, Christmas carols, nursery tunes, and so on. I would not claim that rhythmic practice is *identical* in all of these styles, but certainly the basic principles are the same: for example, the general restriction to duple and triple meters, the tendency for note-onsets to be aligned with relatively strong beats, and the role of various kinds of phenomenal accent such as note length, harmonic change, and parallelism. With some other styles—for example, rock—one might find that rather different models were required. In fact, one of the benefits of the probabilistic approach is that it provides a systematic, quantitative way of describing stylistic differences; we will return to this issue in chapter 9.

# 4
# Melody II: The Pitch Model

In this chapter, we turn our attention from the temporal dimension of music to the pitch dimension, and in particular, to the concept of *key*. In many ways, key plays an analogous role in the pitch dimension to that of meter in the temporal dimension. The key of a piece provides the framework for our interpretation and understanding of pitches; this is evident in any music theory textbook, where notes and chords are generally discussed in terms of their relationship to the key, rather than in absolute terms. Experimental work has confirmed both the psychological reality of key and its important role in music perception (this research will be discussed further below). As with meter, the key of a piece is not usually acoustically indicated in any obvious way, but must be inferred by the listener. For that reason, the way that listeners identify key is an issue of great musical and psychological interest.

In this chapter, I present a probabilistic model of key perception, which I simply call the "pitch model." The model infers the key of a melody from the pitches; as such, it offers an account of this important cognitive process. The model also incorporates two other important principles of pitch organization, *pitch proximity* and *range*. As well as performing key identification, the pitch model—like the rhythm model presented earlier—can also be used to calculate the probability of a surface pattern (in this case, a sequence of pitches rather than a sequence of note-onset times). The implications of this will be explored in chapter 5.

Bear in mind that the model proposed here is concerned only with monophonic input. In chapter 6, I present a model of key perception in polyphonic music, where a rather different approach is required.

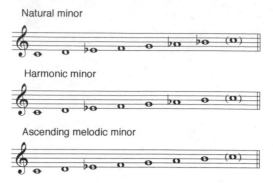

Natural minor

Harmonic minor

Ascending melodic minor

**Figure 4.1**
Three different "minor scales" (for the key of C minor).

**4.1**
**Previous Models of Key-Finding**

Since the modeling of key perception is one of the primary concerns of this book, we begin with a review of the extensive research on this subject. Experimental studies have shown, first of all, that listeners are sensitive to key and that there is a good deal of agreement in the way key is perceived. This has been shown, for example, in "probe-tone" studies where subjects are played a musical context (establishing a key) followed by a pitch and are asked to judge how well the tone fits the context; both musically trained and untrained listeners show sensitivity to which notes belong or do not belong in the key (Krumhansl 1990; Brown et al. 1994; Cuddy 1997). Studies have also explored the effect of key on other aspects of music cognition: it has been shown that key context determines the stability and hierarchical importance of pitches (Krumhansl and Kessler 1982; Palmer and Krumhansl 1987), affects the memory and recognition of melodies (Cuddy, Cohen, and Miller 1979; Cuddy, Cohen, and Mewhort 1981), and conditions our expectations for future events (Schmuckler 1989; Cuddy and Lunney 1995).

Other research has focused on the question of how listeners infer a key from a pattern of notes—a process sometimes known as "key-finding." A number of models of key-finding have been put forth, both in psychology and in artificial intelligence. Perhaps the first key-finding model was that of Longuet-Higgins and Steedman (1971), who proposed an algorithm for determining the key of a monophonic piece. Longuet-Higgins and Steedman's model is based on the conventional association between keys and scales. (This is problematic in minor keys, as there is more than one possible "minor scale"—see figure 4.1; Longuet-Higgins and Steedman assume the harmonic minor scale.) The model proceeds

A.

B.

**Figure 4.2**
(A) "The Star-Spangled Banner"; (B) "Ta-Ra-Ra-Boom-De-Ay."

left-to-right from the beginning of the melody; at each note, it eliminates all keys whose scales do not contain that note. When only one key remains, that is the chosen key. If the model gets to the end of the melody with more than one key remaining, it looks at the first note, and chooses the key of which that note is the tonic pitch (or, failing that, the dominant pitch). If at any point all keys have been eliminated, the "first-note" rule again applies. Longuet-Higgins and Steedman tested their model on the 48 fugue subjects of Bach's *Well-Tempered Clavier* and achieved correct results on every case. In many other cases, however, the model would not fare so well. In "The Star-Spangled Banner," for example (figure 4.2A), the first phrase seems to imply Bb major quite strongly, but the model would be undecided between Bb major, F major, and several other keys in terms of scales, and would choose F major based on the first-note rule. The model would also have trouble with chromatic notes (notes outside the scale); for example, the traditional melody "Ta-Ra-Ra-Boom-De-Ay" (figure 4.2B) clearly conveys a tonal center of C despite the chromatic F♯ and D♯.

A more robust approach to key-finding was proposed by Krumhansl and Schmuckler. The Krumhansl-Schmuckler (hereafter K-S) key-finding algorithm, described most fully by Krumhansl (1990), is based on a set of "key-profiles" representing the stability or compatibility of each pitch class relative to each key. The key-profiles are based on experiments by Krumhansl and Kessler (1982), in which subjects were played a key-establishing musical context such as a cadence or scale, followed by a probe-tone, and were asked to judge how well the probe-tone "fit" given the context (on a scale of 1 to 7, with higher ratings representing better fitness). This data was averaged across different contexts and keys to create a single major key-profile and minor key-profile, shown in

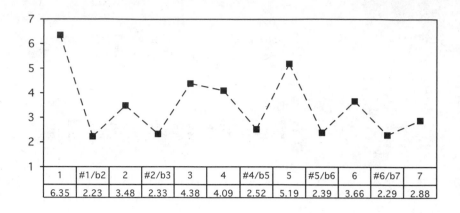

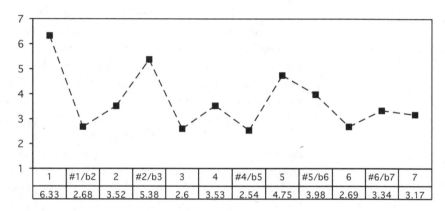

**Figure 4.3**
Key-profiles for major keys (above) and minor keys (below). From Krumhansl and Kessler 1982.

figure 4.3 (we will refer to these as the K-K profiles). Pitch-classes are identified in relative or "scale-degree" terms. In relation to C major, for example, C would be scale-degree $\hat{1}$, with a value of 6.35; C♯ would be $\sharp\hat{1}/\flat\hat{2}$, with a value of 2.23. The K-K key-profiles reflect well-established principles of music theory: in both the major and minor profiles, the tonic pitch is rated most highly, followed by other notes of the tonic triad, followed by other notes of the scale, followed by chromatic notes. (Notice that the minor-key profile seems to reflect the "natural minor" scale, as $\flat\hat{7}$ has a higher value than $\hat{7}$, though the difference is small.)

Given these profiles, the K-S algorithm judges the key of a piece by generating an "input vector"; this is, again, a twelve-valued vector, showing the total duration of each pitch-class in the piece. The correlation value, $r$, is then calculated between each key-profile vector and the input vector, using the standard correlation formula:

$$r = \frac{\sum (x - \bar{x})(y - \bar{y})}{\left(\sum (x - \bar{x})^2 \sum (y - \bar{y})^2\right)^{1/2}} \tag{4.1}$$

where $x$ = input vector values; $\bar{x}$ = the average of the input vector values; $y$ = the key-profile values for a given key; and $\bar{y}$ = the average key-profile value for that key. The key whose profile yields the highest correlation value is the preferred key. Essentially, the correlation formula takes the product of each input vector value with the corresponding key-profile value, and sums these products; this means that a key will score higher if the peaks of its key-profile (such as the tonic-triad notes) have high values in the input vector.

The key-profile paradigm has generated a great deal of interest and further research, and also raises some questions. First of all, we might ask whether the probe-tone responses in Krumhansl and Kessler's experiments (and others like them) really reflect listeners' internal representation of key. One might wonder if subjects are simply responding to the distribution of tones in the context—giving high ratings to tones that often occurred. However, this is clearly not the case; the response profiles in probe-tone studies are not usually a simple reflection of the distribution of tones in the context, and indeed, profiles very similar to those in figure 4.3 have been generated using quite different contexts, such as a scale, a major or minor triad, or a IV–V–I cadence (Krumhansl and Kessler 1982; Cuddy and Badertscher 1987). Thus key-profiles seem to represent a kind of permanent schematic knowledge that may be invoked by a musical context. This is not to say, however, that listeners are insensitive to pitch-class distribution; indeed, according to Krumhansl and Schmuckler, it is this that determines which key-profile will be invoked. This raises a further question: Assuming listeners possess internal key-profiles, how is this knowledge acquired? As Krumhansl (1990) has noted, the most plausible answer seems to be that it is acquired from statistical regularities in tonal music: the C major key-profile reflects the typical pitch-class distribution for C major. Again, this fits in well with the logic of the K-S algorithm; the algorithm only works because the

K-K key-profiles correspond fairly well with scale-degree distribution in actual music. We will return to this point in later sections.

Several variants of the K-S model have been proposed. One question left open by the model is how to handle modulation: the model can output a key judgment for any segment of music it is given, but how is it to detect changes in key? Krumhansl herself (1990) proposes a simple variant of the K-S model for this purpose, which outputs key judgments for each measure of a piece, based on the algorithm's judgment for that measure (using the basic K-S algorithm) combined with lower-weighted judgments for the previous and following measures. Huron and Parncutt (1993) present an "exponential decay" version of the K-S model, where the input vector at a given point in time represents all events of the piece so far, weighted under an exponential curve. Toivianen and Krumhansl (2003) adopt a similar approach; an input vector is created with events weighted under an exponential decay, and this is then used to plot the course of a piece through a four-dimensional space of keys (first proposed in Krumhansl and Kessler 1982). Shmulevich and Yli-Harja (2000) offer a different solution. Under their model, the piece is divided into very small slices, and key judgments are made for each slice using the usual K-S method. Slices are grouped together to form larger sections, the average position of all the slices in each section is calculated in Krumhansl and Kessler's four-dimensional key space, and the key is chosen that is closest to that average position.

A further variant of the K-S model was proposed in my book *The Cognition of Basic Musical Structures* (2001a), which I will call the "CBMS model." A number of revisions to the original K-S model were suggested. The original profiles of the model seemed problematic in certain respects—particularly the higher value for $\flat\hat{7}$ as opposed to $\hat{7}$ in the minor profile—and some adjustments were made, leading to improved performance. Another problem with the K-S model was that intensive repetition of a pitch-class within a short time-span seemed to give too much weight to that pitch-class (this point will be further discussed in chapter 6). To address this, I argued that the input should be divided into small segments, and an input vector calculated for each segment, in which each pitch-class gets a 1 if it is present and 0 if it is not. To calculate the match between an input vector and a key-profile, we simply add the key-profile values for the pitch-classes that score 1 in the input vector. The division of the piece into segments also allows the model to handle modulation. The CBMS model makes a key judgment for each segment, but imposes a change penalty if the key for one segment differs from the key for the previous segment. These penalties are then combined additively with the key-profile scores to choose the best key for each segment. This model actually relates very closely to the polyphonic key-finding model I present in chapter 6, and I will discuss it more fully there.

Several other key-finding models require brief mention. In Chew's (2002) model, pitches are located in a three-dimensional space, the "spiral array," formed by bending an infinite line of fifths into a spiral so that major thirds are vertically aligned. Every key is given a characteristic point in this space; the key of a passage of music can then be identified by finding the average position of all events in the space, and choosing the key whose "key point" is closest. Vos and Van Geenen's (1996) model, which only handles monophonic input, processes a melody in a left-to-right fashion; each pitch contributes points to each key whose scale contains the pitch or whose I, IV, or V7 chords contain it, and the highest-scoring key is the one chosen. (The key judgment at each point only considers the previous 40 notes; thus the model is capable of modulation.) Finally, Leman's (1995) model differs from the others presented so far, in that it derives key directly from an acoustic signal, rather than from a representation where notes have already been identified. The model is essentially a key-profile model, but in this case the input vector represents the strength of each pitch-class (and its harmonics) in the auditory signal. Key-profiles are generated in a similar fashion, based on the frequency content of the primary chords of each key. Input vectors are generated from short segments, and are then integrated over time; this allows the wider context to influence the model's judgments, and also allows changes in key. The model was tested on two pieces, scoring correct rates of 75–80% when compared against experts' key analyses.[1]

The models discussed so far might all be called "distributional" models, in that they focus on the frequency of occurrence of pitch-classes without much regard for their temporal placement or the patterns they form (though Longuet-Higgins and Steedman's "first-note" rule is an exception to this). While many have pursued the distributional approach, it is not without its critics. Some authors have argued that key identification involves a search for certain conventional patterns of pitches, in which temporal ordering is crucially important. Brown (1988) and Butler (1989) argue that tritone intervals are a powerful cue to key detection, and that this depends on the ordering of the pitches in time: the tritone F–B conveys a tonal center of C (implying scale-degrees "fa–ti") much more than B–F ("ti–fa").[2] Similarly, Vos (1999) suggests that an ascending fourth or descending fifth at the beginning of a melody is an important cue to key. While such cues may, indeed, play some role in key-finding, they are certainly not sufficient for a key-finding algorithm; many melodies contain neither a "fa–ti" tritone nor an opening ascending fourth or descending fifth. And there is, as yet, no proposal as to how such ordering cues might be integrated into a more general model of key identification. We will return to the issue of temporal ordering in section 6.5.

As can be seen from this survey, most work on key-finding has in some way been influenced by the "key-profile" idea. The two key-finding models presented in this book—the monophonic model in this chapter and the polyphonic model in chapter 6—continue in this tradition, but from a rather different perspective, the perspective of Bayesian probabilistic modeling.

## 4.2
## The Pitch Model

In this section, I present a probabilistic model of key-finding in monophonic music, which can also be used to evaluate the probability of a sequence of pitches. The input to the model is simply an ordered sequence of pitches; no timing information is used. (For convenience, we use the same input format as the rhythm model presented in chapter 3—showing pitch, ontime, and offtime for each note—but the ontime and offtime information is ignored.) Like the rhythm model, the pitch model uses Bayesian reasoning: we infer a structure (a key, in this case) from a surface (a sequence of pitches), based on assumptions about how surfaces are generated from structures. The model therefore assumes a certain generative process, which I will now describe.

To understand the logic of the generative process, let us begin with a very basic question: What kind of pitch sequence makes a likely melody? Perhaps the first principle that comes to mind is that a melody tends to be confined to a fairly limited range of pitches. Data was gathered about this from the Essen Folksong Collection—a corpus of 6,217 European folk songs, encoded with pitch and rhythmic information as well as key labels. As with the rhythm model, we use the entire Essen corpus (*except* for a 65-song test set) to set the parameters for the model. If we examine the overall distribution of pitches in the corpus (figure 4.4), we find a roughly bell-shaped or "normal" distribution, with the majority of pitches falling in the octave above C4 (middle C). (Following the usual convention, pitches are represented as integers, with C4 = 60.) Beyond this general constraint, however, there appears to be an additional constraint on the range of individual melodies. While the overall variance

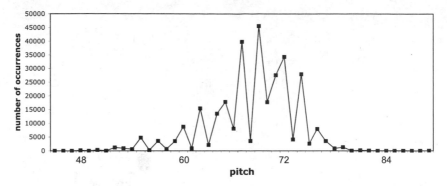

**Figure 4.4**
The distribution of pitches in the Essen Folksong Collection (middle C = 60).

A.

B.

**Figure 4.5**
(A) A stochastic melody generated from a "range profile." (B) A stochastic melody generated from an RPK key-profile like that in figure 4.8 (in this case the profile is generated anew at each note).

of pitches in the Essen corpus is 25.0, the variance of pitches within a melody—that is, with respect to the mean pitch of the melody—is 10.6. We can model this situation in a generative way by first choosing a central pitch $c$ for the melody; this is randomly chosen from a normal distribution, which we call the *central pitch profile*. (The central pitch of a melody is not the *tonal* center, but rather the center of the range.) We then create a second normal distribution centered around $c$, called the *range profile*. A melody can be constructed as a series of notes generated from the range profile.

A melody generated from a range profile—assuming a central pitch of 68 and variance of 10.6—is shown in figure 4.5A. While this melody is musically deficient in many ways, two problems are particularly apparent. One problem is that the melody contains a number of wide leaps be-

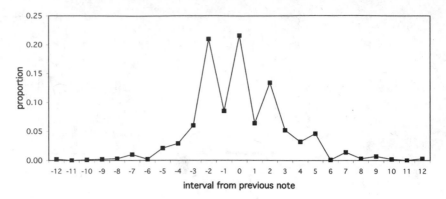

**Figure 4.6**
The distribution of melodic intervals in the Essen corpus. (For example, a value of −2 indicates a note two semitones below the previous note.)

tween pitches, especially toward the end. In general, intervals between adjacent notes in a melody are small; this phenomenon of *pitch proximity* has been amply demonstrated as a statistical tendency in actual melodies (von Hippel and Huron 2000; von Hippel 2000) and also as an assumption and preference in auditory perception (Miller and Heise 1950; Schellenberg 1996; Deutsch 1999). Figure 4.6 shows the distribution of "melodic intervals" in the Essen corpus—pitches in relation to the previous pitch; it can be seen that more than half of all intervals are 2 semitones or less. We can approximate this distribution with a *proximity profile*—a normal distribution centered around a given pitch, indicating the pitch probabilities for the following note. We then create a new distribution which is the product of the proximity profile and the range profile. In effect, this "range × proximity" profile favors melodies which maintain small note-to-note intervals, but also remain within a fairly narrow global range.

Before proceeding, a word is needed here about normal distributions. A normal distribution is defined mathematically as follows:

$$N(\mu, \sigma^2) = \frac{1}{\sigma(2\pi)^{1/2}} \exp(-(x - \mu)^2 / 2\sigma^2) \tag{4.2}$$

A normal distribution can be construed as a probability function, which takes a value of a variable ($x$ in the expression above) and returns its probability; in this case, the values of $x$ are integers representing pitches.[3] As seen in the equation above, a normal distribution has two parameters: the mean $\mu$, which is the center of the "bell curve," and the variance $\sigma^2$,

**Table 4.1**
The parameters used by the pitch model.

---

Central pitch profile $= N(68, 13.2)$
Range profile $= N(c, 29.0)$, where $c$ is the central pitch
Proximity profile $= N(p_{n-1}, 7.2)$, where $p_{n-1}$ is the previous pitch
Key profiles (see figure 4.7)
RPK profile $=$ product of key, range, and proximity profiles
$P(\text{key}) = (1/12) \times 0.88$ for major keys
$\qquad\qquad (1/12) \times 0.12$ for minor keys

---

which controls the width of the curve. We now consider how to set these parameters for the three normal distributions proposed above—the central pitch profile, the range profile, and the proximity profile. The parameters for the central pitch profile can be set straightforwardly from the Essen corpus. The mean of mean pitches in the corpus is roughly 68 (A♭4), and the variance of mean pitches is 13.2; thus the central pitch profile is $N(68, 13.2)$. (Here we take the observed mean pitch of each melody as an estimate of its central pitch.[4]) As for the range profile, the mean (the central pitch) varies from song to song; similarly, the mean of the proximity profile varies from one note to the next. The variances of the range and proximity profiles, however, do not appear to vary greatly across songs; for simplicity, we will assume that they are constant. The values used for these parameters are shown in table 4.1; the values were estimated from the Essen data using a rather complex procedure that is not of central importance here.[5]

The melody in figure 4.5A has another glaring problem: The pitches of the melody are more or less uniformly distributed across the chromatic scale. In a real melody, by contrast (at least in the tradition of Western tonal music), melodies tend to adhere to the scale of a particular key. We incorporate this using the concept of key-profiles. As discussed in the previous section, a key-profile is a twelve-valued vector, representing the stability or appropriateness of pitch-classes in relation to a key. In this case, the key-profiles are based on the actual distribution of scale-degrees in the Essen corpus. We count the occurrences of each scale-degree in each song; we sum these counts over all songs (grouping major-key and minor-key songs separately), and express the totals as proportions. This then tells us the probability of a note being a certain scale-degree. The resulting key-profiles are shown in figure 4.7. The profiles show that, for example, 18.4% of notes in major-key melodies are scale-degree $\hat{1}$. The profiles reflect conventional musical wisdom, in that pitches belong-

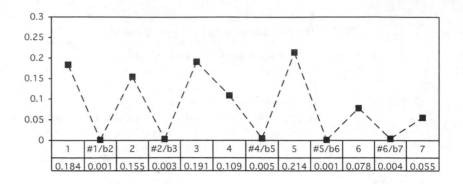

| | 1 | #1/b2 | 2 | #2/b3 | 3 | 4 | #4/b5 | 5 | #5/b6 | 6 | #6/b7 | 7 |
|---|---|---|---|---|---|---|---|---|---|---|---|---|
| | 0.184 | 0.001 | 0.155 | 0.003 | 0.191 | 0.109 | 0.005 | 0.214 | 0.001 | 0.078 | 0.004 | 0.055 |

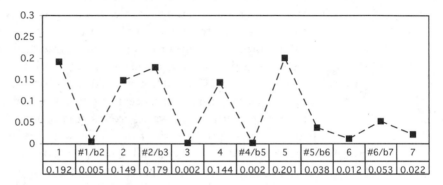

| | 1 | #1/b2 | 2 | #2/b3 | 3 | 4 | #4/b5 | 5 | #5/b6 | 6 | #6/b7 | 7 |
|---|---|---|---|---|---|---|---|---|---|---|---|---|
| | 0.192 | 0.005 | 0.149 | 0.179 | 0.002 | 0.144 | 0.002 | 0.201 | 0.038 | 0.012 | 0.053 | 0.022 |

**Figure 4.7**
Key-profiles for major keys (above) and minor keys (below), generated from the Essen corpus.

ing to the major or minor scale of the key have higher values than other pitches, and pitches of the tonic chord (the $\hat{1}$, $\hat{3}$, and $\hat{5}$ degrees in major or the $\hat{1}$, $b\hat{3}$, and $\hat{5}$ degrees in minor) have higher values than other scalar ones.

The key-profiles in figure 4.7 capture the fact that the probability of pitches occurring in a melody depends on their relationship to the key. However, we also wish to incorporate the principles of range and pitch proximity discussed earlier. To do this, we duplicate the key-profiles over many octaves; we can then multiply a key-profile together with the range and proximity profiles. We will call the resulting distribution the *RPK profile*. (To be interpretable as probabilities, the RPK profile values must be normalized to sum to 1.) In generating a melody, we must construct the RPK profile anew at each point, since the proximity profile

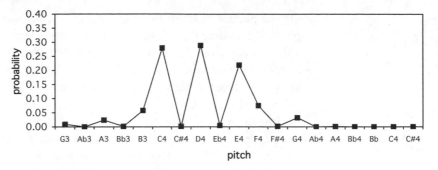

**Figure 4.8**
An RPK profile, assuming a central pitch of A♭4, a previous pitch of C4, and a key of C major.

depends on the previous pitch. (For the first note, since there is no previous pitch, we simply use the product of the range and key profiles.)

Figure 4.8 shows an RPK profile, assuming a key of C major, a central pitch of 68 (A♭4), and a previous note of C4. One can discern a roughly bell-shaped curve to this profile (though with smaller peaks and valleys). The proximity profile pulls the center of the curve toward C4, but the range profile pulls it toward A♭4; the result is that the actual center is in between the two. The key-profile gives higher values to pitches that are within the C major scale, thus accounting for the local peaks and valleys. Figure 4.5B shows a melody generated by this method, again assuming a key of C major and a central pitch of A♭4.

The generative process thus operates by choosing a key and a central pitch, and then generating a series of pitches. (The process does not decide how many pitches to generate; this is assumed to be given.) The probability of a pitch occurring at any point is given by its RPK profile value: the normalized product of its range-profile value (given the central pitch), its proximity-profile value (given the previous pitch), and its key-profile value (given the chosen key). The probability of a series of pitches is the product of their RPK profile values. We express the joint probability of a pitch sequence with a key $k$ and a central pitch $c$ as follows:

$$P(\text{pitch sequence} \cap k \cap c) = P(\text{pitch sequence} \,|\, k \cap c)P(k \cap c)$$

$$= P(k)P(c) \prod_n RPK_n \qquad (4.3)$$

where $P(k)$ is the probability of a key being chosen, $P(c)$ is the probability of a central pitch being chosen, and $RPK_n$ are the RPK-profile values for the pitches of the melody given the key, central pitch, and previous pitch. We assume that all keys of the same mode are equal in prior probability, since most listeners are incapable of identifying keys in absolute terms. However, we assign major keys a higher probability than minor keys, reflecting the higher proportion of major-key melodies in the Essen collection (see table 4.1).

How do we calculate the overall probability of a pitch sequence? For the moment, let us think of the structure as the combination of a key and a central pitch; the surface is a sequence of pitches. From equation 2.8, we know that

$$P(\text{surface}) = \sum_{\text{structure}} P(\text{surface} \cap \text{structure}) \qquad (4.4)$$

Now we can define the probability of a pitch sequence as the expression in equation 4.3, summed over all keys and central pitches.

$$P(\text{pitch sequence}) = \sum_{k,c} \left( P(k)P(c) \prod_n RPK_n \right) \qquad (4.5)$$

This can be calculated quite easily by considering each $(k, c)$ pair and calculating the joint probability of the pitch sequence with that pair.

**4.3 Testing the Model on Key-Finding**

We now consider how the generative process described above might be incorporated into a key-finding model. The task is simply to choose a single key for a given melody. (We do not allow the possibility of modulations—changes of key; this issue will be addressed in chapter 6.) Let us now define the key alone as the structure. From equation 2.19, we know that, for a key $k$,

$$P(k \,|\, \text{pitch sequence}) \propto P(k \cap \text{pitch sequence}) \qquad (4.6)$$

To calculate the right-hand side of this expression, let us consider "$k \cap$ pitch sequence" as one variable and $c$ (central pitch) as another. From equations 2.8 and 4.3:

$$P(k \cap \text{pitch sequence}) = \sum_c (\text{pitch sequence} \cap k \cap c)$$

$$= \sum_c \left( P(k)P(c) \prod_n RPK_n \right) \qquad (4.7)$$

**Figure 4.9**
A "modal" melody from the Essen corpus ("Czech01"). This melody is identified in the collection as being in G major.

Thus the most probable key given a pitch sequence is the one maximizing this expression.[6]

Our key-finding process thus proceeds as follows. For each key, we calculate the joint probability of the melody with that key and each central pitch, and sum this over all central pitches. The probability of a pitch at a given point in the melody depends only on its value in the RPK profile at that point; the RPK profile can be recreated at each note, just as it was in the generative process. We perform this process for all keys, and choose the key yielding the highest value; this is the most probable key given the melody.

To test the model's key-finding ability, we use a sample of 65 songs from the Essen collection—the same sample used in the test of the rhythm model in chapter 3. (This sample was not included in the corpus used for setting the model's parameters.) Each song in the corpus is annotated with a single key label; these labels provide a set of "correct" judgments against which the model can be evaluated.

The model judged the key correctly for 57 of the 65 melodies (87.7%). The errors were inspected to see how the model's performance might be improved. Figure 4.9 shows one melody analyzed incorrectly by the model. This is a *modal* melody: the "tonal center," the pitch-class which is most emphasized, and which begins and ends the melody, is G, but the scale used is that of C major. The correct key here was indicated as G major, but the model chose C major. In fact, all but one of the model's errors were on modal melodies, in which the model chose the key favored by the scale, but the correct key reflected a pitch emphasized by repetition and prominent placement. Perhaps the model could be improved by giving extra weight to pitches occurring at structurally important points. We should note, however, that the identification of "key" in modal melodies is problematic. One might argue that such melodies are really ambiguous in key, or indeed that the concept of key is not really relevant. In cases where the melody reflects a more conventional "tonal" organization, the model seems to perform extremely well.

By way of comparison, two other key-finding models were also tested on the Essen sample (using my own implementations): the Longuet-Higgins/Steedman model and the Krumhansl-Schmuckler model, both discussed in section 4.1 above. The Longuet-Higgins/Steedman model guessed the correct key on 46 out of 65 melodies, or 70.8% correct; the Krumhansl-Schmuckler model guessed the correct key on 49 out of 65, or 75.4% correct. In fairness to Longuet-Higgins and Steedman, their model was specifically designed for Bach fugues, not folk melodies. As for the Krumhansl-Schmuckler model, this was not designed for or trained on any particular corpus, but rather was based on experimental perception data; a further test of this model will be reported in the next chapter.

The Bayesian model was also tested on another monophonic corpus which has been widely used for testing—the 48 fugue subjects of Bach's *Well-Tempered Clavier*. This corpus was first used by Longuet-Higgins and Steedman, whose model chose the correct key in all 48 cases. Using my own implementation, I also tested the Krumhansl-Schmuckler model, which chose the correct key in 32 cases (66.7% correct). Vos and Van Geenen's (1996) model chose the correct key in 39 cases (81.2% correct); the model of Temperley (2001a) chose the correct key in 43 cases (89.6% correct).[7] The current probabilistic model chose the correct key in 40 of the 48 fugue subjects (83.3% correct). Inspection of the results showed that many of the model's errors were due to a problem with the key-profiles: in minor, the $\flat\hat{7}$ degree has a higher value than $\hat{7}$, whereas in the Bach corpus (as in "common-practice" music generally), $\hat{7}$ is much more commonly used in minor keys than $\flat\hat{7}$. When scale-degree $\flat7$ was given a value of .015 in the minor profile and scale-degree 7 was given .060, and the preference for major keys was removed, the correct rate of the model was increased to 44 out of 48 cases (91.7% correct).[8]

These tests suggest that a probabilistic approach to key-finding can yield quite successful results. In chapter 6, I present a model of key-finding in polyphonic music; there, we will consider some further comparisons between different key-finding models and some other factors that may be involved in key perception. Before proceeding to this topic, however, we will consider some further issues in melody and how they might be addressed by the monophonic rhythm and pitch models.

# 5
# Melody III: Expectation and Error Detection

**5.1**

**Calculating the Probability of a Melodic Surface**

So far, our main concern in this book has been with problems of information retrieval—the identification of underlying structures from monophonic musical surfaces. The rhythm model of chapter 3 infers a metrical structure from a pattern of note-onset times; the pitch model of chapter 4 infers a key from a sequence of pitches. As well as modeling these analytical processes, I have suggested that these models could also be used to measure the overall probability of a musical surface. We can define a musical surface as either an onset pattern or a sequence of pitches. In section 3.5, we saw that the probability of an onset pattern can be expressed as $\sum P(\text{onset pattern} \mid \text{grid}) P(\text{grid})$, summed over all metrical grids. In section 4.2, we derived an expression for the probability of a pitch sequence (equation 4.5, reprinted here):

$$P(\text{pitch sequence}) = \sum_{k,c} \left( P(k) P(c) \prod_n RPK_n \right) \tag{5.1}$$

Given expressions for $P(\text{onset pattern})$ and $P(\text{pitch sequence})$, one could combine them to calculate the probability of an entire melody—a combined pattern of pitch and rhythm. (In generative terms, the rhythm model decides how many notes there are and when they occur; the pitch model then assigns pitches to the notes.) If we assume that pitch and rhythm are independent, the probability of a melody is simply $P(\text{onset pattern}) \times P(\text{pitch sequence})$.[1] In what follows, however, we will generally consider the rhythmic and pitch dimensions separately.

One of the main theses of this book is that the probability of a musical surface—defined either as pitch pattern or an onset pattern—is an important concept that sheds light on a variety of phenomena in music perception and cognition. In what follows we will examine this idea with regard to two important "surface-level" processes: expectation and error detection.

## 5.2
## Pitch Expectation

One very important aspect of melody perception is expectation. It is well known that in listening to music, listeners form expectations as to what will happen next; the creation, fulfillment, and denial of such expectations has long been thought to be an important part of musical affect and meaning (Meyer 1956; Narmour 1990). Expectation could well be considered a fundamentally probabilistic phenomenon: A judgment of the "expectedness" of a note could be seen as an estimate of its probability of occurring in that context. While this point has been observed before—for example, Schellenberg et al. (2002) define expectation as "anticipation of an event based on its probability of occurring"—the possibility of modeling melodic expectation using probabilistic methods has been little explored.

We could divide melodic expecation into two issues: pitch expectation is the issue of *what* notes will occur; rhythmic expectation is the issue of *when* notes will occur. Most research on melodic expectation has focused on the pitch dimension (though there has been some work on rhythm, as discussed in the next section). With regard to experimental work, most pitch expectation studies have used one of two paradigms: a perception paradigm, in which subjects are played musical contexts followed by a continuation tone and are asked to judge the expectedness of the tone (Schmuckler 1989; Cuddy and Lunney 1995; Schellenberg 1996; Krumhansl et al. 1999); and a production paradigm, in which listeners are given a context and asked to produce the tone (or series of tones) that they consider most likely to follow (Carlsen 1981; Lake 1987; Unyk and Carlsen 1987; Povel 1996; Thompson et al. 1997; Larson 2004). For our purposes, perception data seems most valuable, since it indicates the relative expectedness of different possible continuations, whereas production data only indicates continuations that subjects judged as most expected. Of particular interest is data from a study by Cuddy and Lunney (1995). In this study, subjects were played a context of two notes played in sequence (the "implicative interval"), followed by a third note (the "continuation tone"), and were asked to judge the third note given the first two on a scale of 1 ("extremely bad continuation") to 7 ("extremely good continuation"). Eight different contexts were used:

**Figure 5.1**
Two-note contexts used in Cuddy and Lunney 1995. (A) ascending major second, (B) descending major second, (C) ascending minor third, (D) descending minor third, (E) ascending major sixth, (F) descending major sixth, (G) ascending minor seventh, (H) descending minor seventh. The continuation tone could be any tone within one octave above or below the second context tone.

ascending and descending major second, ascending and descending minor third, ascending and descending major sixth, and ascending and descending minor seventh (see figure 5.1). Each two-note context was followed by 25 different continuation tones, representing all tones within an octave above or below the second tone of the context (which was always either C4 or F♯4). For each condition (context plus continuation tone), Cuddy and Lunney reported the average rating, thus yielding 200 data points in all. This data will be considered further below.

A number of models of pitch expectation have been proposed, both in psychology and music theory (Schmuckler 1989; Narmour 1990; Cuddy and Lunney 1995; Krumhansl 1995; Bharucha 1996; Schellenberg 1996, 1997; Lerdahl 2001; Larson 2004; Margulis 2005). We will focus here on models that have been tested on experimental perception data. Such models generally employ the technique of multiple regression. Given a context, each possible continuation is assigned a score which is a linear combination of several variables; multiple regression is used to fit these variables to experimental judgments in the optimal way. Schmuckler (1989) played excerpts from a Schumann song followed by various possible continuations (playing melody and accompaniment separately and then both together); regarding the melody, subjects' judgments correlated with Krumhansl and Kessler's (1982) key-profiles and with principles of melodic shape proposed by Meyer (1973). Other work has built on the Implication-Realization theory of Narmour (1990), which predicts expectations as a function of the shape of a melody. Narmour's theory was quantified by Krumhansl (1995) and Schellenberg (1996) to include five factors: registral direction, intervallic difference, registral return, proximity, and closure (these factors are difficult to describe succinctly and I will not attempt to do so here). Schellenberg (1996) applied this model to experimental data in which listeners judged possible continuations of excerpts from folk melodies. Cuddy and Lunney (1995) modeled their expectation data (described above) with these five factors; they also included predictors for pitch height, "tonal strength" (the degree to which the pattern strongly implies a key—quantified using Krumhansl and Kessler's key-profile values), and "tonal region" (the ability of the final tone to serve as a tonic, given the two context tones). On Cuddy and Lunney's experimental data, this model achieved a correlation of .80. Schellenberg (1997) found that a simpler version of Narmour's theory achieved equal or better fit to expectation data than the earlier five-factor version. Schellenberg's simpler model consists of only two factors relating to melodic shape—a "proximity" factor, in which pitches close to the previous pitch are more likely, and a "reversal" factor which favors a change of direction after large intervals—as well as the predictors of pitch height, tonal strength, and tonal region used by Cuddy and Lunney. Schellenberg reanalyzed Cuddy and Lunney's data and found a correlation of .851. Krumhansl et al. (1999) gathered melodic expectation data using Finnish folk hymns (using both Finnish and foreign subjects) and found that the original five-factor version of Narmour's model fit the data better than Schellenberg's two-factor model; Schellenberg et al. (2002) once again argue for the superiority of the two-factor model.

We now consider a test of the pitch model presented in chapter 4, using Cuddy and Lunney's (1995) experimental data. Recall that, in Cuddy and Lunney's study, subjects judged the expectedness of different melodic continuations on a scale of 1 to 7. To test the current model, we must we must reinterpret Cuddy and Lunney's data in probabilistic terms. There are various ways that this might be done. One could interpret subjects' ratings as probabilities (or as proportional to probabilities) for different continuations given a previous context; one could also interpret the ratings as logarithms of probabilities, or as some other function of probabilities. There seems little *a priori* basis for deciding this issue. Initially, ratings were treated as directly proportional to probabilities, but this yielded poor results; treating the ratings as logarithms of probabilities gave much better results, and we adopt that approach in what follows. Specifically, each rating is taken to indicate the log probability of the continuation tone given the previous two-tone context. Under the current model, the probability of a pitch $p_n$ given a previous context $(p_0 \ldots p_{n-1})$ can be expressed as

$$P(p_n \mid p_0 \ldots p_{n-1}) = P(p_0 \ldots p_n)/P(p_0 \ldots p_{n-1}) \qquad (5.2)$$

where $P(p_0 \ldots p_n)$ is the overall probability of the context plus the continuation tone, and $P(p_0 \ldots p_{n-1})$ is the probability of just the context. An expression indicating the probability of a sequence of tones was given in equation 5.1 above; this can be used here to calculate both $P(p_0 \ldots p_{n-1})$ and $P(p_0 \ldots p_n)$. For example, given a context of (B♭4, C4) and a continuation tone of D4, the model's expectation judgment would be $\log(P(\text{B♭4, C4, D4})/P(\text{B♭4, C4})) = -1.955$.

The model was run on the 200 test items in Cuddy and Lunney's data, and its outputs were compared with the experimental ratings for each item.[2] Using the parameters gathered from the Essen Folksong Collection (shown in table 4.1), the model yielded the correlation $r = .729$. It seemed reasonable, however, to adjust the parameters to achieve a better fit to the data. This is analogous to what is done in a multiple regression—as used by Cuddy and Lunney (1995), Schellenberg (1997), and others—in which the weight of each factor is set so as to optimally fit the data. It was found that better performance could be achieved by using different variance values for the three normal distributions used in the model: 40.0 for the central pitch profile, 16.0 for the range profile, and 25.0 for the proximity profile. It was apparent from the experimental data, also, that many highly-rated patterns were ones in which the final tone could be interpreted as the tonic of the key. (This trend was also noted by Cuddy and Lunney and Schellenberg, who introduced a special "tonal region" factor to account for it.) This factor was incorporated into the current model by using a special key-profile for the continuation tone, in which the value for the tonic pitch is much higher than usual (its usual key-profile value was multiplied by 20). With these adjustments, the model achieved a score of $r = .870$, exceeding both Cuddy and Lunney's model (.80) and Schellenberg's (.851).[3] Figure 5.2 shows Cuddy and Lunney's data along with the model's output, using the optimized parameters, for two of their eight context intervals (ascending major second and descending major sixth).

One interesting emergent feature of the current model is its handling of "post-skip reversal" or "gap-fill." It is a well-established musical principle that large leaps in melodies tend to be followed by a change of direction. Some models incorporate post-skip reversal as an explicit preference: it is reflected, for example, in the "registral direction" factor of Narmour's model, and in the "reversal" factor of Schellenberg's two-factor model. However, von Hippel and Huron (2000) have suggested that post-skip reversal might simply be an artifact of "regression to the mean." A large interval is likely to take a melody close to the edge of its

**Ascending major second**

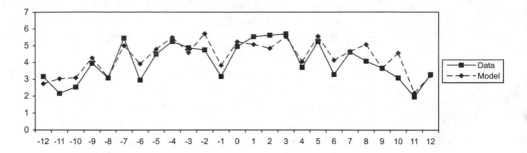

**Descending major sixth**

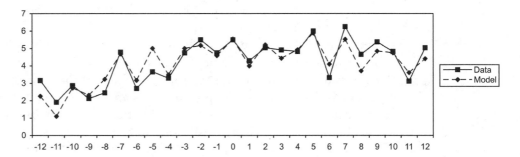

**Figure 5.2**
Expectation data from Cuddy and Lunney 1995 and the pitch model's predictions. Data is shown for two two-tone contexts, ascending major second (Bb3–C4) and descending major sixth (A4–C4). The horizontal axis indicates continuation tones in relation to the second context tone. The vertical axis represents mean judgments of expectedness for the continuation tone given the context, from Cuddy and Lunney's experimental data and as predicted by the pitch model. (The model's output here has been put through a linear function which does not affect the correlation results, but allows easier comparison with the experimental data.)

range; the preference to stay close to the center of the range will thus exert pressure for a change of direction. The current model follows this approach. While there is no explicit preference for reversal, a context consisting of a large descending interval like A4–C4 is generated with highest probability by a range centered somewhat above the second pitch; given such a range, the pitch following C4 is most likely to move closer to the center, thus causing a change in direction. The preference for ascending intervals following an descending major sixth, though slight, can be seen in figure 5.2 in Cuddy and Lunney's data as well as in the model's predictions. (Values for ascending—positive—intervals are somewhat higher than for descending ones.) It appears that such an indirect treatment of reversal as an artifact of range and proximity constraints can model experimental expectation data quite successfully.

The influence of key on the model's behavior is also interesting to consider. For example, given the ascending-major-second context (figure 5.2), compare the model's judgments (and the experimental data) for continuations of a descending major second ($-2$) and descending minor second ($-1$). Proximity would favor $-1$, and range would seem to express little preference. So why does the model yield a much higher value for $-2$? The reason surely lies in the influence of key. Note that the model does not make a single, determinate key judgment here, nor should it. A context such as B♭4–C4 is quite ambiguous with regard to key; it might imply B♭ major, B♭ minor, E♭ major, G minor, or other keys. In each of these cases, however, a continuation of $-2$ (moving back to B♭4) remains within the key, whereas a continuation of $-1$ (moving to B4) does not. Thus key plays an important role in the model's expectation behavior, even when the actual key is in fact quite ambiguous. The fact that the experimental data also reflects a higher rating for $-2$ than for $-1$ suggests that this is the case perceptually as well.

## 5.3 Rhythmic Expectation

There is also a rhythmic dimension to melodic expectation. Given a musical context, we expect subsequent notes to happen at certain times. While rhythmic expectation has not been studied as much as pitch expectation, some important work has been done here, notably that of Jones and her colleagues (Large and Jones 1999; Jones et al. 2002). This research has shown that a regular rhythmic pattern creates a strong expectation for the pattern to continue. For example, when a series of note-onsets is regularly spaced by a certain time interval $T$, listeners expect the next note to occur at an interval of (roughly) $T$ after the last one.

This is reflected in judgments of time intervals, and in pitch judgments as well: when a note occurs at its most expected position, its pitch is judged more accurately than if it occurs a bit earlier or later. Large and Jones (1999) model these phenomena with an "oscillator" model, in which pulses of attention entrain to the period and phase of a rhythmic pattern. They note that the model can be interpreted probabilistically, in that its attentional pulses represent the probability of an event occurring at different time points.

How could phenomena of rhythmic expectation be captured by the rhythm model of chapter 3? Our basic approach is the same as in the previous section. We are given a certain context—a pattern of onsets in time—and we want to know the probability of different continuations. The expectedness of a continuation is just $P(\text{continuation} \mid \text{context})$. The problem is more complex than in the case of pitch expectation, however. Our approach in the previous section took advantage of the fact that the expression in equation 5.1 defines the probability of a sequence of pitches, regardless of whether those pitches form a complete melody or part of a melody. In the case of the rhythm model, however, the expression derived in section 3.5 indicates the probability of an onset pattern as a *complete* pattern. What we need to know is the probability of an onset pattern as an incomplete (or possibly incomplete) pattern which might be continued in various different ways. This can be calculated under the current approach, but it is rather complicated. Fortunately, there is a simpler solution. It is a simple mathematical fact that for any context and continuation, $P(\text{continuation} \mid \text{context}) \propto P(\text{continuation} \cap \text{context})$ (assuming the context is held constant). And the right-hand side of this expression *can* be calculated—it is simply the probability of the entire onset pattern of context and continuation combined, as defined in section 3.5. Using this logic, we can compare the expectedness of different continuations of a given context, even though we cannot really compare across contexts.

Figure 5.3 shows a simple example of how this might be done. We have four patterns, each with eight onsets. Let us define the context as everything up to and including the seventh onset; the continuation is then the final onset, which may occur at different times. Given a context of 600-msec intervals, we would expect the final interval to be 600 msec as well; a continuation interval of 700 msec would be less expected. By contrast, if the context featured 700-msec intervals, then a 700-msec interval would be a more expected continuation than a 600-msec interval. (This is essentially the finding of Jones et al. 2002.) The rhythm model

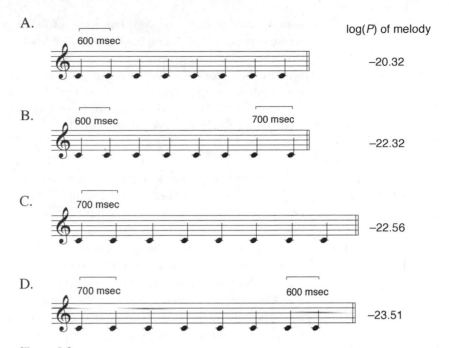

A.
600 msec

log(*P*) of melody

−20.32

B.
600 msec          700 msec

−22.32

C.
700 msec

−22.56

D.
700 msec          600 msec

−23.51

**Figure 5.3**
Four rhythmic patterns, showing the log probability assigned to each one by the rhythm model.

captures these phenomena well. Figure 5.3 shows the probability assigned by the rhythm model to each entire pattern; recall that this is proportional to *P*(continuation | context) for a given context. (Again, we use logarithms here, since the probabilities themselves are extremely small numbers.) Given a context of 600-msec intervals, a 600-msec continuation interval yields a higher probability than the 700-msec continuation; given a context of 700-msec intervals, however, the 700-msec continuation yields the higher probability. The fact that the model finds a higher probability for the 600-msec interval continuation in the first context, but the 700-msec continuation in the second, shows that it is not simply treating tactus intervals in isolation, but is considering the context as well.

To understand the model's behavior here, we should note that the overall probability of an onset pattern is likely to be greatly affected by its probability in combination with its best (most probable) metrical analysis. In all four examples, the best analysis assigns a tactus beat to each onset. In figures 5.3A and 5.3C, however, the regularity of the final note gives this analysis maximal joint probability with the melody, whereas in figures 5.3B and 5.3D its probability is lower.

In short, the rhythm model proposed here seems to hold considerable promise as a model of rhythmic expectation, or at least as one component in such a model. While its ability to predict experimental data in detail remains to be tested, it can at least accommodate an important qualitative finding of expectation research.

## 5.4 Error Detection

Another kind of phenomenon that is illuminated by the current model could be broadly described as "note error detection." It seems uncontroversial that most human listeners have some ability to detect errors—"wrong notes"—even in an unfamiliar melody. However, the idea of error detection proves to be quite complex and encompasses a variety of different phenomena. Let us confine ourselves to the case of classical music, where the score prescribes fairly clearly what the correct notes are. On some instruments, such as the piano, the issue of what notes were played, and thus which notes were errors, can be resolved fairly objectively, at least in the domain of pitch (not rhythm). On other instruments, it may sometimes be more appropriate to speak of ambiguities as opposed to errors: for example, when a singer or a violinist renders a note a quarter-tone sharp, halfway between two idealized pitches; or when a flute player "overblows" a note, momentarily sounding the pitch an octave above the intended one. Errors may also vary in the extent to which the listener is aware of them; some errors may enter the listener's consciousness, while others might be unconsciously corrected without even being noticed. (The phenomenon of unconscious error correction is well documented in music performance; see Sloboda 1976.) As yet another category of error, we might consider "deliberate errors" on the part of the composer—for example, the famous moment in Beethoven's "Eroica" Symphony where the horn enters with the theme four measures early (figure 5.4); this category shades into phenomena which are not really errors at all but rather deliberate surprises or denials of expectation.[4] The important point about all these types of errors, ambiguities, and surprises is that the listener is (at least to some extent) able to detect them—to identify the error, and perhaps also to guess which note was "correct." This ability depends on knowledge of the probabilities of different notes occurring; and it seems plausible that knowledge of musical structure—the principles of key and pitch proximity, for example—is brought to bear in this process. (All of this would seem to apply to

**Figure 5.4**
Beethoven, Symphony No. 3 ("Eroica"), I, mm. 396–403. The horn melody in mm. 398–399 is a "deliberate error."

rhythm as well, at least to some extent; for example, there are times when we hear a note in a piece as the correct note but occurring early or late in relation to its expected position.)

The ability of the pitch and rhythm models to detect errors was tested using the 65-song Essen test set described in chapter 3. The models were given the original Essen melodies (as represented by the keyboard performances used in chapter 3) as well as randomly distorted versions of the same melodies; the question was whether they could reliably assign a higher probability to the correct versions as opposed to the distorted versions. The pitch and rhythm models were tested separately. In both cases, the deformed version of a melody was produced by randomly choosing one note and changing it in some way. For the pitch model, the note's pitch was replaced by a random pitch within the range of the melody (between the lowest and highest pitch). For the rhythm model, the note's ontime was replaced by a random time between the ontimes of the two notes on either side. Each of the 65 melodies in the sample was randomly deformed in both pitch and rhythm. The process was repeated 10 times, yielding a total of 650 trials for the pitch model and 650 for the rhythm model. In each trial, the model's analyses for the correct version and the deformed version were compared simply with regard to the total probability given to each melody, to see which version was assigned higher probability. In effect, then, the model simply judged which of a pair of melodies was more likely to contain an error, without expressing any opinion as to exactly where the error was.

On the pitch model test, the model assigned the correct version of the melody higher probability than the deformed version in 573 out of 650 trials (88.2%). On the rhythm model test, in 49 of the 650 cases, the deformed melody was treated as equivalent to the original by the model (because the deformed note was quantized to the same pip as the original

Melody III: Expectation and Error Detection

note); out of the remaining 601 cases, the model judged the correct version higher in probability in 493 cases (82.0%). This level of performance seems promising. Probably, not all random "errors" of this type would be identifiable as errors even by humans; whether the models' ability is comparable to that of human listeners remains to be tested.

A further aspect of melody perception deserving brief mention here is the actual identification of notes. The process of extracting note information from an auditory signal, sometimes known as "transcription," is highly complex, involving the grouping of partials (individual frequencies) into complex tones, and the correct categorization of these tones into pitch categories. It seems likely that the models proposed above (both the rhythm and pitch models) could contribute to this task, by evaluating the probability of different possible note patterns (as in the error-detection task above). These judgments could then be used in a "top-down" fashion—in effect, bringing to bear musical considerations such as key, pitch proximity, and meter on the transcription process. We will return to this issue in chapter 8.

## 5.5
## Further Issues

In this chapter and the previous two, I have proposed models of pitch and rhythm perception. The models perform meter identification and key identification; they also perform the surface-level tasks of expectation and error detection. On balance, where comparison is possible, the models are at least competitive with other models in their level of performance. Beyond the issue of performance, however, I will argue here that the current models have several important advantages over others that have been proposed.

One important feature of the current models is that they are able to perform both the structural tasks of meter and key identification and the surface-level tasks of expectation and error detection within a single framework. This sets them apart from most prior models, which have addressed these problems separately. One exception in the rhythmic domain is Large and Jones's oscillator model, which offers a framework for modeling both meter perception and expectation (Large and Jones 1999; Jones et al. 2002). The connection between expectation and key-finding is also indirectly reflected in some earlier work—notably in the fact that Krumhansl and Kessler's key-profiles have been incorporated into both expectation models (e.g., Cuddy and Lunney 1995) and key-finding models (Krumhansl 1990). But this connection is brought out much more clearly in the current approach. Key-finding is a matter of finding the key with which the note pattern achieves the highest joint probability; expectation is a matter of judging the probability of the note pattern itself (given a prior context), which is the joint probability of the note pattern with all possible keys. This points to another advantage of the current approach: Because it offers a way of calculating the overall probability of a surface pattern, it provides a method for performing error detection (and could also, potentially, contribute to the transcription task). By contrast, regression-based and oscillator-based models of expectation do not appear to offer any natural way of modeling error detection or transcription, as they provide no measure of the overall probability of a surface pattern.

Undoubtedly, the performance of the current models on surface-level tasks could be improved. In chapter 3, we considered several further factors in meter perception that might be incorporated into the rhythm model, such as note length; incorporation of these factors would probably improve the model's performance in rhythmic error detection as well. With regard to the pitch model, one might consider further factors of melodic "shape" besides range and pitch proximity. One example is the tendency for melodies to follow small intervals with another small interval in the same direction—a phenomenon that has sometimes been called "process" (Narmour 1990) or "inertia" (Larson 2004). This factor is clearly evident in Cuddy and Lunney's data: for example, given a context of an ascending major second Bb4–C4 (see figure 5.2), the highest ratings are for continuation intervals of +1 (Db4), +2 (D4), and +3 (Eb4), creating another small interval in the same direction. This tendency is not predicted by the current model, nor by Schellenberg's two-factor model; it *is* predicted by the "registral direction" factor of Cuddy and Lunney's model, but this model performed less well than the current model or Schellenberg's model overall. Clearly, there is further work to be done in combining the strengths of the various pitch expectation models.

Other kinds of musical knowledge would require a more integrated treatment of pitch and rhythm. An example is parallelism—the use of repeated patterns. As noted in section 3.7, there is a preference to align strong beats with repeated patterns, but the identification of such patterns requires consideration of both pitch and rhythm; to address this issue satisfactorily would probably require a generative model in which pitches and rhythms were generated in combination. A similar point could be made about harmony. Melodies normally have some kind of implied harmonic structure, forming a coherent progression and ending in a conventional cadence. Harmonic structure is closely tied to metrical

Melody III: Expectation and Error Detection

structure, in that changes of harmony tend to occur on strong beats; harmony then serves as in important cue to meter perception (Temperley 2001a). Again, an adequate treatment of this issue would require a generative model in which rhythmic and tonal structures were combined, giving rise to a combined pitch and rhythmic surface pattern.

Before we leave the topic of surface-level processes, one further issue deserves discussion. Up to now, following the usual Bayesian reasoning, we have defined the probability of a pitch or onset pattern, $P$(surface), as its probability in combination with a structure, summed over all structures: $\sum P$(surface $\cap$ structure). An alternative, however, would be to define the probability of a surface pattern as its probability in combination with its most probable structure; I will refer to this quantity as $max(P$(surface $\cap$ structure)). While $max(P$(surface $\cap$ structure)) is, strictly speaking, a poor approximation to $P$(surface) (it is often less by many orders of magnitude), it generally seems to be roughly *proportional* to $P$(surface); among many surface patterns, the one with the highest value for $max(P$(surface $\cap$ structure)) is also generally the one with the highest value for $P$(surface). (This seems to be true in many cases, but has not yet been systematically examined.) From a practical viewpoint, one advantage of using $max(P$(surface $\cap$ structure)) is that this is *precisely* the quantity that needs to be calculated in order to determine the most likely surface given the structure. The quantity $\sum P$(surface $\cap$ structure), while it emerges somewhat naturally out of the structure-finding process, still requires a good deal of extra computation, especially in the case of the rhythm model (as discussed in section 3.5 above).

Using $max(P$(surface $\cap$ structure)) as an indicator of $P$(surface) is also an interesting possibility to consider with regard to perception. In the case of the rhythm model, for example, we have assumed that listeners judge the probability of an onset pattern by summing its joint probability with all possible metrical structures. But another possibility is that they simply calculate the melody's joint probability with its most probable structure, and take that to indicate the surface probability. With regard to pitch expectation, it seems clear from Cuddy and Lunney's data that key plays a role; but do listeners really consider all possible keys in judging the probability of different continuations, or only the most probable key given the context? These are open questions. Thus the possibility of using $max(P$(surface $\cap$ structure)) as an indicator of $P$(surface) may have interesting implications for the modeling of music perception and cognition.

# 6
# A Polyphonic Key-Finding Model

**6.1**

**A Pitch-Class-Set Approach to Key-Finding**

In exploring the perception of meter and key, we have so far limited ourselves to monophonic music. However, this is a major oversimplification of musical experience; the vast majority of music that we hear (in Western society at least) is polyphonic, with multiple notes or voices present simultaneously. In this chapter I propose a probabilistic model for key-finding in polyphonic music (first presented in Temperley 2002 and Temperley 2004b). As we will see, the most obvious way of extending the monophonic key-finding model of chapter 4 to polyphonic music does not work very well; a rather different approach is required. As for the musical style under investigation, our focus will shift from folk music to art music—specifically Western art music of the eighteenth and nineteenth centuries, sometimes known as "common-practice" music.

As with the monophonic pitch model, the current model proves to have implications for a number of issues besides key-finding itself. A separate chapter (chapter 7) will be devoted to these further issues; the current chapter is concerned only with key-finding.

The monophonic key-finding model was based on key-profiles representing the pitch-class probabilities for an event given a key. To judge the key of a pitch sequence, the model calculated the probability of the pitch sequence being generated given each key, also taking into account range and pitch proximity. We will no longer consider the factors of range and pitch proximity (which are separate issues from key-finding in any case); such factors are very problematic in polyphonic music, as they require the grouping of notes into contrapuntal lines. This leaves us with the key-profiles shown in figure 4.7, simply representing the

**Figure 6.1**
Haydn, String Quartet Op. 74 No. 3, II, m. 30.

probability of each scale-degree. In theory, we could apply these key-profiles to key-finding in polyphonic music, much as we did with mono-phonic music. The notes of a piece (or rather, the pitch-classes of the notes) could be treated as independent decisions generated from a key-profile; the most probable key would be the one that generated the notes with the highest probability. However, I believe that this approach would not be very successful, for reasons which I now explain.

Consider a segment such as figure 6.1, from a Haydn string quartet. Here, we have a clear implication of C major. If we examine the pitch-class distribution for this segment, however, we find eight Es and seven Gs but only two Cs. Under the model suggested above—and given ap-propriate key-profiles gathered from common-practice music—this dis-tribution favors a key of E minor over C major. And yet perceptually, all the repetitions of E and G do not seem to have much effect on the ton-al implications of the passage. This brings up an important point about key-finding: the perception of key over a short segment of music (say, a few seconds) does not seem to be greatly affected by immediate repeti-tions or doublings of pitch-classes, but is mainly sensitive to the pitch-classes that are present. Of course, this criticism could also be made with regard to the monophonic model proposed earlier; even with melodies, the counting of individual notes might sometimes give too much weight to repetitions. But the problem is much more severe in polyphonic music, given the frequent doublings of pitch-classes in different voices. Prelim-inary tests showed that the performance of an "event-counting" key-finding model on polyphonic music was greatly hindered by the problem of repeated and doubled pitch-classes. A better approach would seem to be to only count each pitch-class as either "present" or "absent" within a short segment of music, ignoring doublings and repetitions.

Another way to view this point is from the generative perspective. The model in chapter 4 presupposes a generative model in which each event

**Figure 6.2**
Three realizations of the C major triad. (A) Mozart, Piano Concerto K. 503, I, m. 1; (B) Mozart, Sonata K. 545, I, m. 1; (C) Chopin, Etude Op. 10 No. 1, m. 1.

is generated independently. But this model is not very plausible for something like figure 6.1. There, a more plausible model would be that the composer decides to use certain pitch-classes—C, E, and G—and then decides to repeat some of them. The surface repetitions of pitches would then be elaborations of some kind of deeper, sparser, representation of events. But what exactly would this underlying pitch representation be like? One possibility that comes to mind is a "middleground" representation like that used in Schenkerian analysis (Schenker 1935/1979) a reduced representation of a piece in which only structurally important events are included, omitting doublings and immediate repetitions as well as many ornamental events (passing tones and the like). But to generate such a representation is an extremely difficult problem (we will return to this in chapter 9). Here we adopt a simpler, and admittedly cruder, solution. We divide the input into short segments, corresponding roughly to measures. In each segment, we simply observe which pitch-classes are used, without regard to how often they are used. In essence, we characterize a piece simply as a series of *pitch-class sets*, one in each segment.

The concept of a pitch-class set—a collection of pitch-classes irrespective of their registral and temporal placement— is an important concept in music theory, widely used in the analysis of atonal twentieth century music (Rahn 1980). Indeed, this concept is rather commonplace in discourse about tonal music as well, though it is not usually described in those terms. For instance, when we speak of a "C major triad," we generally have in mind a set consisting of the pitch-classes C, E, and G, so that for example the passage in figure 6.1 as well as the passages in figure 6.2 are all realizations of the set. Also of relevance is the concept

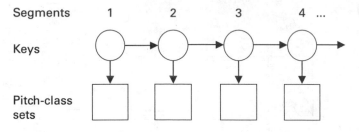

Segments   1        2        3        4 ...

Keys

Pitch-class
sets

**Figure 6.3**
A hidden Markov model for polyphonic key-finding. Key nodes (circles) are
"hidden"; pitch-class-set nodes (squares) are "observed."

of a "pitch-class set-type"—an equivalence-class of all pitch-class sets
that are related by transposition, as reflected for example in the term
"major triad." One advantage of basing a key-finding model on pitch-
class sets is that we can then use this model to examine theoretical
assumptions that are generally presented in pitch-class-set terms—
assumptions about chords, scalar collections, and the like; we will return
to this topic in chapter 7.

Dividing the piece into short segments has a further benefit which has
not yet been mentioned. Since we are choosing not a single global key,
but rather a key for each segment, we have the possibility of changing
keys from one segment to another—so-called *modulations*. This is a desirable feature for handling common-practice polyphonic music, where
changes of key within a piece are a frequent and important occurrence.

For the current model, we can, as usual, define the problem as one of
recovering a structure from a surface. We assume some kind of prior division of the piece into short segments (this will be explained more precisely below). The surface can then be regarded as a series of pitch-class
sets, one in each segment; the structure is a labeling of each segment with
a key. Our model can be represented graphically as in figure 6.3: a network consisting of "key nodes" and "pitch-class-set nodes" for each segment. This model is a simple example of a family of models called *hidden
Markov models* (discussed briefly in chapter 2). A hidden Markov model
is a network of interconnected variables in which certain variables are
observable (the pitch-class-set nodes in this case) and others are hidden
(the key nodes); using Bayesian logic, the hidden values can be inferred
from the observed ones. The model entails two important assumptions:
that each pitch-class set depends only on the current key, and that each
key choice depends only on the key of the previous segment (these

dependencies are represented by the arrows in figure 6.3). We discuss these assumptions further in the next section.

<table>
<tr>
<td>

6.2
The Generative
Process

</td>
<td>

We begin by describing the generative process assumed by the key-finding model. This process involves two stages. First, the structure must be created. In this case, this is not merely a choice of a single key (as it was in chapter 4), but rather a choice of key for each segment. As usual, these choices are made using probability distributions. We will assume that, for the initial segment of a piece, all 24 keys (12 major and 12 minor) are equally probable. We could then generate keys for subsequent segments in a similar, independent fashion; however, this would not be very true to musical practice. Generally, a piece will stay in one key for a number of measures, changing key only occasionally: key has a kind of "inertia," and our probability distribution should reflect that. (This assumption is reflected in perception, also; we tend to assume that the current key remains in force, unless there is strong evidence to the contrary. For example, a G major triad in the context of C major will normally be heard as V of C rather than I of G.) For now, let us assume, for any segment except the first, a probability of .8 of remaining in the same key as the previous segment; this leaves a probability of .2 for moving to one of the other 23 keys, or a probability of $.2/23 = .0087$ for each key. (We consider all key changes to be equally likely, though this is undoubtedly an oversimplification; I discuss this further below.) Given this distribution, a complete key structure can be generated in a left-to-right fashion, choosing the key for each segment based on the previous one.

</td>
</tr>
</table>

The next task is to generate a surface given a structure. Recall that this simply involves generating a series of pitch-class sets, one for each segment. Let us assume that, in each segment, the composer makes twelve independent decisions as to whether or not to use each pitch-class. Given a key (C major for example), some pitch-classes (such as C) have a high probability of being generated; for others (such as C♯), the probability is much lower. The probability of each pitch-class given the key can be represented in a key-profile. Notice this is a very different way of constructing a key-profile from that proposed in chapter 4, where each key-profile reflected a single probability function in which all values summed to 1. In this case, the values of the key-profile are independent and need not sum to 1. As with previous models, this proposal may seem wholly implausible as a model of the compositional process. But it is not intended as a model of the compositional process, only as a model of how listeners might represent the compositional process for the purpose of key-finding. (The model may well have *some* bearing on composition, however, as I will discuss in later chapters.)

As in chapter 4, it is possible and desirable to base the key-profiles on actual compositional practice. For this, I used the Kostka-Payne corpus, a set of 46 excerpts (a total of 9057 notes) from the common-practice repertoire, taken from the workbook accompanying Stefan Kostka and Dorothy Payne's textbook *Tonal Harmony* (1995a, 1995b) (this corpus was also used in Temperley 2001a). The workbook is accompanied by an instructors' manual (Kostka 1995) containing harmonic analyses with chord symbols and modulations; thus data can be gathered on pitch-class distribution relative to the *local* key—something that has not been possible in previous studies of this kind (Youngblood 1958; Knopoff and Hutchinson 1983). Using this corpus, I gathered data as to the proportion of segments in major-key sections containing each scale-degree—simply noting each scale-degree as "present" or "absent," and ignoring any repetitions or doublings. A similar count was then performed for minor-key sections. In defining "segments," it seemed wise to maintain a fairly consistent length in terms of absolute time; it also seemed sensible to use segments defined by the metrical structure. Thus I defined a segment as the shortest metrical unit that was greater than 1 second (using whatever tempo seemed reasonable). The data is shown in figure 6.4; we will call these the "K-P" key-profiles. As an example, scale degree $\hat{1}$ (the tonic) occurs in .748 (74.8%) of segments in major keys; scale degree $\sharp\hat{4}$, by contrast, occurs in only .096 (9.6%) of segments. In many ways, these profiles are similar to the original Krumhansl-Kessler profiles (shown in figure 4.3) and also those derived from the Essen Folksong Collection (figure 4.7); table 6.1 shows all of these key-profiles in a comparative fashion. In both major and minor profiles, scalar degrees have higher values than chromatic ones, and notes of the tonic triad score higher than other notes of the scale. One feature of the Kostka-Payne profiles worth noting is the strong presence of the harmonic minor scale—in particular, the high frequency in minor keys of $\hat{7}$ compared to $\flat\hat{7}$. In this respect, the Kostka-Payne minor profile differs from the K-K and Essen minor profiles. This seemingly small difference will prove to have very significant consequences.

Using the Kostka-Payne profiles, a pitch-class set can be generated by deciding whether or not to include each pitch-class. To summarize, then, the generative process consists of (a) generating a series of keys for segments, using a probability distribution which favors remaining in the

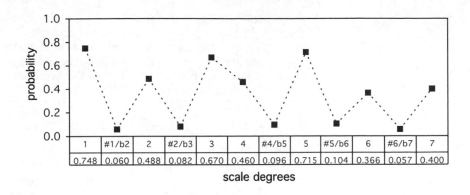

| scale degrees | 1 | #1/b2 | 2 | #2/b3 | 3 | 4 | #4/b5 | 5 | #5/b6 | 6 | #6/b7 | 7 |
|---|---|---|---|---|---|---|---|---|---|---|---|---|
| | 0.748 | 0.060 | 0.488 | 0.082 | 0.670 | 0.460 | 0.096 | 0.715 | 0.104 | 0.366 | 0.057 | 0.400 |

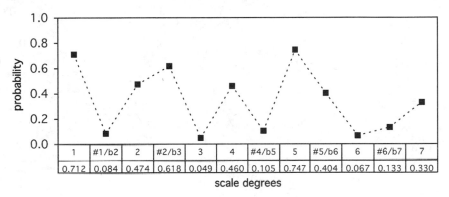

| scale degrees | 1 | #1/b2 | 2 | #2/b3 | 3 | 4 | #4/b5 | 5 | #5/b6 | 6 | #6/b7 | 7 |
|---|---|---|---|---|---|---|---|---|---|---|---|---|
| | 0.712 | 0.084 | 0.474 | 0.618 | 0.049 | 0.460 | 0.105 | 0.747 | 0.404 | 0.067 | 0.133 | 0.330 |

**Figure 6.4**
Key-profiles for major keys (above) and minor keys (below), based on the Kostka-Payne corpus.

same key; and (b) generating a series of pitch-class sets, one for each segment, using the key-profile for the chosen key of each segment.

**6.3
The Key-Finding
Process**

We now turn to the key-finding process. Given a surface pattern of pitches, we must find the most probable key structure—a labeling of each segment of the piece with a key. (We will assume the segmentation as given.) Let us assume for now that the model considers all possible key structures and evaluates the probability of each structure given the surface pattern. The usual Bayesian logic applies:

$$P(\text{key structure} \mid \text{surface}) \propto P(\text{surface} \mid \text{key structure})P(\text{key structure})$$

$$(6.1)$$

A Polyphonic Key-Finding Model

**Table 6.1**

Five sets of key-profile values, for major keys (above) and minor keys (below). The five columns represent (from left to right) the Krumhansl-Kessler profiles (1982), the profiles derived from the Essen folksong collection, the CBMS profiles (Temperley 2001a), the profiles derived from the Kostka-Payne corpus, and the profiles derived from the Temperley corpus.

| Scale-degree | K-K | Essen | CBMS | Kostka-Payne | Temperley corpus |
|---|---|---|---|---|---|
| *Major keys* | | | | | |
| 1 | 6.35 | 0.184 | 5.0 | 0.748 | 0.811 |
| ♯1/♭2 | 2.23 | 0.001 | 2.0 | 0.060 | 0.024 |
| 2 | 3.48 | 0.155 | 3.5 | 0.488 | 0.659 |
| ♯2/♭3 | 2.33 | 0.003 | 2.0 | 0.082 | 0.074 |
| 3 | 4.38 | 0.191 | 4.5 | 0.670 | 0.721 |
| 4 | 4.09 | 0.109 | 4.0 | 0.460 | 0.616 |
| ♯4/♭5 | 2.52 | 0.005 | 2.0 | 0.096 | 0.117 |
| 5 | 5.19 | 0.214 | 4.5 | 0.715 | 0.835 |
| ♯5/♭6 | 2.39 | 0.001 | 2.0 | 0.104 | 0.088 |
| 6 | 3.66 | 0.078 | 3.5 | 0.366 | 0.430 |
| ♯6/♭7 | 2.29 | 0.004 | 1.5 | 0.057 | 0.031 |
| 7 | 2.88 | 0.055 | 4.0 | 0.400 | 0.544 |
| *Minor keys* | | | | | |
| 1 | 6.33 | 0.192 | 5.0 | 0.712 | 0.786 |
| ♯1/♭2 | 2.68 | 0.005 | 2.0 | 0.084 | 0.058 |
| 2 | 3.52 | 0.149 | 3.5 | 0.474 | 0.618 |
| ♯2/♭3 | 5.38 | 0.179 | 4.5 | 0.618 | 0.734 |
| 3 | 2.60 | 0.002 | 2.0 | 0.049 | 0.052 |
| 4 | 3.53 | 0.144 | 4.0 | 0.460 | 0.618 |
| ♯4/♭5 | 2.54 | 0.002 | 2.0 | 0.105 | 0.185 |
| 5 | 4.75 | 0.201 | 4.5 | 0.747 | 0.763 |
| ♯5/♭6 | 3.98 | 0.038 | 3.5 | 0.404 | 0.497 |
| 6 | 2.69 | 0.012 | 2.0 | 0.067 | 0.104 |
| ♯6/♭7 | 3.34 | 0.053 | 1.5 | 0.133 | 0.139 |
| 7 | 3.17 | 0.022 | 4.0 | 0.330 | 0.399 |

First, how do we calculate $P$(key structure)? We assume, as before, that each key has an initial probability of 1/24; for subsequent segments, there is a probability of .8 of staying in the same key as the previous segment, and .2/23 of moving to any other key. The probability of a complete key structure can then be calculated as the product of these probabilities—we will call them "modulation scores" ($M$)—for all segments ($seg$):

$$P(\text{key structure}) = \prod_{seg} M \qquad (6.2)$$

For a key structure of four segments, C major–C major–C major–G major, the probability will be $= 1/24 \times .8 \times .8 \times .2/23 = .000232$.

To calculate $P$(surface | key structure), we begin by identifying the set of pitch-classes in each segment. Given a key, we can interpret these pitch-classes as scale-degrees and use the key-profiles in figure 6.4 to calculate the probability of each scale-degree given the key. The probability of a scale-degree *not* occurring in a segment is 1 minus the key-profile value: for scale-degree $\hat{1}$ in major keys, $1 - .748 = .252$. The probability of a certain pitch-class set (pcset) being used is then given by the product of the key-profile values, $K_{pc}$, for all pitch-classes present in the segment ($p$), multiplied by the product of $(1 - K_{pc})$ for all pitch-classes not present ($\sim p$):

$$P(\text{pcset} \mid \text{key}) = \prod_{p} K_{pc} \prod_{\sim p} (1 - K_{pc}) \qquad (6.3)$$

The probability of a complete surface (a series of segments) given a complete key structure is the product of these scores over all segments.

$$P(\text{surface} \mid \text{key structure}) = \prod_{seg} \left( \prod_{p} K_{pc} \prod_{\sim p} (1 - K_{pc}) \right) \qquad (6.4)$$

Now we can calculate the most probable key structure given the surface. From equations 6.1, 6.2, and 6.4 above:

$$P(\text{key structure} \mid \text{surface}) \propto \prod_{seg} \left( M \prod_{p} K_{pc} \prod_{\sim p} (1 - K_{pc}) \right) \qquad (6.5)$$

The key structure maximizing the expression on the right will be the most probable structure given the surface. We can also express this as a logarithm (this will be useful to us later on):

A Polyphonic Key-Finding Model

$$\log\left(\prod_{seg}\left(M\prod_{p}K_{pc}\prod_{\sim p}(1-K_{pc})\right)\right)$$

$$=\sum_{seg}\left(\log M+\sum_{p}\log K_{pc}+\sum_{\sim p}\log(1-K_{pc})\right) \qquad (6.6)$$

I have said how the probability of key structures can be calculated, but not how the most probable key structure of a piece could actually be found. (One could theoretically generate and evaluate all possible complete key structures for a piece, but this would be computationally impractical due to the huge number of possible structures.) Here, we can employ the technique of dynamic programming (already discussed in chapter 3 with regard to the rhythm model). Under the dynamic-programming approach, the model proceeds through the piece in a left-to-right fashion (just as a listener would). At each segment, it keeps a small number of analyses of the portion of the piece heard so far. Specifically, at the first segment, it generates analyses of that segment for each key. At the second segment, it considers each key for that segment, and considers combining each of these segment 2 analyses with each segment 1 analysis (factoring in the appropriate modulation score). For each key $X$ at segment 2, some key $Y$ at segment 1 will yield the highest score for the two segments; key $Y$ is then stored as the key that key $X$ at segment 2 "points back to" (we call $Y$–$X$ the "best-so-far" analysis ending with key $X$ at segment 2). Continuing to segment 3, the process is repeated; this time, for each key $X$, the key-$X$ analysis of segment 3 is combined with each best-so-far analysis ending at segment 2; the one yielding the highest score becomes the one that key $X$ at segment 3 points back to. This process is then continued in a similar way up to the end of the piece. At the final segment $S_f$, the highest-scoring key $X$ can be traced back to yield the best analysis. (First we find the key $Y$ that key $X$ at segment $S_f$ points back to at segment $S_{f-1}$, then we find the key $Z$ that key $Y$ at segment $S_{f-1}$ points back to at segment $S_{f-2}$, and so on.)

This approach has several nice consequences. At each segment $S_n$, we have 24 analyses of the entire piece so far: the "best-so-far" analysis ending in each key. The highest-scoring best-so-far analysis at that point can be viewed as the preferred analysis of everything up to that point. In this way, we can capture the process of building up a key analysis as the piece unfolds in time. There is another interesting aspect to this process as well. The overall best-so-far analysis at segment $S_n$ entails a certain key for each previous segment ($S_{n-1}$, $S_{n-2}$, etc.). But the key for segment

$S_{n-1}$ that is entailed by this analysis may not be the one that was originally chosen. In this way, the model naturally captures the process of "revision": changing one's initial interpretation of a segment based on subsequent events. (See Temperley 2001a for further discussion of revision in key perception.)

<table>
<tr><td>

6.4
Comparing
Distributional
Models of Key-
Finding

</td><td>

The Bayesian key-finding model presented above has much in common with two other models of polyphonic key-finding: the Krumhansl-Schmuckler (K-S) model and my own model from Temperley 2001a, what I have called the CBMS model (these models were described in section 4.1). All three of these models are based on the concept of key-profiles, though each one uses key-profiles in a slightly different way. The key-profiles used in the three models are also quite similar, though there are some subtle differences; table 6.1 shows the key-profiles of all three models. (Recall that the K-S model uses the Krumhansl-Kessler profiles, and the Bayesian model uses the Kostka-Payne profiles.) The CBMS model and the Bayesian model are particularly similar. Both models involve a division of the piece into segments; key judgments are made for each segment, choosing the key whose profile best matches the pitch-classes in the segment and also factoring in a penalty for key changes between segments. (In the Bayesian model, this penalty is reflected in the fact that the probability of remaining in the same key is higher than the probability of modulating.) If we pretend that the key-profile values and modulation penalties from the CBMS model are really logarithms of other numbers, then the two models are virtually identical. There is one significant difference: in the CBMS model, the score for a key on a segment is produced by summing the key-profile scores for the pitch-classes that are present; in the Bayesian model, we also add "absent-pc" scores for pitch-classes that are absent.

</td></tr>
</table>

The three models were subjected to an empirical test, using the Kostka-Payne corpus discussed earlier. (It may seem questionable to use this corpus for testing, as it was also used for setting the parameters of the Bayesian model; I will return to this issue.) The corpus contains 896 segments and a total of 40 modulations (as indicated by the authors' analyses). The output of the models was compared with the correct analyses; each model was simply scored on the proportion of segments that were labeled correctly.[1] (It was necessary to modify the K-S model somewhat, since the original model has no mechanism for handling modulations. In this test, the K-S model evaluates each segment independently

**Table 6.2**
Tests of key-profile models on the Kostka-Payne corpus.

| Model | Optimal change penalty | Percentage of segments correct |
|---|---|---|
| K-S model (using K-K profiles) | 2.3 | 67.0% |
| CBMS model (using CBMS profiles) | 12.0 | 83.8% |
| Bayesian model (using Kostka-Payne profiles) | 0.998 | 86.5% |
| K-S model (using Kostka-Payne profiles) | 1.8 | 80.4% |
| CBMS model (using Kostka-Payne profiles) | 2.5 | 86.3% |
| Bayesian model (using Temperley corpus profiles) | 0.98 | 84.9% |

using the correlation formula, and imposes a change penalty for changes between segments.) With each model, different values of the change penalty were tried, and the value was used that yielded the best performance. (In the case of the Bayesian model, the change penalty is the probability of not modulating from one segment to the next.) This seemed justified, since key structure is generally assumed to be hierarchical, and the level of key represented in a key analysis is therefore rather subjective; what is considered a modulation by one analyst might be considered a mere "tonicization" by another.

Table 6.2 shows the results. The Bayesian model judged 86.5% of segments correctly, slightly better than the CBMS model (83.8%) and significantly better than the K-S model (67.0%). It seemed likely, however, that some of this difference in performance was due simply to differences between the key-profiles. For this reason, the same test was run using the Kostka-Payne profiles with all three models. This improved the performance of the CBMS model to 86.3% and the K-S model to 80.4%.

The approach to testing used here—in which the Bayesian key-finding model (and other models) are tested on the Kostka-Payne corpus, using key-profiles derived from the same corpus—is problematic. Ideally, one would derive the model's parameters from one data set and then test it on another (as we did earlier using the Essen corpus). This is difficult at present, due to the small amount of encoded data available. (As emphasized earlier, it is important to have data in which *local* keys are encoded, not merely the global key of the piece.) One could use one part of the Kostka-Payne corpus for parameter setting and another part for testing, but this would result in even smaller data sets for both parameter setting and testing. To address this, I created another corpus, consisting of 10 long (1 minute or more) excerpts from pieces by a variety of common-practice composers, with local keys analyzed; I will (immodestly) call this the Temperley corpus. The key-profiles generated from the corpus were qualitatively similar to those of the Kostka-Payne corpus, reflecting the same three-level hierarchy of chromatic, diatonic, and tonic-triad scale-degrees (see table 6.1). When the profiles of this corpus were used as the parameters for the Bayesian model, the model labeled 84.9% of segments correctly on the Kostka-Payne corpus, only slightly lower than the rate of 86.5% obtained using the Kostka-Payne parameters. This suggests that the tests reported previously were not greatly biased by the use of the same dataset for training and testing.

At this point, the reader may be feeling somewhat overwhelmed by the proliferation of key-profiles in this study (see table 6.1). In chapter 4, I presented the Krumhansl-Kessler profiles (derived from probe-tone experiments) and the key-profiles from the Essen Folksong Collection; in this chapter, we have added the CBMS profiles (from Temperley 2001a), the Kostka-Payne profiles, and the Temperley corpus profiles. Thus we have seen five sets of key-profiles (major and minor) in all. Let us step back and consider the big picture. First of all, note that all of these key-profile sets are really in very close agreement. All of them reflect a clear three-level structure, with tonic-triad notes rated most highly, other notes within a seven-note (major or minor) scale collection given intermediate values, and chromatic notes given the lowest values. One significant difference is that the CBMS, Kostka-Payne, and Temperley corpus profiles reflect the harmonic minor scale (with $\hat{7}$ as scalar), while the K-K profiles and Essen profiles reflect the natural minor scale (with $\flat\hat{7}$ as scalar—though in both cases the difference is quite small). This seems to indicate a significant difference in compositional practice between folk music (reflected in the Essen corpus) and common-practice music (reflected in the Kostka-Payne and Temperley corpora). It is noteworthy that $\flat\hat{7}$ has a higher value than $\hat{7}$ in the K-K profiles; this may tell us something interesting about key perception among modern Western listeners (as represented by the subjects in Krumhansl and Kessler's experiments). Most Western listeners have heard much music besides common-practice music; many contemporary popular musical styles reflect a modal or blues-based orientation in which $\flat\hat{7}$ is treated as scalar. For common-practice music, however, both the Kostka-Payne and Temperley corpora point strongly to the primacy of $\hat{7}$ over $\flat\hat{7}$ in minor; as we will see, this has important consequences for other musical issues as well.

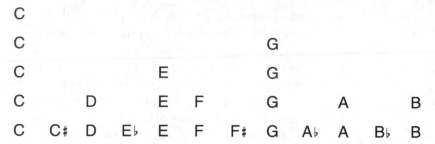

**Figure 6.5**
Lerdahl's "basic space" for C major (2001).

Regarding finer distinctions within levels, there is little agreement among the models, nor is there strong agreement in music theory about such distinctions.[2] Indeed, one might well argue that these distinctions (both in compositional practice and in perceptual data) are just statistical "noise," and that cognitive key-profiles are best represented by eliminating them—giving the same high value to all tonic-triad notes, the same intermediate value to other scalar notes, and the same low value to all chromatic notes. This brings to mind the model of Lerdahl (2001), who reinterprets the key-profile as a structure of discrete levels or "alphabets" (figure 6.5), such that all scale-degrees at the same level are equal in stability. (Lerdahl does make distinctions within the tonic-triad degrees, however, positing a "tonic-fifth" level containing $\hat{5}$ and $\hat{1}$ and a "tonic" level containing just $\hat{1}$.) Such an approach might well be worth pursuing. In what follows, however, we will generally use the Kostka-Payne profiles, simply because they represent the most systematically gathered sample of scale-degree distribution in common-practice music.

**6.5
Further Issues in
Key-Finding**

In this section, we examine some of the errors made by the polyphonic key-finding model, and possible ways of improving it. We then we address several further issues, such as the relationship between the monophonic and polyphonic key-finding models, the hierarchical nature of key, and the general plausibility of the "distributional" approach with regard to human key perception.

In the tests reported in the previous section, the Bayesian key-finding model labeled 86.5% of segments correctly. This level of performance is encouraging, but certainly leaves room for improvement; inspection of the model's errors suggests some ways that it might be improved.[3] Probably the model's most frequent type of error was that its rate of modula-

Chapter 6

A.

B.

**Figure 6.6**
(A) Two different arrangements of the pitches E–F–B–C. (B) A French augmented sixth chord.

tion was not correct; it sometimes modulated at points where the correct analysis did not, or failed to modulate when it should have. As noted earlier, this is a frequent source of "judgment calls" and differences of opinion between analysts. In most of these cases, the model's errors seemed quite reasonable and arguably correct—for example, the model might find a modulation where the correct analysis only indicated a tonicization, or vice versa.

One possible way of improving the model would be to give more consideration to how the pitches in a passage are arranged temporally and registrally. Certainly, there are cases where the arrangement of pitches can affect their tonal implications. One example was suggested by Butler (1989); both of the patterns in figure 6.6A contain the pitches E–F–B–C, but the first seems to strongly imply C major, while the second is much more ambiguous in its implications. Such phenomena could be explained by positing harmony as a factor in key-finding; the first pattern clearly implies a G7–C progression, favoring C major, while the second implies a more ambiguous E–F progression. Inspection of the Bayesian model's errors revealed only a few cases where it seemed that consideration of harmony would help; these mostly involved chromatic chords such as augmented sixths (figure 6.6B). The reason for the model's poor performance on such chords is fairly clear. A French augmented sixth chord Ab–C–D–F♯ is normally assumed to imply a key of C major or minor; but the chord contains an F♯, which is foreign to these keys. Perhaps special rules for such chromatic chords would be needed to handle them effectively.

A further factor one might consider is pitch-spelling information. The model assumes that pitches are sorted into twelve pitch-class categories, which I have elsewhere called "neutral pitch-classes" (Temperley 2001a).

In music notation, however, pitches are further categorized with names like A♭ and G♯—what I have called "tonal pitch-classes." It may be that introducing tonal-pitch-class distinctions in the input and giving the model knowledge of these distinctions—so that, for example, E was more compatible with C major than F♭ was—would improve the model's performance. With regard to the CBMS model, it was found that introducing pitch-spelling distinctions improved performance on the Kostka-Payne corpus from 83.8% to 87.4%; no doubt this would also yield an improvement for the Bayesian model. This would, of course, mean that pitch-spellings would have to be identified in the input before key analysis could take place—a major practical complication and perhaps a questionable assumption from a perceptual viewpoint as well.[4]

The Bayesian perspective suggests other possible ways of improving the model. One way concerns the "modulation scores"—the probability of modulating or not modulating. One could set this parameter empirically, by observing the actual number of modulations in a corpus. Since the Kostka-Payne corpus contains 40 modulations and 850 segments (excluding the initial segment of each excerpt), the probability of a modulation should be $40/850 = .047$. (By contrast, the value for this parameter found to be optimal through trial-and-error adjustment was .002.) As an experiment, the modulation scores were set to reflect this, adding a score of $\log(.047/23)$ for each modulating segment (assuming again that moves to any of the other 23 keys are equally likely), and $\log(1 - .047)$ for nonmodulating segments. This produced a score of only 81.9% correct—somewhat less than the optimal performance of 86.5%. A second possible improvement would be to modify the assumption that all keys are equally likely. Major keys are undoubtedly more commonly used than minor keys; in the Kostka-Payne corpus, 70.0% of the segments are in major keys. Thus it might be advantageous to give them a higher probability. However, analysis of the Bayesian model's output showed that, even without a special preference for major keys, the model was achieving almost exactly the right proportion of major segments (68.7%); this suggests that adding a preference for major keys is unlikely to improve performance very much.

A more promising area for incorporating probabilistic information concerns transitions between keys. It is well known that keys have varying degrees of relatedness to each other: with respect to C major, G major is a closely related key while F♯ major is not. It seems likely that this plays a role in key-finding, in that we tend to favor moves to closely related keys. The common-practice repertoire contains some passages

**Figure 6.7**
Handel, "Hallelujah Chorus" (from *Messiah*), mm. 57–63.

where such a relational factor seems to influence key perception. Consider figure 6.7, from the "Hallelujah Chorus" in Handel's *Messiah*. The first three-measure phrase (indicated by a square bracket above the score) clearly implies D major, forming a I–IV–I harmonic pattern on the "Hallelujah's"; this seems fairly clear even when the passage is heard out of context. The following three-measure phrase features almost exactly the same pattern, except transposed up a whole-step. (The inner voices are slightly rearranged, but I doubt very much that this would affect the passage's tonal implications.) But the second phrase seems to imply A major, not E major as one might expect; thus the implied harmony of the "Hallelujah's" is V–I–V in A. This could be explained by the fact that the phrase itself is somewhat ambiguous between E major and A major, and given that the previous context establishes D major, we favor A major as it is more closely related. Another well-known example is the opening of Beethoven's *Waldstein* sonata (figure 6.8); here again, we have a phrase (mm. 1–4) repeated in exact transposition (mm. 5–7 —the fourth measure of the phrase is altered). But whereas mm. 1–4 imply C major, perhaps with a tonicization of G at the end, mm. 5–7 seem to imply F major much more than B♭ major. Again, we can explain this in terms of key relations: given the larger context of C major, F major seems a much more appropriate key to tonicize than B♭. (See Lerdahl

A Polyphonic Key-Finding Model

**Figure 6.8**
Beethoven, Sonata Op. 53 ("Waldstein"), I, mm. 1–8.

2001 for a more thorough discussion of the complex key structure of this passage.) In cases such as this, key relations seem to have a significant influence on key-finding.

In principle, information about key relations could be incorporated into the Bayesian key-finding model rather easily, by adjusting the modulation score depending on the relationship between the two keys in question. This has not yet been attempted; to construct such a model based on empirical values would require more data, as the Kostka-Payne corpus itself provides only 40 modulations. One could also derive the values theoretically; this would require a quantitative theory of key relations, a topic that I will address in chapter 7.

Overall, the polyphonic key-finding model seems quite promising in its key-finding performance; further refinements—such as the incorporation of key-transition information—seem likely to improve it further. At this point, we should perhaps step back and reconsider what the model might tell us about *human* key perception. As noted in chapter 1, the mere fact that a model performs well at a task does not prove that humans perform it the same way. Some may find the distributional approach of this model (and many other key-finding models) counterintuitive, as it ignores many kinds of important musical knowledge—knowledge about

**Figure 6.9**
Stravinsky, *Sonata for Two Pianos*, I, mm. 1–9.

conventional melodic patterns, harmonic progressions and cadences, and so on. To exclude knowledge of this kind from a key-finding model is not, of course, to deny its general importance, but merely to suggest that it may not play much role in key perception. One source of *positive* evidence for the distributional view of key perception comes from so-called "pan-diatonic" music, which uses a diatonic scale collection but in nontraditional ways. A case in point is shown in figure 6.9, the opening of Stravinsky's *Sonata for Two Pianos*. This excerpt projects an unmistakable sense of an F major tonality in mm. 1–4 modulating to C major in mm. 5–9, despite the general absence of conventional harmonic and melodic patterns. This suggests that such patterns are not necessary to project a sense of tonality; pitch-class distribution alone has surprising power as an indicator of key.[5] What the current tests have shown is that the identification of key from distributional information is, to a large extent, possible in common-practice music as well. Taken together, then, the evidence seems to point strongly toward an important role for distributional information in key perception.

One important aspect of key which has only been mentioned briefly so far is its hierarchical nature. The key structure of an extended piece may have several levels: there is generally one main or "top-level" key, with secondary key sections within it, and perhaps with smaller (third-level or even fourth-level) key areas within those. These lower-level key sections may be quite fleeting—perhaps consisting only of a V–I progression in the implied key—and are often labeled only as tonicizations or "applied chords" rather than as true modulations. We have focused here on what might be called the "basic level" of keys, those that are likely to be represented as modulations in a harmonic analysis. But it is an interesting question whether the probabilistic approach proposed here might somehow be used to generate a hierarchical key structure. The hierarchical aspect of key structure has barely been studied—either in music theory or music psychology—and we will not pursue it further here.

One might wonder about the relationship between the polyphonic key-finding model presented here and the monophonic one presented in chapter 4. It would seem odd to propose that key-finding worked by quite different principles in monophonic and polyphonic music; and I do not wish to imply this. Rather, we can view the monophonic model of chapter 4 as a simple, preliminary proposal for probabilistic key-finding; what I have proposed in this chapter is a more sophisticated approach (providing a better handling of repeated pitch-classes and allowing for modulation), which could be applied to both polyphonic and monophonic music. The monophonic model does have one important advantage, however: since it generates actual pitches, it can be used to assess the probabilities of actual pitch sequences. The polyphonic model, which only generates pitch-class sets, cannot be used in this way. However, the idea of "surface probability" does have some interesting implications with regard to the polyphonic model, though it must be construed in a rather different way. This, along with some other applications of the polyphonic model, will be the subject of the next chapter.

# 7
# Applications of the Polyphonic Key-Finding Model

In chapter 6, I proposed a Bayesian model of key-finding in polyphonic music and showed that it was quite successful in predicting human key judgments. In the current chapter, I will examine the implications of the model for issues beyond key-finding, focusing on three issues in particular. The first is key relations—relations of similarity or closeness between keys. The second is what I will call "tonalness"—the degree to which a segment of music is characteristic of the language of common-practice tonality. The third is ambiguity—the degree to which a musical segment is clear or equivocal in its tonal implications. Both ambiguity and tonalness can fruitfully be examined with regard to abstract sets of pitch-classes, and also with regard to actual musical passages. In these areas, the Bayesian model sheds light on basic matters of music perception and tonal theory, as well as providing analytical insights into specific musical pieces.[1]

In what follows, we will assume the key-finding model presented in the previous chapter, along with the key-profiles generated from the Kostka-Payne corpus (see figure 6.4). As emphasized earlier, I do not claim that these are the ultimate, ideal key-profiles. However, they seem to be the best available profiles for our purposes, as they represent common-practice music (which will be our main concern in this chapter) and were set in a systematic, empirical way.

**7.1**
**Key Relations**

It is generally assumed in music theory that keys have relations of closeness or similarity with one another. G major is a closely related key to C

**Figure 7.1**
Mozart, Symphony No. 40, I, mm. 99–105.

major; C major and F♯ major are much more distantly related. This is reflected in common patterns of modulation—a piece in C major is much more likely to modulate to G major than to F♯ major. Key relations are also exploited by composers for dramatic effect—for example, the wrenching shift from B♭ major to the distant key of F♯ minor in the first movement of Mozart's Fortieth Symphony (figure 7.1). Experiments have shown that listeners, even those without musical training, are sensitive to key relations, and can distinguish between modulations to closely or distantly related keys (Thompson and Cuddy 1992).

This section explores the possibility of using the probabilistic key-finding model of chapter 6 to predict key relations in common-practice music. The idea of using key-profiles to model key relations was explored in some depth by Krumhansl and Kessler (1982) (see also Krumhansl 1990); the work of Lerdahl (2001) in this area is also important. My treatment of this topic builds on this earlier work in many respects, but I will suggest that the probabilistic approach sheds light on some further musical issues.

Krumhansl and Kessler proposed to quantify the relationship between two keys by calculating the correlation between their key-profiles. Recall that the correlation method was also the basis for the Krumhansl-Schmuckler key-finding algorithm, discussed in chapter 4. As explained there, correlation is a kind of "template-matching"; if two key-profiles have high values for many of the same pitches, the correlation between them should be high. (Correlation produces a value between −1.0 and 1.0, with 1.0 indicating a perfect match between the two vectors.) Table 7.1, column A, shows the correlation values for all keys in relation to C major and A minor, using Krumhansl and Kessler's original key-profiles (shown in figure 4.3); we will call these the "K-K" correlations. Column B shows the correlations for the same key relations, using the Kostka-Payne key-profiles; we will call these the "K-P" correlations. Recall that

**Table 7.1**
Distances from C major and A minor to all other keys, using three different distance models.

| Key | A. K-K profiles, correlation method (from Krumhansl 1990) | | B. K-P profiles, correlation method | | C. K-P profiles, cross-entropy method | |
|---|---|---|---|---|---|---|
| | C major | A minor | C major | A minor | C major | A minor |
| C | 1.000 | .651 | 1.000 | .646 | 5.888 | 7.243 |
| C♯/D♭ | −.500 | −.508 | −.575 | −.488 | 12.754 | 12.313 |
| D | .040 | .241 | .146 | .198 | 9.658 | 9.466 |
| D♯/E♭ | −.105 | −.369 | −.065 | −.421 | 10.337 | 11.696 |
| E | −.185 | .215 | −.224 | .251 | 11.471 | 9.359 |
| F | .591 | .536 | .638 | .521 | 7.318 | 7.919 |
| F♯/G♭ | −.683 | −.654 | −.840 | −.709 | 13.972 | 13.106 |
| G | .591 | .237 | .638 | .343 | 7.472 | 8.659 |
| G♯/A♭ | −.185 | −.298 | −.224 | −.355 | 11.028 | 11.738 |
| A | −.105 | .511 | −.065 | .436 | 10.691 | 8.385 |
| A♯/B♭ | .040 | −.158 | .146 | −.009 | 9.417 | 10.199 |
| B | −.500 | −.402 | .575 | −.414 | 12.855 | 12.099 |
| Cm | .511 | .055 | .436 | .072 | 8.584 | 10.551 |
| C♯m/D♭m | −.298 | .003 | −.355 | −.002 | 11.388 | 9.886 |
| Dm | .237 | .339 | .343 | .374 | 8.568 | 8.568 |
| D♯m/E♭m | −.654 | −.673 | −.709 | −.542 | 13.191 | 12.030 |
| Em | .536 | .339 | .521 | .374 | 7.856 | 8.517 |
| Fm | .215 | −.003 | .251 | −.002 | 9.135 | 10.297 |
| F♯m/G♭m | −.369 | .055 | −.421 | −.072 | 11.434 | 9.906 |
| Gm | .241 | .160 | .198 | −.165 | 9.464 | 10.846 |
| G♯m/A♭m | −.508 | −.394 | −.488 | −.364 | 12.156 | 11.689 |
| Am | .651 | 1.000 | .646 | 1.000 | 7.258 | 5.979 |
| A♯m/B♭m | −.402 | −.394 | −.414 | .364 | 11.945 | 11.360 |
| Bm | −.158 | −.160 | −.009 | −.165 | 9.926 | 10.590 |

A.

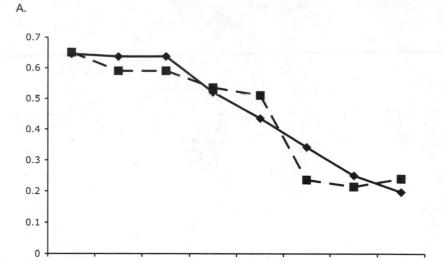

B.

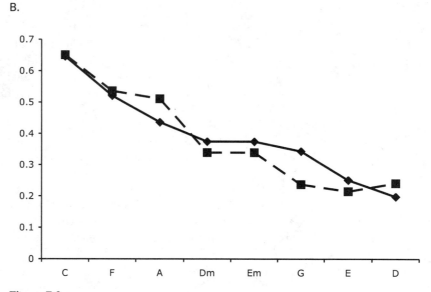

**Figure 7.2**
The eight closest keys to C major (A) and A minor (B), in order of closeness, according to the K-P correlation values; the solid line represents these values. The dotted line represents the K-K correlation values for these key relationships. (F major and G major are equal in closeness to C major, under both models; similarly, D minor and E minor are equal in closeness to A minor.)

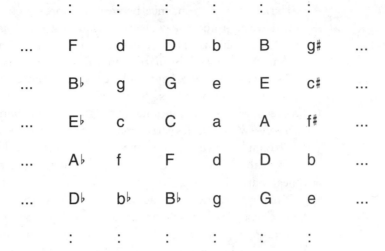

|     |     |     |     |     |     |     |     |     |
| --- | --- | --- | --- | --- | --- | --- | --- | --- |
| ⋮ | | ⋮ | | ⋮ | | ⋮ | | ⋮ | | ⋮ | |
| ... | F | d | D | b | B | g♯ | ... |
| ... | B♭ | g | G | e | E | c♯ | ... |
| ... | E♭ | c | C | a | A | f♯ | ... |
| ... | A♭ | f | F | d | D | b | ... |
| ... | D♭ | b♭ | B♭ | g | G | e | ... |

**Figure 7.3**
Schoenberg's "Chart of Regions" (1954/1969: 20). Upper-case letters represent major keys; lower-case letters represent minor keys.

the Kostka-Payne profiles were derived from scale-degree distributions in a corpus of common-practice excerpts taken from the Kostka-Payne theory textbook. Figure 7.2 shows the "closest" keys in relation to C major and A minor, according to the K-P correlation values; the K-K correlation values for these keys are also shown.

It can be seen that the K-K and K-P correlation values are in many ways similar. The "top five" keys in terms of closeness are the same in both models, in both major and minor keys. These rankings also correspond well with music-theoretical assumptions about key relations. For C major, the five most closely related keys (in order) are the relative minor (Am), major dominant (G), major subdominant (F), mediant (Em), and parallel minor (Cm). If we consider a well-known spatial representation of keys in music theory—Schoenberg's "Chart of Regions"—we find that the closest four keys to C major in the space include four of these five: Am, Cm, G, and F (see figure 7.3). For A minor, the five most closely-related keys according to both the K-K and K-P profiles are the relative major (C), submediant (F), parallel major (A), minor dominant (Em), and minor subdominant (Dm); here again, these five keys include the four closest keys on Schoenberg's chart (C, A, Dm, and Em). Krumhansl and Kessler (1982) note this similarity as well, and show how a four-dimensional spatial representation of keys derived from their correlation values closely resembles the Chart of Regions.

Applications of the Model

The close correspondence between key-profile correlations and theoretical wisdom about key relations can largely be understood in terms of scale collections. The usual theoretical explanation for key relations is that they depend primarily on the overlap between scales (Piston 1978: 221–222): two keys will be closely related if their scales share many of the same tones. Since scales are also reflected in the key-profiles—with scalar tones having higher values than chromatic ones—two keys whose scales share many tones will have a high correlation. For example, if we consider just major keys, the scales sharing the most tones with C major are F major and G major (both share 6 out of 7 tones); naturally, then, these keys yield a high correlation with C major.[2]

When we include minor keys, the situation becomes more complicated; here it depends on which "minor scale" is being assumed. Recall that the Kostka-Payne minor-key profile reflects the harmonic minor scale, in that $\hat{7}$ has a higher value than $\flat\hat{7}$. Consider the number of scale-degrees each scale shares with every other scale, assuming the harmonic minor scale for minor keys; this is shown in table 7.2. It can be seen that C major shares 6 degrees with three other keys (F major, G major, and A minor), whereas A minor shares 6 degrees with only one other key (C major). A key whose scale shares 6 degrees with that of another key will be called a "nearest neighbor"; thus each major key has three nearest neighbors, while each minor key has just one. We might characterize this difference by saying that minor keys are more "remote" from other keys than major keys are, in terms of the overlap between scales. This difference is reflected in the correlation values as well, and can be clearly seen in figure 7.2 (here we focus on the Kostka-Payne correlations). C major has three very closely related keys; A minor, G major, and F major are all almost equally close. By contrast, A minor has only one very closely related key, C major. (The difference is not reflected as strongly in the K-K distance values, which is not surprising, as the K-K profiles do not really reflect the harmonic minor scale; $\flat\hat{7}$ has a slightly *higher* value than $\hat{7}$ in minor.) I will suggest below that the greater "remoteness" of minor keys has some interesting musical implications.[3]

The fact that the relative major is predicted to be the most closely related key to a minor key accords well with compositional practice. It is well known that minor-key pieces tend to modulate to the relative major key more than any other. The predictions of the model regarding major-key pieces are not quite so successful. Major-key pieces tend to favor the major dominant as the most common secondary key. The major dominant is one of the three closest keys to a major key, but the model does

Chapter 7

**Table 7.2**
Pitch-classes (pcs) shared between C major/A minor and all other keys (assuming the harmonic minor scale for minor keys).

| Key | Number of pcs shared with C major | Key | Number of pcs shared with A minor |
|---|---|---|---|
| C | — | C | 6 |
| C♯ | 2 | D♭ | 3 |
| D | 5 | D | 4 |
| E♭ | 4 | E♭ | 4 |
| E | 3 | E | 4 |
| F | 6 | F | 5 |
| F♯ | 2 | F♯ | 3 |
| G | 6 | G | 5 |
| A♭ | 3 | A♭ | 3 |
| A | 4 | A | 5 |
| B♭ | 5 | B♭ | 4 |
| B | 2 | B | 3 |
| Cm | 5 | Cm | 5 |
| D♭m | 3 | D♭m | 4 |
| Dm | 5 | Dm | 4 |
| E♭m | 3 | E♭m | 4 |
| Em | 5 | Em | 4 |
| Fm | 4 | Fm | 4 |
| F♯m | 4 | F♯m | 5 |
| Gm | 4 | Gm | 3 |
| A♭m | 3 | A♭m | 3 |
| Am | 6 | Am | — |
| B♭m | 3 | B♭m | 3 |
| Bm | 4 | Bm | 3 |

not predict why it should be favored over the (almost equally close) relative minor and subdominant. However, if we allow that there might be other reasons for the preference for the major dominant—for example, regarding it as an expansion of the dominant harmony within the key—then the model at least explains why this preference might be overruled in minor keys, due to the greater closeness of the relative major.

Another factor affecting these correlation values is overlap between tonic triads. Recall that members of the tonic triad have higher values than other scalar tones, in both major and minor, in both the K-P and K-K profiles. A major triad such as C major shares two tones with three

**Figure 7.4**
Brahms, Sonata for Violoncello and Piano Op. 38, I, mm. 1–8.

other tonic triads: C minor (the parallel minor), A minor (the relative minor), and E minor (the mediant). No doubt this partly explains why C minor and E minor achieve relatively high correlation values in relation to C major. Similarly, with regard to A minor, C major (the relative major), A major (the parallel major) and F major (the submediant) share two tonic-triad tones and also have relatively high correlations. Lerdahal (2001) proposes a theoretical model of key relations incorporating both scale overlap and tonic-triad overlap, and shows how Schoenberg's Chart of Regions can be derived in this manner.

One further, subtle, issue to consider is the "parallel dominant." Which is closer: the minor dominant of a major key (we will call this relationship "M-Dm") or the major dominant of a minor key ("m-DM")? While one can certainly find examples of both "moves" in tonal pieces, I would argue that the m-DM relationship is closer. Moves from a minor key to the dominant major are not uncommon, and can be viewed simply as tonicizing the major V chord, which is the normal dominant chord in the minor key; we see this, for example, in the opening of Brahms's Cello Sonata Op. 38 (figure 7.4), which begins in E minor and moves

**Figure 7.5**
Chopin, Prelude Op. 28, No. 15, mm. 9–12.

directly to B major. By contrast, direct moves from a major key to the dominant minor are much rarer and can seem quite peculiar—for example, the move to A♭ minor in Chopin's D♭ Major Prelude (figure 7.5). If we consider the K-P correlation values in table 6.1, it can be seen that m-DM is indeed closer than M-Dm: the correlation for the m-DM relationship (A minor to E major) is .251, while the correlation for M-Dm (C major to G minor) is .198. This result cannot be explained in terms of scale overlap: Both the M-Dm and the m-DM pairs have 4 scale-degrees in common. It seems to be due, rather, to the overlap between the tonic-triad of one key and the scale of another (assuming, as always, the harmonic minor scale). In the case of A minor and E major, the three tonic-triad notes of E major are all within the scale of A minor. In the case of C major and G minor, by contrast, only two tonic-triad tones of each key are scalar in the other key. This is essentially just a rephrasing of the musical explanation offered at the beginning of the paragraph: the m-DM relationship is close because the tonic triad of the major dominant is a normal triad (within the scale) of the tonic key. Thus, this subtle distinction in key relations seems to be captured well by the K-P correlation values.

This discussion has evaded a number of complexities in the modeling of key relations. First of all, key relations are asymmetrical. The most closely related key to a major key is usually assumed to be the dominant, and this is surely the most common secondary key in major-key pieces. But in terms of correlations, the tonic-dominant relationship is the same as the subdominant–tonic relationship, so their distances will be the same; the correlation measure of closeness is not well suited to representing such asymmetries. One possible approach to this problem is to view key relations from the perspective of harmonic progressions—treating key areas, in effect, as expanded harmonies (see for example Aldwell and Schachter 2003). (I suggested earlier that this might explain the preference for modulations to the dominant.) There is certainly some merit to this idea, but it too encounters problems: the most common chord progressions are not necessarily common key progressions, and vice versa. Another complication is that compositional practice with regard to key relations changes significantly within the common-practice period. It is generally agreed that "parallel" keys (e.g., C major and C minor) become more closely related in the nineteenth century; shifts between parallel keys become much more common, as do shifts from one key to the closely related keys of the parallel key (for example, from C major to E♭ major or A♭ major). In short, there are many further issues that a comprehensive model of key relations would have to address. Still, the K-P correlation measures seem to provide a good "first approximation" to key distances in common-practice music.

Since we are interpreting key-profiles probabilistically in this study, one might also wonder if there was a probabilistic method of calculating the closeness or similarity between two keys. One possible method is *cross-entropy*. We introduced cross-entropy in chapter 2 as a way of calculating the degree to which a model fits a body of data (see equation 2.24). We can actually think about it in a similar way here. Suppose we had a piece consisting of many segments, whose pitch-class distribution exactly reflected the C major key-profile: that is to say, .748 of segments contained C, .060 of segments contained C♯, and so forth. We can then ask: What is the probability that such a distribution would be produced by a generative model using the G major profile? This is essentially what cross-entropy tells us. This method was applied to calculate the distance between C major and all other keys, and between A minor and all other keys; the resulting values are shown in column C of table 7.1. (In this case, unlike in the correlation values, a *lower* value represents a closer relationship.) The cross-entropy method yields very similar results to the correlation method (in terms of the ranking of different keys), so it will not be discussed in detail here; but it is worth noting that the probabilistic approach does provide a way of calculating key distances.[4]

**7.2
Tonalness**

As we have seen in earlier chapters, one attractive aspect of the Bayesian "structure-and-surface" approach is the possibility of calculating the probability of a surface itself:

$$P(\text{surface}) = \sum_{\text{structure}} P(\text{surface} \cap \text{structure})$$

$$= \sum_{\text{structure}} P(\text{surface} \mid \text{structure})P(\text{structure}) \tag{7.1}$$

In chapter 5, I argued that this concept of "surface probability" was relevant to a number of aspects of melody perception: expectation, error detection, and pitch identification. In what follows, we will explore the implications of this concept with respect to the polyphonic key-finding model. One problem here is that, whereas the combined rhythm/pitch monophonic model calculates the probability of actual note patterns, the polyphonic model does not; it essentially represents a pattern of notes as a series of pitch-class sets. Thus the model cannot make precise predictions about expectation or error detection in polyphonic music. However, I will argue that the concept of surface probability is still of considerable interest, though we must think of it in a rather different way.

Let us consider how surface probability might be defined, just for a single segment. The surface of a segment can be represented simply as the set of pitch-classes (pcset) that it contains; the structure is the key of the segment. If we ignore the context (so that there is no "modulation factor"), and assume that all keys are equally likely, the prior probability of each key—$P(\text{structure})$—is 1/24. Then, from equations 7.1 and 6.3:

$$P(\text{pcset}) = \sum_{\text{key}} P(\text{pcset} \mid \text{key})P(\text{key})$$

$$= \sum_{\text{key}} \left( \prod_{p} K_{pc} \prod_{\sim p}(1 - K_{pc}) \right)(1/24) \tag{7.2}$$

Table 7.3 shows this quantity for certain well-known pitch-class sets (using the Kostka-Payne key-profiles). The table shows, first, the overall probability of each set. It can be seen that, among three-pc sets, the major and minor triad have higher probability than the diminished triad, which in turn has higher probability than C–C♯–D. No doubt this is because the major and minor triad are highly probable in combination with certain keys, namely keys in which they are diatonic triads (and the tonic triad in particular). By contrast, the set C–C♯–D is not particularly probable given *any* key, as it will always contain at least one chromatic note. This is made clear by the second column, which shows the joint probability of each set with its most probable key.

**Table 7.3**
Tonalness of some common pitch-class sets.

| Pitch-class set | Overall probability of set ("tonalness") | Probability of set combined with most probable key | Number of distinct transpositions of set | Total probability of $T_n$ set-type |
|---|---|---|---|---|
| C–E–G (major triad) | .00173 | .00103 (C) | 12 | .02080 |
| C–E♭–G (minor triad) | .00178 | .00098 (Cm) | 12 | .02137 |
| C–E♭–G♭ (dim. triad) | .00032 | .00004 (B♭m) | 12 | .00382 |
| C–C♯–D ([012]) | .00022 | .00002 (Gm) | 12 | .00261 |
| C–D–E–F–G–A–B (major scale) | .00049 | .00032 (C) | 12 | .00590 |
| C–D–E♭–F–G–A♭–B (harmonic minor scale) | .00028 | .00025 (Cm) | 12 | .00332 |
| C–D–E–F♯–A♭–B♭ (whole-tone scale) | .00001 | .000001 (Gm*) | 2 | .00002 |
| C–D–E♭–F–G♭–A♭–A–B (octatonic scale) | .000004 | .0000007 (E♭m*) | 3 | .00001 |
| C–C♯–D–E♭–E–F–F♯ ([0123456]) | .000006 | .000001 (D♭) | 12 | .00007 |

* Symmetrical sets (such as the whole-tone scale and octatonic scale) yield equal probability judgments for multiple keys; in this case the model makes an arbitrary decision.

Table 7.3 also shows the probabilities of several larger pitch-class collections. It can be seen that the major (or "diatonic") scale is somewhat more probable than the harmonic minor scale; both are much more probable than the six-note whole-tone scale, the eight-note octatonic scale, or the set C–C♯–D–E♭–E–F–F♯ (seven pitch-classes spaced by half-steps, which we call by its pitch-class set-theory name, [0123456]). Notice that the overall probability figures in table 7.3 tell us only the probability of one particular transposition of each set: for example, the C major scale. We could also consider the probability of a certain *type* of set, or "$T_n$ set-type" (Rahn 1980)—for example, major scales in general. This would be given by the probability of one transposition of the set, multiplied by the number of distinct transpositions; this is shown in the rightmost column of table 7.3. In the case of the major scale, the set-type probability is .00049 × 12; in the case of the whole-tone scale, it is .00001 × 2, since there are only two distinct whole-tone scales. We will focus on particular transpositions of sets here, rather than set-types, though the two approaches usually lead to quite similar results; the major scale is far more probable than the whole-tone scale, whether one considers a single transposition of the set or all transpositions.

Essentially, the numbers in table 7.3 tell us the probability of different pitch-class sets occurring (within a short span of time) in a piece—specifically, a *tonal* piece, a piece using the musical language from which the current key-profiles were generated. To put it a slightly different way, they tell us how characteristic each pitch-class set is of the language of common-practice tonality—how tonal the set is, one might say. Certainly, we are capable of making such judgments as listeners. If we turn on the radio and hear a diatonic scale, we are likely to suspect that the piece is tonal; if we hear a whole-tone scale or [0123456], our estimate of that probability will be significantly less (though one must also take into account the extremely low *prior* probability of hearing a nontonal piece on the radio!). Of course, this would depend on the way the pitches were arranged; no doubt the set [0123456] could be compositionally realized in such a way as to sound unproblematically tonal. There is more to tonality, and judgments of tonality, than sheer pitch-class content. But the pitch-class content of a passage surely *contributes* to its tonalness, and this aspect of tonality appears to be captured rather well by the Bayesian model.[5]

The method of measuring tonalness presented here can be used only for a single pitch-class set. Let us consider how this approach might be applied to longer musical passages. The logical way would be to estimate the surface probability of a sequence of segments—again, treating each segment as a pitch-class set. To do this, according to equation 7.1, one must calculate the probability of all possible key structures for the passage (all ways of labeling segments with keys) in combination with the surface, and sum these together: $\sum P(\text{structure} \cap \text{surface})$. Such calculations do not emerge very naturally out of the current model, and require a good deal of extra computation. An alternative approach would be to take the joint probability of a passage with its most probable analysis—that is, the *maximum* value of $P(\text{structure} \cap \text{surface})$—as representative of the overall probability of the passage. This possibility was discussed earlier, in section 5.4; it was suggested there that, in many situations, $max(P(\text{structure} \cap \text{surface}))$ might actually be quite a good indicator of $P(\text{surface})$.

With this assumption in mind, consider the kinds of passages that would be judged as probable by the model. Recall that

$$P(\text{structure} \cap \text{surface}) = P(\text{surface} \mid \text{structure})P(\text{structure}) \qquad (7.3)$$

Applications of the Model

**Figure 7.6**
Chopin, Mazurka Op. 6, No. 1, mm. 1–10.

A probable passage would therefore be one for which the value of $P(\text{surface} \mid \text{structure})P(\text{structure})$ was high, for some structure. For $P(\text{surface} \mid \text{structure})$ to be high, there must be some sequence of keys such that the key of each segment is relatively compatible with the pitches of the segment. For $P(\text{structure})$ to be high, the number of modulations must be relatively low. Consider an excerpt consisting of an alternating pattern of C major and G major triads (each one occupying a segment). In this case, a key analysis which maintains C major throughout allows good compatibility between the key of each segment and the pitches, and also avoids modulations. Now imagine a series of segments consisting of alternating C major and F♯ major triads. In this case, the model would either have to incorporate all of the segments within a single key, such as C major, in which case the F♯ major segments would have a low probability, or it would have to change key at each segment, in which case the probability of the structure would be low. Neither of these analyses would be especially high-scoring, thus the probability of the passage as a whole would be judged as relatively low. A passage which contained many chromatic pitch-class sets—so that no compatible key could be found even for individual segments—would be assigned a low probability also.

A model such as this might yield revealing judgments, not only of the tonalness of an entire piece, but of fluctuations in tonalness within pieces. Consider figure 7.6, mm. 1–10 of Chopin's Mazurka Op. 6 No. 1. The

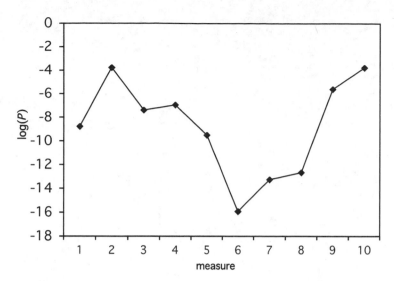

**Figure 7.7**
The model's probability scores for the Chopin Mazurka excerpt in figure 7.6.

model's preferred analysis here is to retain F♯ minor throughout the entire passage. The probability of each segment of the passage (treating measures as segments), in combination with the preferred analysis, is shown in figure 7.7 (note that in this case a logarithmic scale is used). Roughly speaking, the first four measures are high in probability, but in mm. 5–8 the probability steeply declines, increasing sharply again in mm. 9–10. Clearly, this trajectory reflects the fact that many of the pitches in mm. 5–8 are chromatic with respect to F♯ minor and thus low in probability given that key. (The probability of the first measure is lowered by the fact that every key has an equal probability of 1/24.)

Figure 7.8 shows a rather different situation—the first movement (excluding the six-measure introduction) of Schumann's *Papillons*. The probability judgments for each measure are shown in figure 7.9. Here, the model's preferred analysis is to remain in D major throughout except for a brief modulation to A♭ major in mm. 15–16. The fact that m. 15 and m. 17 are both low in probability reflects the fact that modulations occur there; in this case, then, the probability of the key structure itself is low. In m. 17, there is chromaticism even with respect to the chosen key (G♯ and A♯ are chromatic in D major), further lowering its probability. The low probability values for this part of the piece reflect its surprising harmonic twists and turns. The model could also have chosen to remain

Applications of the Model

**Figure 7.8**
Schumann, *Papillons*, No. 1, mm. 7–22. The model's key analysis is shown above the staff.

in D major for the entire passage; but then, there would have been even more extreme chromaticism in mm. 15–16 relative to the key.[6]

I submit that these probabilistic scores relate in an interesting way to musical perception and experience—though it is not exactly clear what dimension of musical experience they correspond to most closely. I suggested earlier that they have something to do with judgments of "tonalness": a kind of grammaticality or normality within the common-practice language. They also have something to do with tension: a passage of low probability is likely to have an effect of tension and instability. This may be partly because unexpected events are more difficult to process, and thus cognitively taxing—a phenomenon known in psychology as *perceptual facilitation* (Swinney 1979; Bharucha 1987). (Low-probability events may also indicate a failure in communication: if the

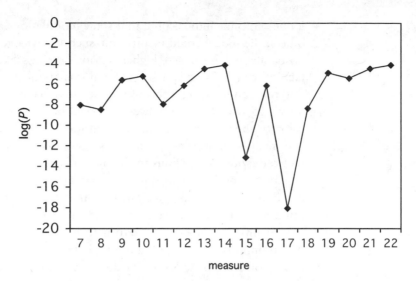

**Figure 7.9**
The model's probability scores for the Schumann excerpt in figure 7.8.

passage seems improbable, this suggests that we may be misanalyzing the structure, or even misperceiving the notes.) The sections yielding low scores in figures 7.6 and 7.8—mm. 5–8 of the Chopin and mm. 15–18 of the Schumann—are, indeed, passages of considerable tension. Of course—to reiterate my earlier caveat—the musical tension of a passage is more than just a simple function of its pitch-class content; all kinds of melodic, harmonic, and rhythmic factors undoubtedly play a role. Yet pitch-class content surely plays *some* role in tension; generally speaking, passages with lots of chromaticism and rapid modulations tend to sound tense and unstable (at least in a common-practice context), no matter how the pitches are arranged. What I am suggesting is that this aspect of musical tension appears to correspond well with surface probability, as judged by the current model. We should note also that this proposed correlate to tension is simply an emergent feature of a model that was proposed for quite a different purpose: modeling judgments of key. The tension of a passage, under the current hypothesis, is given by the maximal value of $P(\text{surface} \mid \text{structure})P(\text{structure})$; but this must be computed anyway (if the Bayesian key-finding model is correct), in order to find the most probable key structure.

Two further points should be made about the model's performance on the Schumann. First, while the model imposes a penalty for modulations, it does not take into account that some modulations are more likely than others; the model could incorporate such knowledge by assigning lower probabilities (and hence, higher tension) for less likely modulations. In fact, moving to A♭ major from D major is about the least likely modulation one can imagine; if this were taken into account, the tonalness score for m. 15 would be even lower. As noted in section 6.5, assigning different probabilities for different key transitions seems desirable in any case, and might well improve the model's key-finding ability. Another point is that the model is oblivious to the hierarchical nature of key, and in particular, has no knowledge that one particular key (D major in this case) is the main one. Thus it assigns the same probability (and therefore the same tension) for a move away from the main key (as in m. 15 of the Schumann) as it does for a return to it (as in m. 17). This may seem counterintuitive; one might, indeed, say that a return to the main key creates a lowering of tension. On the other hand, a return to the tonic—particularly an abrupt return from a distant key, as in this case—surely can create a momentary sense of surprise and confusion; is this not a kind of tension? This is a tricky issue; perhaps what it tells us is that there are different kinds of tension (even within the fairly narrow aspect of "key tension" at issue here) that cannot be adequately described on a single dimension.[7]

## 7.3 Tonal Ambiguity and Clarity

We now turn to another aspect of tonality that is illuminated by the Bayesian key-finding model: ambiguity. Ambiguity plays an important role in many dimensions of music—key, harmony, meter, and form—and has been widely discussed in music theory, the writings of Meyer (1956, 1973) being perhaps the most notable example. With regard to key, the ambiguity of a passage is simply the degree to which it clearly implies a single key, or is equivocal between two or several keys. As with our exploration of tonalness, we begin by examining ambiguity in the relatively abstract domain of pitch-class sets, and then move toward more complex situations of real music.

Let us first consider how ambiguity might be calculated with regard to a single segment. Using Bayes' rule (equation 2.9), we can calculate the probability of a key given the pitch-class set in the segment:

$$P(\text{key} \mid \text{pcset}) = \frac{P(\text{pcset} \mid \text{key})P(\text{key})}{P(\text{pcset})} \tag{7.4}$$

**Table 7.4**
The probability of each key given two pitch-class sets, C–E–G and C–C#–D.

| Key | $P(\text{key} \mid \text{C–E–G})$ | $P(\text{key} \mid \text{C–C#–D})$ |
| --- | --- | --- |
| C | .597 | .057 |
| C#/Db | .000 | .040 |
| D | .002 | .038 |
| D#/Eb | .003 | .007 |
| E | .001 | .001 |
| F | .063 | .053 |
| F#/Gb | .000 | .010 |
| G | .058 | .071 |
| G#/Ab | .006 | .058 |
| A | .001 | .049 |
| A#/Bb | .002 | .054 |
| B | .000 | .002 |
| Cm | .018 | .078 |
| C#m/Dbm | .004 | .043 |
| Dm | .006 | .071 |
| D#m/Ebm | .000 | .002 |
| Em | .130 | .003 |
| Fm | .063 | .055 |
| F#m/Gbm | .000 | .089 |
| Gm | .007 | .112 |
| G#m/Abm | .001 | .002 |
| Am | .035 | .027 |
| A#m/Bbm | .000 | .029 |
| Bm | .003 | .051 |

The three terms on the right are all familiar to us. We already derived an expression for $P(\text{pcset} \mid \text{key})$ (see equation 6.3); this is calculated as part of the key-finding process. As for $P(\text{key})$, we assume once again that each key has a prior probability of 1/24. The value $P(\text{pcset})$ is the overall probability of the set; a way of calculating this was proposed in section 7.2. Thus we can easily calculate $P(\text{key} \mid \text{pcset})$. Table 7.4 shows, for two pitch-class sets (C–E–G and C–C#–D), the probability of each key given the set. As $P(\text{key} \mid \text{pcset})$ represents a conditional probability function, the values for all 24 keys must add up to 1.

From a glance, it is clear that the distribution of values is much more even in the case of C–C#–D than C–E–G. For C–E–G, one key's value (C major) is far higher than any other, and a number of keys have values of .000; for C–C♯–D, the "probability mass" is more evenly divided. In this way, the model's judgments seem to reflect the greater ambiguity of C–C♯–D. It is not immediately obvious, however, how to represent the ambiguity of a set with a single number. One way would just be to consider the probability of the most probable key; if a single key was very probable, the set would be judged as unambiguous. However, this is not very satisfactory. If, for a certain pitch-class set, two keys have probabilities of .5 and all other keys have probabilities of 0, this should surely be considered a highly ambiguous set; by contrast, if a set yields a probability of .4 for one key and the other 23 keys have probabilities of .6/23, the ambiguity seems lower. But the measure just considered would judge the second set as *more* ambiguous than the first. Intuitively, the ambiguity of a set seems to depend on the ratio in probability between the most probable key and the next most probable; if this value is close to 1 the set is ambiguous (it can never be *less* than 1), while if it is much greater than 1 the set is unambiguous. Even this measure, which we will call the "top-two-ratio" measure, is not perfect: it considers only the top two keys, while the probabilities of lower-ranked keys might also have some impact on ambiguity. But the top-two-ratio method appears to be the best among the simple alternatives, and we will employ it here. It is important to note that a *higher* top-two ratio indicates *lower* ambiguity; rather than describing this as an indicator of tonal ambiguity, it would be more precise to call it an indicator of *tonal clarity*, and I will henceforth do so here.

Table 7.5 shows this measure of tonal clarity for certain basic pitch-class sets. The first two columns show the most probable and second-most probable keys, with their probabilities; the third column is the ratio between the two, yielding the "tonal clarity score" for the set.[8] We can see that C–E–G is, indeed, judged to have higher clarity (lower ambiguity) than C–C♯–D by this measure. Turning to larger pitch-class collections, we find that the octatonic and whole-tone sets and [0123456] are very low in clarity, close to or at the minimum score of 1. (In fact, an octatonic scale has four keys that are tied for top rank, and a whole-tone scale has six; it is arbitrary in such cases to decide which of the keys are first- and second-ranked, but whichever ones are, the ratio between their probabilities is clearly 1.) The major scale has much higher clarity, and the harmonic minor scale has the highest of all.

In some respects, these results are unsurprising. It is common knowledge that the whole-tone scale and octatonic scale are highly ambiguous:

**Table 7.5**
Tonal clarity and tonalness of some common pitch-class sets.

| | Best key (with $P(\text{key}|\text{pcset})$) | Second-best key (with $P(\text{key}|\text{pcset})$) | Tonal clarity score | Tonalness score |
|---|---|---|---|---|
| **Chords** | | | | |
| C major triad | C (.597) | Em (.130) | 4.60 | .00173 |
| C minor triad | Cm (.550) | Eb (.134) | 4.11 | .00178 |
| C diminished triad | Bbm (.136) | Cm (.122) | 1.11 | .00031 |
| C–C♯–D | Gm (.112) | F♯m (.089) | 1.26 | .00022 |
| **Larger sets** | | | | |
| C major scale | C (.658) | Am (.159) | 4.14 | .00049 |
| C harmonic minor scale | Cm (.908) | Eb (.054) | 16.78 | .00028 |
| Whole-tone scale (C–D …) | Gm (.100) | C♯m (.100) | 1.00 | .00001 |
| Octatonic scale (C–D …) | Ebm (.190) | Cm (.190) | 1.00 | .000004 |
| [0123456] (C–C♯ …) | Db (.218) | Bbm (.214) | 1.02 | .000006 |
| **Other sets** | | | | |
| C–Eb–F♯–A | Em (.192) | C♯m (.192) | 1.00 | .00012 |
| C–D–E–G–B | C (.481) | G (.373) | 1.29 | .00137 |
| C–D–F–G–A–B | G (.438) | C (.342) | 1.28 | .00111 |
| C–D–Eb–F–G–Ab | Cm (.713) | Eb (.180) | 3.95 | .00071 |
| D–Eb–F–G–Ab | Eb (.460) | Cm (.425) | 1.08 | .00049 |
| **Cadence sets** | | | | |
| V–I (C–D–E–G–B) | C (.481) | G (.373) | 1.29 | .00137 |
| V7–I (C–D–E–F–G–B) | C (.832) | Am (.047) | 17.71 | .00067 |
| V–i (C–D–Eb–G–B) | Cm (.684) | G (.161) | 4.25 | .00064 |
| V7–i (C–D–Eb–F–G–B) | Cm (.842) | C (.056) | 15.03 | .00044 |

they are symmetrical scales, formed by a repeating intervallic pattern, thus they yield the same degrees in several different keys. For example, the whole-tone scale C–D–E–F♯–Ab–Bb contains $\hat{1}$–$\hat{2}$–$\hat{3}$–$\sharp\hat{4}$–$\flat\hat{6}$–$\flat\hat{7}$ of C major, and the same scale-degrees in D major, E major, F♯ major, Ab major, and Bb major. It is generally agreed that the widespread use of such scales in the late nineteenth and early twentieth centuries by composers such as Rimsky-Korsakov, Scriabin, Debussy, Stravinsky, and Bartok contributed to (or perhaps reflected) the gradual dissolution of tonality in Western art music (Kostka 1990: 34–37; Aldwell and Schachter 2003: 582). By contrast, the major scale is not symmetrical:

each major scale contains the scale-degrees of just one major key. Harmonic minor scales, too, are asymmetrical, each one corresponding to the key-profile of a single minor key.

One aspect of table 7.5 that is surprising, and *not* part of conventional wisdom, is the greater clarity of the harmonic minor scale compared to the major scale. Closer examination proved that this was due to two factors. One—already noted—concerns the degree of overlap between scales of different keys. In our discussion of key relations above, we observed that a major key has three "nearest neighbors" (keys that share 6 out of 7 of its scale-degrees), while a minor key (represented by the harmonic minor scale) has just one. Thus a minor key has only one key—the relative major—that is maximally close to it in scalar terms. There is another factor as well, relating specifically to the relationship between relative keys. In the case of C major, the three tonic-triad notes of all three nearest-neighbor keys (G major, F major, and A minor) are all within the scale; this means these keys have reasonably high probability given the C major scale. In the case of A minor, however, C major—the only nearest-neighbor key—has only *two* tonic-triad notes within the A minor scale. Together, these two factors explain why a major scale is judged by the model as more ambiguous than a harmonic minor one.

An interesting issue that arises here is the relationship between clarity and tonalness. Table 7.5 gives both tonalness and clarity ratings for the same sets, so that these values can be compared. One might assume, at first thought, that clarity and tonalness usually go together. Famously ambiguous (low-clarity) sets such as the octatonic scale and whole-tone scale are low in tonalness; highly tonal scale collections such as the major and harmonic minor scales are high in clarity. However, consider the set C–D–E–G–A–B—sometimes known as the diatonic hexachord (this is shown further down in table 7.5). This set is very low in clarity, but it is rather high in tonalness—much higher than the whole-tone scale, which also has six notes. The high tonalness of this set is due to the fact that it is highly probable given two different keys (C major and G major), but this also accounts for its low clarity. (The major scale and harmonic minor scale offer an interesting comparison in this regard as well, as we will see in the next section.) Could there also be pitch-class sets which are low in tonalness, but high in clarity? This is more difficult to imagine; if a set is low in tonalness, it unlikely to be contained in any major or harmonic minor scale, but any such set would probably tend to be low in clarity as well.

In many respects, the predictions of the current model have been much as we would expect—simply confirming well-established truths about key relations and the tonal properties of basic pitch-class sets. In a few cases, however, it has yielded rather unexpected outcomes. Some of the most surprising results concern the differences between major and minor keys. It is worth taking a closer look at these results to see if they shed any explanatory light on the perception and compositional use of major and minor in common-practice music.

The first issue concerns the status of the "minor scale." As noted earlier, there are three forms of the minor scale (see figure 4.1), and the question arises as to which if any should be treated as the primary or most basic form; contemporary theory texts differ on this issue (Piston 1978; Kostka and Payne 1995; Aldwell and Schachter 2003). Evidence reported in chapter 6 suggests that the harmonic minor scale represents the most common scale-degrees in minor; this is reflected very clearly in both the Kostka-Payne corpus and the Temperley corpus.[9] However, to simply regard the degrees within the harmonic minor scale as "scalar," and everything else as "chromatic," may seem oversimplified. In certain minor-key situations, the $\hat{6}$ and $\flat\hat{7}$ degrees are routinely used: the $\flat\hat{7}$ in descending melodic contexts and the $\hat{6}$ in ascending contexs. One might argue for these degrees as being scalar or at least "quasi-scalar" on this basis. (The minor-key Kostka-Payne distribution gives partial support for this: out of the five degrees not contained in the harmonic-minor scale, the $\flat\hat{7}$ degree is the most common; $\hat{6}$ is the fourth most common.) On the other hand, certain nonscalar degrees are routinely used in certain situations in major as well. For example, the $\sharp\hat{4}$ is so often used (rather than $\hat{4}$) as a lower neighbor to $\hat{5}$ that it is sometimes described as normative in this situation (see for example Forte and Gilbert 1982: 18). Yet no one has suggested considering $\sharp\hat{4}$ part of the major scale for this reason. Rather, most would probably say that the major scale represents the normative scale collection for major keys, but certain chromatic degrees may be favored in certain melodic situations; we might well account for the use of $\hat{6}$ and $\flat\hat{7}$ in minor keys in a similar way. In any case, if one *is* going to choose a certain seven-tone collection as the primary "minor scale," the harmonic minor would appear to be the most sensible choice.

Treating the harmonic minor as the primary minor scale sheds light on several issues in tonal harmony. One such issue is the status of the III chord in minor—for example, a C major chord in the context of A minor. Traditionally, the III chord in minor has been treated as a

**Figure 7.10**
(A) Antonio Caldara, "Sebben, crudele," mm. 1–2. (B) A major-mode "recomposition" of the same excerpt.

diatonic chord (a chord within the key) as opposed to a chromatic chord (a chord that goes outside the key). From the current perspective, however, the III chord contains the ♭7 scale-degree, which goes outside the primary minor scale. In this sense, it is really a chromatic chord; we would therefore expect it to undercut the current minor key and to imply another key. The key it implies is, of course, the relative major key (C major in the context of A minor), of which it is the tonic chord. I would argue that this is true to experience: a III chord in a minor context often seems to assert itself as a tonic chord even without any other support. For example, consider figure 7.10A, from the beginning of a Baroque aria. The piece is in C minor, but moves in the second measure to a III chord (E♭ major); the mere presence of this III chord suggests a brief "tonicization" of the relative major key. Notice that the III chord is not preceded by its dominant (as normally occurs in tonicizations); it is tonicized only by the chord itself. (This is despite the fact that the ♭7 degree in the melody is used in a "descending-melodic" pattern which is a standard minor-mode usage.) Compare this with the major-mode recomposition of the passage shown in figure 7.10B. In this case, we have a iii chord (E minor) in the second measure, but the sense of tonicizing E minor is much less strong; this is just as the model predicts, because the second measure remains entirely within the C major scale.

A second issue concerns the expressive properties of major and minor keys. It is well known that major and minor keys have different emotional connotations in Western music: roughly speaking, major is happy and minor is sad. These connotations date back at least to the sixteenth century, when Zarlino contrasted the "gay and lively" character of modes built on the major triad with the "sad and languid" character of minor-based modes (1558/1968: 21–22). Experiments have shown that these implications are also widely understood by listeners; in a study where children were played melodies and shown cartoon faces, subjects as young as three years old showed a reliable ability to associate major melodies with happy faces and minor melodies with sad ones (Kastner and Crowder 1990). A number of explanations for these associations have been put forth. Some have focused on the acoustic differences between the major and minor triads—particularly the fact that the major triad is more strongly supported by the overtone series.[10] But this explanation suggests that the expressive differences between major and minor should be universal, and this seems doubtful. In classical Indian music, for example—which has many different scales with different expressive associations—scales with the major third do not generally seem to have more positive connotations than those with the minor third (Danielou 1968). Thus acoustic explanations for the meanings of major and minor do not seem very promising, though they cannot be discounted.

One interesting explanation for the expressive differences between major and minor has been put forth by Meyer (1956). Meyer suggests that the negative implication of minor is largely due to what he calls its "ambiguity"—in particular, the variable nature of its scale. As we have noted, in major keys, the $\hat{6}$ and $\hat{7}$ degrees are almost always used, but in minor, either $\hat{6}$ or $b\hat{6}$ may be used and either $\hat{7}$ or $b\hat{7}$.

Melodically the minor mode differs from most other modes in that it is quasi-chromatic and changeable, appearing in several different versions, while other modes, whether the major mode of Western music, the modes of oriental music, or those of folk music and primitive music, are essentially diatonic and stable.... In other words, the minor mode is by its very nature more ambiguous than modes with a more limited repertory of tones. (1956: 224–226)

Meyer's explanation fits in nicely with his general theory that musical emotional response has much to do with the creation and fulfillment of expectations: situations where expectations are weak or uncertain are generally unpleasant for the listener. Thus minor mode has negative connotations because we have high uncertainty as to which scale-degrees will be used. The theory also shifts the focus away from the major and minor triads; thus it has no problem with the fact that, cross-culturally, scales with the minor third do not seem to have more negative associations than those with the major third. One might question Meyer's use of the term "ambiguity." To say that something is ambiguous usually means that it has multiple meanings or can be construed in different ways, but that is not really Meyer's point: rather, his point is that the minor mode is more variable in the way it is musically realized, and thus creates uncertainty for the listener in this regard. (Whether minor really *is* more ambiguous than major, I will consider below.)

Probability theory allows us test Meyer's claim: Does minor really have higher uncertainty (variability) than major? As discussed in chapter 2, the uncertainty of a distribution can be measured using the concept of entropy (see equation 2.26). We can use the Kostka-Payne corpus to find scale-degree distributions for major and minor keys. (In this case, we count the 9057 notes of the corpus separately, rather than judging scale-degrees as present or absent in each segment as we did in chapter 6.) We then calculate the entropy of the major and minor distributions:

$$H(P) = -\sum P(s) \log(P(s)) \tag{7.5}$$

where *s* indicates the 12 scale-degrees. The result: the major-key profile yields an entropy of .310; the minor-key profile yields an entropy of .309. The entropy of minor keys is actually (marginally) *lower* than that of major keys. It appears, then—based on one fairly large sample of common-practice music—that minor keys do not have any higher uncertainty than major keys.

Let us now revisit the issue of ambiguity. What does it really mean (or what *should* it mean) to say that minor keys are more ambiguous than major keys? It means, I suggest, that a piece (or passage) in a minor key is more likely to be ambiguous with regard to key than a piece in a major key. If minor keys really are more ambiguous in this way, this might offer an explanation for the expressive associations of major and minor. While Meyer does not appear to have advocated this idea, he certainly maintained—and I think many people would agree—that musical ambiguity in general tends to cause anxiety and apprehension for the listener. Thus, the possibility that minor keys are more ambiguous than major keys seems to be worth testing.

If we inspect the data presented in earlier sections, we find that minor keys are *not* more ambiguous than major keys; indeed, the opposite is true. A highly ambiguous key would seem to be one whose typical pitch-class distribution is very similar or close to that of another key or keys. It was shown in section 7.1, however, that minor keys are generally more "remote" from other keys than major keys are. For both major and minor keys, the most closely related key is the "relative" key; but a major key has two other keys that are almost equally close, whereas a minor key does not.[11] Another way of approaching this issue was suggested in section 7.3: We can treat the major and harmonic minor scales as pitch-class sets, and measure their ambiguity using the top-two-ratio method. Here again, we find that in fact the harmonic minor scale is considerably higher in clarity—lower in ambiguity—than the major scale (see table 7.5). Thus, all the evidence suggests that minor keys are less ambiguous than major keys: Rather than creating tonal uncertainty, minor keys should evoke a sense of confidence and security.

This discussion has cast doubt on two possible explanations for the expressive meanings of major and minor. Minor keys do not appear to have higher uncertainty than major keys; nor do they appear to be more ambiguous. So, what *is* the reason for these expressive differences? They could simply be arbitrary meanings that have developed by historical accident; indeed, this seems quite a likely possibility. The current approach holds out one further possibility, however, which relates to the idea of "tonalness," discussed in section 7.2. I argued there that we can take the overall probability of a pitch-class set as a measure of its tonalness, and that sets that are low in tonalness tend to convey a sense of tonal tension and instability. We saw that the harmonic minor scale is significantly lower in tonalness than the major scale (see table 7.3); no doubt, part of the reason for this is the relatively low overlap between the harmonic minor scale and other scales (which also accounts for its high clarity). Also of interest is the fact that some of the sets contained by the harmonic minor scale are low in probability as well: for example, the set B–C–D–E♭ occurs only in C minor (whereas the major equivalent, B–C–D–E, occurs in C major, G major, and A minor). As noted in section 7.2, low-probability sets might cause tension simply because they are generally unexpected and, thus, more difficult to process. Thus, the negative emotional effect of the minor scale may be due to the fact that the scale and some of its subsets are relatively rare and thus cognitively taxing.[12] While this explanation is for now quite conjectural, it is (I would argue) as plausible as any other, and perhaps a solution worth exploring to what remains a vexing musical mystery.

**7.5
Ambiguous Pitch-Collections in Common-Practice Music**

In section 7.3, I proposed a probabilistic measure of the ambiguity (clarity) of a pitch-class set. One might wonder how this approach could be applied to measuring the tonal ambiguity of an actual musical passage. An ambiguous passage might be defined as one where multiple analyses of the passage are roughly equal in probability (where an "analysis" is some labeling of all the segments of the passage with keys). However, this measure is in some ways problematic. In the first place, it is difficult to calculate, due to the exponentially large number of different possible analyses. But in any case, I would argue that this is not really the way the term "tonal ambiguity" is usually used. A passage in which there was clearly a modulation from key X to key Y, but it was not exactly clear where the modulation occurred, would probably not be considered ambiguous; indeed, this is a very common situation in tonal music. Rather, tonal ambiguity usually suggests a situation where a passage as a whole is ambiguous between two different keys. In what follows, we will consider some passages of this type, and examine the model's ability to detect their ambiguity. We make the further simplifying assumption of treating the entire passage as a single segment. (This assumption is not too far from our practice in chapter 6, since the passages considered below are all only 2–4 measures long.)[13] In that case, we can proceed much as we did in section 7.3. We simply consider the pitch-class set of the entire passage, calculate $P(\text{pcset} \mid \text{key})$ for all keys, and find the ratio between the top two keys; an ambiguous passage is one in which this ratio is low.

As noted earlier, it is well established that certain scalar collections are highly ambiguous, such as the whole-tone and octatonic scales. Also well known is the ambiguity of certain tonal chords, such as the diminished seventh chord. This, too, is a symmetrical pitch-class set; the chord C–E♭–F♯–A contains the scale degrees $\hat{7}$–$\hat{2}$–$\hat{4}$–♭$\hat{6}$ in E minor, and contains the same degrees in C♯ minor, G minor, and B♭ minor. Naturally, then, the model assigns it the minimal clarity score of 1.0 (see table 7.5). A passage built on a diminished seventh chord gives an effect of extreme tonal instability and disorientation; an example is seen in figure 7.11, from the development section of Beethoven's *Appassionata* sonata.

Common-practice composers sometimes also employ ambiguous pitch-class sets in more subtle ways. Consider the set C–D–E–G–B. This set is fully contained in two major scales, C major and G major (and no harmonic minor scales); moreover, it contains the tonic triads of both keys. Since the set is equally compatible with the two keys at both scalar and triadic levels, we would expect it to be highly ambiguous; the model confirms this, assigning a clarity value of just 1.29. A very simple use of this set—one which seems to maximize its tonal ambiguity—is found in the opening of Chopin's Mazurka Op. 24 No. 2 (figure 7.12). The passage alternates beween a C major triad and a G major triad, both in root position—thus even harmonic factors cannot really tip the balance to

**Figure 7.11**
Beethoven, Sonata Op. 57 ("Appassionata"), I, mm. 123–126.

**Figure 7.12**
Chopin, Mazurka Op. 24, No. 2, mm. 1–4.

one key or the other. (Even the metrical placement of the chords seems deliberately even-handed: the "cross-rhythm" pattern places C major on the downbeat in mm. 1 and 3, and G major in mm. 2 and 4.) The progression begins on a C major chord, perhaps slightly favoring C major—but one might just as well say that ending on a G major chord favors that key. The piece proves to be in C major, in fact, but one could just as easily imagine it continuing in G major.

If one adds an A to the set discussed above, this produces C–D–E–G–A–B, sometimes known as a "diatonic hexachord." This set, too, occurs in two major scales, C major and G major, and contains both complete tonic triads; not surprisingly, it is low in clarity, with a value of 1.28. An

**Figure 7.13**
Bach, Goldberg Variations, Aria, mm. 1–8.

example of this set (except transposed to G–A–B–D–E–F♯, implying G major or D major) is seen in the first two measures of Bach's Goldberg Variations (figure 7.13). As in the Chopin Mazurka, the harmony is also equivocal between these two keys: G major in m. 1 followed by D major in m. 2, with the root featured prominently in the melody in both cases. The following two measures introduce C♯, tonicizing D major; but the following four measures (mm. 5–8) replace C♯ with C, and establish G major beyond all doubt. One might question whether mm. 1–2 are really ambiguous. Of course, we know (if we know the piece) that it is in G major, and that may bias us toward a G major interpretation over a D major one. I would argue, however, that mm. 1–2 do contain a subtle element of ambiguity. A I–V6 progression, though perhaps favoring the first chord as tonic because of its primacy, can also be interpreted as IV–I6 (favoring the second chord as tonic) without difficulty.[14] Admittedly, the effect of the ambiguity in the Bach is very different from that of the *Appassionata* example (figure 7.11). The feeling here is not one of complete disorientation, as in that case, but rather a subtle undercurrent of indecision or equivocation between two clear alternatives, followed by a leaning toward one (D major in mm. 3–4) and then a much stronger commitment to the other (G major in mm. 5–8).

A similar kind of ambiguity, also involving a diatonic hexachord, is found in the middle section of Brahms's Clarinet Sonata Op. 120 No. 1, second movement (figure 7.14). The passage in mm. 23–24 uses A♭–B♭–

**Figure 7.14**
Brahms, Clarinet Sonata Op. 120, No. 1, II, mm. 21–32.

**Figure 7.15**
Schoenberg, *Verklärte Nacht*, mm. 1–4.

C–Db–Eb–F, implying either Ab major or Db major. Here, as in the previous two examples, the composer creates a delicate balance between the two keys. The harmony alternates Db major and Ab major (though the Bb in m. 24 hints just slightly at a Bbm6/5 chord). The previous context has strongly established Ab major—note the perfect cadence in Ab in mm. 21–22—but the last beat of m. 22 brings in a Gb, introducing a slight leaning toward Db. The following context is also of little help in resolving the uncertainty: Brahms simply shifts the pattern down a whole step (in mm. 25–26), denying both Ab and Db and creating a new ambiguity between Cb and Gb. The next four measures lead strongly toward Db (C#) minor, however, and when the phrase repeats in varied form mm. 31–32, the previous context favors the Db interpretation.

Several other pitch-collections deserve consideration with regard to ambiguity. One is C–D–Eb–F–G–Ab—sometimes called a minor hexachord. In scalar terms, this set is ambiguous between two "relative" keys, C minor and Eb major in this case. However, there is an important difference between this and the diatonic hexachord; in this case, the C minor tonic triad is fully included in the set, while the Eb major triad is not. Thus we would expect the model to favor C minor quite strongly, and it does, assigning a clarity value of 3.95. This seems true to perception. Even in cases where the set is presented in such a way that does not strongly outline a particular harmony, the minor key seems to prevail over the major one. The opening of Schoenberg's *Verklärte Nacht* is one example, where a downward scalar presentation of the hexachord (Bb–A–G–F–E–D) seems to favor D minor over F major (figure 7.15). Of course, this is reinforced by the D pedal tone; but even disregarding this, the D minor implication seems to prevail. (Another factor in this case is that the D in the descending hexachord is not followed closely by step; this tends to favor it as a chord-tone, thus implying D minor harmonically. If we imagine the pattern in reverse, D–E–F–G–A–Bb,

**Figure 7.16**
Brahms, Clarinet Quintet, I, mm. 1–5.

the leaning toward D minor is indeed somewhat less strong, but still present, in my opinion.)

A more ambiguous case is the set D–E♭–F–G–A♭, the same as the minor hexachord except with the C deleted. This set is still ambiguous between the same two keys (C minor and E♭ major) in scalar terms, but now has exactly two notes from the tonic triad of each (E♭ and G from C minor, and E♭ and G from E♭ major)—though the fact that it contains the tonic of E♭ major and not of C minor may slightly favor the former. We would therefore expect the set to be quite evenly balanced between these two keys, and the model agrees, assigning a clarity score of 1.08. The ambiguity of this set is sometimes exploited quite effectively; a well-known example is the opening of Brahms's Clarinet Quintet, using C♯–D–E–F♯–G (implying D major or B minor) (figure 7.16). The harmony in this passage is also equivocal between the two keys, but in a different way from the examples considered earlier: in this case, the harmony *itself* is ambiguous, as the root of mm. 1 and 2 could be either B or D. Having presented these two tonalities, the piece as a whole unfolds as a series of ever larger oscillations between them: to B minor in m. 3, then to D major in mm. 4–8, then to B minor in mm. 9–28, then to D major for the second half of the exposition and finally returning to B minor in the recapitulation.[15]

**7.6**
**Explaining**
**Common Strategies**
**of Tonal Harmony**

In chapter 1, I suggested that a probabilistic model might predict certain aspects of compositional practice, and thus, might claim to characterize cognitive processes of composition. Such predictions might concern aspects of compositional practice that are already well known; alternatively, one could test a theory by examining its predictions about phenomena not previously observed. In this section I will explore these

Applications of the Model

**Figure 7.17**
Mozart, Sonata K. 545, I, mm. 11–12.

possibilities, in a small way, with regard to the theory of tonal ambiguity proposed above and its predictions regarding certain strategies of common-practice composition.

We have seen that composers sometimes use extreme tonal ambiguity as a means of creating instability or disorientation, as in figure 7.11. Another place where ambiguity might serve a useful function is at points of modulation. By creating a short section of music that was ambiguous between two keys, the composer could create a smooth transition from one to another. This is, indeed, a well-recognized phenomenon, reflected in the concept of "pivot chord" (Piston 1978). Typically, though by no means always, a point of modulation between two keys will feature a chord which is contained in the scales of both the previous and following keys: for example, one might modulate from C major to G major via an A minor chord. I wish to suggest, however, that this "pivot" idea might be applied to larger pitch-class sets as well. An interesting example in this regard is the "neighbor 6/4 progression"; an example is shown in figure 7.17. Such a progression is commonly understood as a root-position triad (typically a major triad), ornamented by a 6/4 chord (whose root is nominally a fifth below): this might be understood as a V–I6/4–V progression (or simply as a V with ornamental neighbor tones), but might also occur as I–IV6/4–I. A particularly common location for this progression is in the transition of a sonata-form exposition, before what Hepokoski and Darcy (1997) have called the "medial caesura"—a strong cadential arrival (usually a half-cadence), just before the second theme enters. Frequently this marks the point of transition between the tonic key and the dominant; in figure 7.17, for example, the previous section has established C major while the following section moves to G major. By the argument advanced earlier, a composer might well favor a tonally ambiguous pitch-collection at this point, so as to effect the transition smoothly. And indeed, the pitch-class set here, C–D–E–G–B, is

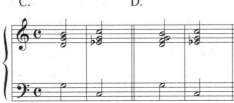

**Figure 7.18**
Cadences in major and minor keys. (A) V–I in C major; (B) V7–I in C major; (C) V–i in C minor; (D) V7–i in C minor.

highly ambiguous: as already discussed, this set favors C major and G major equally in terms of both scales and tonic triads, and the Bayesian model ranks them almost equally in preference (see table 7.5). Perhaps the tonal ambiguity of the neighbor 6/4 progression accounts for its frequent use at points of tonal transition.

A second prediction of the model concerns cadences. It is well known that most tonal pieces (and large sections of pieces) end with a "perfect authentic cadence": a root-position V chord followed by a root-position I, with the tonic pitch in the melody of the I chord. This is almost required at the end of a piece—at least, if the composer intends to create a sense of full closure in the tonic key. The key of the piece may be either major or minor, and the V chord may be either a V triad or a V7 chord; this creates four possibilities, as shown in figure 7.18. The four progressions shown in the figure yield four different pitch-class sets, with differing degrees of ambiguity (see the final section of table 7.5, "cadence sets"). Both progressions involving V7 are extremely high in clarity, as is the V–i progression in minor, employing C–D–E♭–G–B.[16] However, the V–I progression in major is quite ambiguous; this employs the set C–D–E–G–B, which (as just mentioned) is ambiguous between C major and G major. This suggests that the V–I progression should seem less decisive than the V–i progression in its key implications. To my ears, this is indeed the case. Admittedly, a progression like that in figure 7.18A (even out of context) implies C major more strongly than G major (probably because this two-chord gesture has strong cadential associations), but it lacks the unshakable confidence and certainty of figure 7.18C. (This point relates to our earlier discussion of major and minor, where we observed that minor keys generally seem to be less ambiguous than major keys.)

These observations suggest a prediction about compositional practice. At the final cadence of a piece, we can assume that composers (at least in the common-practice period) generally sought to achieve a maximal sense of tonal stability and closure. Thus we might expect, in final cadences of major-key pieces, that composers would tend to favor V7–I over V–I cadences, given the rather low clarity of the V–I variant. In minor-key pieces, by contrast, both the V7–i and V–i variants of the cadence are very high in clarity; thus the current theory does not predict any strong preference for the V7–i variant.

This prediction was tested with regard to three corpora: the piano sonatas of Haydn, Mozart, and Beethoven. All movements in all sonatas of all three composers (with the exception of Haydn's early piano sonatas) were examined to see if the key was major or minor and if the final cadence contained a V or V7 chord. Table 7.6 shows the results. For all three composers, it can be seen that the proportion of V–I cadences in minor-key movements is much higher than in major-key movements; in all three corpora, this difference is statistically significant. Thus, for the classical-period composers at least, there does indeed seem to be a stronger preference for V7 over V with major-key pieces, just as the current model predicts.

The line of reasoning advanced here might be applied also to "predominant" chords. V–I cadences in common-practice music are most often preceded by one of a group of harmonies known as predominants—usually (in major) IV, ii, or ii6 (figure 7.19). Why these particular chords are preferred as predominants has long been a topic of debate in music theory. The preference for ii (and ii6) before V could be attributed to the general preference for descending-fifth root motion; but what about IV? Rameau viewed the IV (when preceding V) as having an implied root of $\hat{2}$, thus providing descending-fifth motion to V (see Lester 1992: 133–138). Schenker, on the other hand, viewed each of the predominant chords as a partial "filling-in" of the ascending interval between scale-degrees $\hat{1}$ and $\hat{5}$ (assuming a preceding tonic chord), either with scale-degree $\hat{4}$ (the bass note of IV and ii6) or $\hat{2}$ (the bass note of

**Table 7.6**
Final cadences in Haydn, Mozart, and Beethoven piano sonatas.

| | Haydn | | Mozart | | Beethoven | |
|---|---|---|---|---|---|---|
| | Major | Minor | Major | Minor | Major | Minor |
| V | 2 (12.5%) | 4 (80.0%) | 5 (23.8%) | 2 (66.7%) | 4 (15.4%) | 8 (72.7%) |
| V7 | 14 (87.5%) | 1 (20.0%) | 16 (76.2%) | 1 (33.3%) | 22 (83.6%) | 3 (27.2%) |
| Total | 16 | 5 | 21 | 3 | 26 | 11 |
| | ($\chi^2 = 8.5$, p $< .01$) | | ($\chi^2 = 4.4$, p $< .05$) | | ($\chi^2 = 11.6$, p $< .001$) | |

Note: This table represents information about the final cadences of movements in piano sonatas by Haydn, Mozart, and Beethoven. All Haydn sonatas from Hob. XIV:27 onwards were examined, as well as all Mozart and Beethoven sonatas. (Haydn's early sonatas were excluded since they tend to have a thin, two-part texture, and often do not use complete harmonies at cadences.) "Major" or "minor" indicates the key of the movement; "V" or "V7" indicates whether the dominant of the final cadence was a V or V7.

Since it is sometimes subjective exactly what constitutes the final cadence of a piece, the following objective algorithm was used:

1. Divide the movement into "segments" defined by the tactus beat of the meter (as indicated in the time signature).

2. Starting from the end of the piece, find the maximal string of segments containing no scale degrees but $\hat{1}$, $\hat{3}$, and $\hat{5}$ (and it must include at least one $\hat{1}$). Define this segment string as the "final tonic span." If no such segment string is found, the movement is disregarded.

3. Starting from the beginning of the final tonic span and working backward: find the maximal string of segments containing no scale degrees but $\hat{5}$, $\hat{7}$, $\hat{2}$, and $\hat{4}$; containing at least one $\hat{5}$ and $\hat{7}$; and featuring a $\hat{5}$ as the lowest pitch. Define this segment string as the "final dominant span." If no such segment string is found, the movement is disregarded.

4. If the final dominant span contains a $\hat{4}$, the final dominant is identified as a V7; if not, it is identified as a V.

A number of movements were eliminated from consideration because they had no "final tonic span" or "final dominant span" satisfying the criteria above: 50 movements in the Haydn corpus were eliminated for this reason, 30 in the Mozart, and 64 in the Beethoven.

**Figure 7.19**
IV and ii as "predominant" chords.

ii) (1935/1979: I, 30). Schenker's explanation is not very satisfactory. The most normal way of filling in the melodic interval $\hat{1}-\hat{5}$ with one note would surely be $\hat{1}-\hat{3}-\hat{5}$, thus one might expect that $\hat{3}$ would be a common bass note for predominant chords; but iii is not a common predominant harmony. Our probabilistic approach suggests an alternative explanation. Assuming (as above) that a composer generally wishes to minimize tonal ambiguity at a cadence, the preferable predominant chords would be those that create a pitch-class set of high tonal clarity. Adding vi to a V–I cadence in C major produces the collection C–D–E–G–A–B, which (as we have seen) is highly ambiguous; adding iii to V–I does not add any new tones, leaving the ambiguous collection C–D–E–G–B. However, adding either IV or ii produces the complete, and unequivocal, C major diatonic collection. Thus, the preference for IV and ii (or their inversions) as predominant harmonies in cadences may be attributable to the desire to minimize tonal ambiguity. This explanation is not perfect; it does not apply as well to minor keys, or to cadences with V7 in major or minor, since in these cases (as we have seen), the dominant–tonic cadence is already unambiguous. But it may add another piece to the puzzle of why certain harmonies are preferred as predominants.

This discussion has suggested that a probabilistic key-finding model may be able to explain certain features of common-practice composition. The reasoning is that composers were sensitive to the ambiguities of different pitch-class sets, and adjusted their practices in light of this—for example, favoring V7 over V with major-key cadences. We should note that the causal pattern proposed here is certainly oversimplified. It implies that composers were faced with a fixed system of probabilities relating pitch-classes to keys (reflected in the distribution of scale-degrees in tonal pieces), and that their compositional practice evolved in response to this. But of course, the system of probabilities itself arose out of the practices of composers; both compositional practice, and the resulting pitch-class distributions, were constantly evolving. Still, it seems reasonable to suggest that considerations of ambiguity and clarity were one factor, among many others, influencing the decisions of common-practice composers. The current approach may provide part of the explanation for this complex historical process.

# 8

# Bayesian Models of Other Aspects of Music

The idea of applying Bayesian probabilistic methods to musical problems seems to have only emerged in the late 1990s; at least, only then was it seriously pursued. Within this short period, however, a number of authors have explored Bayesian approaches to music research. In previous chapters, I have discussed work by Cemgil et al. (2000a, 2000b), Raphael (2002a), and myself on the modeling of meter perception; I have also presented my own work on modeling key perception. In this chapter I survey several other studies that apply Bayesian strategies to musical problems. My goal is to summarize this work, offer some critical commentary, and provide a synthetic and comparative view of the approaches taken by different scholars.

## 8.1 Probabilistic Transcription Models

We begin with an aspect of music perception that we have hardly considered in this study so far, but which is, in a way, the most basic aspect of all. This is the process of identifying notes from an auditory signal. That listeners are able to perform this process, at least in many situations, seems self-evident. Listeners can, for example, sing back the notes of a melody they hear, even the melody of a complex polyphonic piece.[1] Developing computational systems that can extract pitch information from audio data is therefore a project of great cognitive interest, and one with many practical applications as well. This problem has been given many names, but is perhaps most widely known as "automatic transcription," and we will use that term here.[2] A great deal of work has been devoted to automatic transcription (for a review, see Klapuri

2004); I will not attempt a general survey here, but will focus on work that has adopted a Bayesian approach to the problem.

To approach the transcription problem from a Bayesian viewpoint, we must conceptualize our "surface-structure" model in a slightly different way. In previous chapters, we defined the surface as a representation of notes, showing the pitch and timepoints of each note. This is the representation that was assumed as input to the meter-finding and key-finding models presented in earlier chapters; the task of these models was to infer a structure (a key or metrical grid) from such a surface. Now, however, we assume such a "pitch-time" representation as the *structure*, the underlying information to be recovered. The surface is the sound itself— an auditory signal or "sound wave." Usually, transcription models convert a sound wave into a *frequency* representation, showing the energy of different periodic components of the sound as they rise and fall over time. This is often represented graphically in a so-called "spectrogram." (Figure 8.1 shows the spectrogram for a bassoon note.) Using a fre-

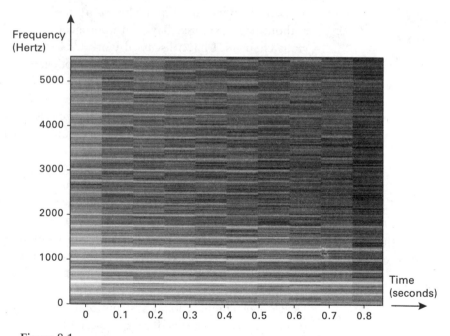

**Figure 8.1**
A spectrogram of a bassoon playing middle C. Lighter shades of gray indicate higher energy. The fundamental of the note (at around 256 Hz) can clearly be seen, as well as the overtones of the fundamental at evenly spaced intervals above it (512 Hz, 768 Hz, etc.). (Spectrogram created by Dave Headlam.)

quency representation makes sense, when we consider the nature of musical sound. Generally speaking, a musical note—such as a bassoon note or piano note—consists of a number of different frequencies: a fundamental plus overtones, where all the overtones are multiples of the fundamental. In a polyphonic piece, the sound signal may contain frequencies from several different notes. The task of transcription, then, is to group the frequencies of the sound into notes in the appropriate way, beginning and ending each note at the correct time and assigning it to the correct pitch category.

With this in mind, consider our usual Bayesian formula:

$$P(\text{structure} \mid \text{surface}) \propto P(\text{surface} \mid \text{structure})P(\text{structure}) \qquad (8.1)$$

Applying our usual approach, we try to find the structure maximizing the left side by finding the one maximizing the right side. $P(\text{surface} \mid \text{structure})$, in this case, is the probability of a certain frequency representation given a pattern of notes. If our pattern of notes is just a single note C4 from time 0 to time 1000 (in milliseconds), then a probable frequency representation will be one with frequencies at about 262 Hz (the frequency of C4) and multiples thereof, starting at about time 0 and ending at about time 1000, with little or no presence of other frequencies.

The second term, $P(\text{structure})$, expresses the probability of a note pattern itself. The Bayesian formula tells us that the probability of a note pattern given a sound signal depends partly on the prior probability of the note pattern. What kinds of things make a note pattern probable? This is essentially what we described in earlier chapters as the problem of determining the probability of a *surface*—since the note pattern was the surface in our earlier models (see chapter 5). I suggested that, for example, a probable pitch pattern (just considering monophonic input for the moment) is one in which intervals between adjacent notes are small, and the notes remain within a fairly narrow range and within the scale of single key. We could also bring in rhythmic and metrical considerations: a more probable note-onset pattern is one which implies a regular and consistent meter. The same methods we used earlier to calculate the probability of a pitch pattern and onset pattern could also be used here. Thus we have, in a sense, already addressed part of the transcription problem. However, we have said nothing about how to calculate $P(\text{surface} \mid \text{structure})$—the probability of an auditory signal given a note pattern.

Two proposals for transcription systems have adopted an explicitly Bayesian approach. The system of Kashino et al. (1998) begins by extracting a spectrogram, as defined above—a representation of frequency components across time. The system then derives a complex representation showing notes as well as chords, with the notes assigned to different instrument categories. The model uses a sophisticated approach to probabilistic modeling, the Bayesian network theory of Pearl (1986), which allows for complex systems of interconnected variables. For example, the system has knowledge of the probable frequency content of sounds generated by different instruments (clarinet, piano, etc.); this allows it to calculate the probability of a frequency pattern given a note, and also allows notes to be assigned to the correct instrument. It also has knowledge about the probability of notes given chords, and about the probability of different chord progressions.

The authors state that many tests of the system have been performed, but they report only one test of one part of the system. In this test, random combinations of notes were played on various instruments and the system had to identify the notes. (As the authors observe, chord knowledge is of little use here since the note patterns are random.) The authors show how knowledge of the characteristic frequency content of instrumental sounds—what they call "tone memory"—helps the system perform better. It will be interesting to see whether other kinds of musical knowledge (such as knowledge of chords and chord progressions) improve the system's transcription performance on real music.

A second model of transcription has been proposed by Raphael (2002b). Raphael's model recovers pitch information from recorded piano music, using the approach of hidden Markov models. As discussed in chapters 2 and 6, a hidden Markov model is a network of variables, connected by probabilistic dependencies, where certain variables are observed and others are "hidden" and must be inferred from the observed ones. In Raphael's model, the observed variables represent segments of sound—we will call these "sound-slices"—each one represented by a set of numerical "features." (Sound-slices are presumably a small fraction of a second, though no precise value is given.) Features represent, for example, whether the segment contains sound or silence and whether it seems to indicate the attack-segment of a note; other features represent the energy content of small frequency bands. The hidden units represent combinations of notes (as well as information about whether the notes are beginning, continuing, or ending at that point); we will call these "score-slices." Score-slices and sound-slices form a network much like that in figure 6.3; score-slices correspond to keys in segments, and sound-slices to pitch-class sets. The problem is to determine, given a series of sound-slices, the underlying pattern of score-slices. The model is trained on statistical data regarding the probability of different transitions between score-slices, and it learns the probabilistic correspondence between score-slices and sound-slices using a form of unsupervised learning called the Baum-Welch algorithm (this will be discussed further below). The model was tested on a Mozart piano sonata recording; it was evaluated simply on whether it identified the correct notes in the correct order, without regard for exact timepoints. The model's performance was measured using a metric based on the number of changes required to turn the model's note sequence into the correct note sequence; this yielded an error rate of 39%.

The application of Bayesian methods to the transcription problem is obviously at a very early stage, but it holds great promise.[3] As noted earlier, the great advantage of this approach is that it provides a natural way of bringing to bear higher-level musical knowledge—in particular, knowledge about the probability of different note patterns—on the transcription process. It may be that certain musical principles are particularly useful in transcription: one example is pitch proximity, the preference for small melodic intervals. A frequent problem with current transcription models is that a note is often mistaken for another note an octave away (due to the similar frequency content of octave-related notes) (Martin 1996; Bello et al. 2000); incorporating knowledge about the probability of different interval sizes should greatly alleviate this problem. Admittedly, the Bayesian approach is not the only way to use higher-level knowledge in transcription, and other models have done this using other methods. For example, Martin's (1996) transcription system employs modules called "knowledge sources" which give preference to certain combinations of notes (chords and harmonic intervals). But the Bayesian approach provides a particularly elegant and logical way of incorporating musical principles and combining them with information of other kinds. Whether such musical knowledge is used in *human* note identification is another question, a very interesting one which has hardly been addressed.

## 8.2 Bod: The Perception of Phrase Structure

A fundamental part of music perception is the identification of phrases. In listening to a melody, we do not simply perceive a continuous, unbroken stream of notes; rather, we group notes into larger units, generally lasting several seconds, and articulated by a variety of musical cues. The factors involved in phrase structure perception have been studied quite

Bayesian Models of Other Aspects of Music

extensively, in music theory (Lerdahl and Jackendoff 1983), psychology (Deliege 1987), and computational modeling (Tenney and Polanksy 1980; Temperley 2001a; Cambouropoulos 2001, 2003). Of interest here is the model of Bod (2002), which adopts a probabilistic approach to modeling phrase perception. While Bod does not use the term "Baye-sian," his approach relates closely to the Bayesian approach of the current study, as I will try to show.

Bod represents phrase structures in terms of "trees." Trees are an important concept in cognitive modeling, particularly in linguistics, where they are used to represent the syntactic structure of a sentence. (Indeed, Bod applies his model to linguistic syntax as well as musical phrase perception, but we will only consider the musical part of his study here.) Tree structures have been used in music theory as well; most notably, Lerdahl and Jackendoff (1983) use them to represent relations of elaboration among pitches. Bod's use of trees is quite different from Lerdahl and Jackendoff's. In this case, trees represent the phrase structure of a song in a very simple way: each tree consists of a top-level "S" node, a level of "P" nodes for phrases, "N" nodes for notes, and "terminal" nodes indicating the pitch and duration of each note. Pitches are indicated in scale-degree notation; duration is represented in relation to the shortest rhythmic value used in the song—a pitch without any duration marker indicates this value, while "_" represents twice this value and "." represents 1.5 times this value (multiple or combined "_" and "." symbols can be used to indicate longer rhythmic values). For example, the terminal symbol "#4._" would indicate a #$\hat{4}$ scale-degree, 3 times as long as the shortest rhythmic unit in the song. Figure 8.2 shows a melody from the Essen Folksong Collection (a particularly short one) represented in Bod's notation. (Phrases are indicated in the score with slurs, as is customary.)

In hearing a melody, we must recover the correct phrase structure tree: essentially, grouping notes under "P" nodes in the correct way. How do we infer the correct phrase structure? In Bod's model, this depends on the concept of a "subtree." A subtree is essentially any part of a tree—a connected subset of nodes and their expansions. A number of possible subtrees can be extracted from a single tree; three possible subtrees for the tree in figure 8.2 are shown in figure 8.3. Bod proposes that the perception of phrase structure involves two main principles. One is likelihood: We prefer to use subtrees that have been often encountered in the past. For example, if many trees contain the subtree 8.3B (a phrase of 5 notes, ending with the tonic pitch, three rhythmic units in length), we

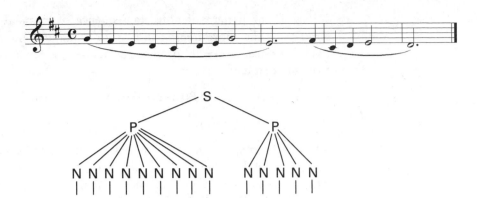

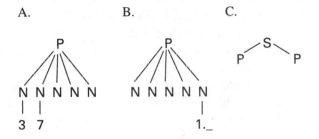

**Figure 8.2**
The melody "Jugos051," from the Essen corpus. The phrase structure is shown below, using Bod's (2002) encoding system.

**Figure 8.3**
Three "subtrees" which could be extracted from the phrase tree in figure 8.2, according to Bod's model.

will prefer to generate new trees that have this feature. (This idea of learning from regularities in the environment should be familiar from earlier chapters.) The second principle is simplicity: we prefer a tree with the minimum number of subtrees seen before. If we can construct a tree for a melody using only 2 large subtrees, this is preferable to a tree involving 10 smaller ones. In testing his model, Bod tried a version using the simplicity criterion, a version using the likelihood criterion, and a version that combined both; the "combined" model proved to yield the best results.

Bod's model could well be viewed in terms of the "surface-structure" framework presented earlier—with one important modification. The

Bayesian Models of Other Aspects of Music

surface is the pattern of notes (a sequence of terminal symbols). The structure is the entire tree, *including* (or "entailing") a surface, so that $P(\text{surface}\,|\,\text{structure}) = 1$ for that surface. Thus, for a surface and any structure that entails it:

$$P(\text{structure}\,|\,\text{surface}) \propto P(\text{surface}\,|\,\text{structure})P(\text{structure})$$

$$= 1 \times P(\text{structure}) \tag{8.2}$$

The most probable tree given a surface, therefore, is simply the most probable tree that entails it. We can then imagine a generative model in which trees are generated in an incremental fashion. Each subtree has a certain probability of being added, conditional on the "parent" node—for example, a parent node of P might generate subtree 8.3A, subtree 8.3B, and many others. The probability of a complete tree, including both nonterminal and terminal nodes, is given by the product of all the subtree probabilities involved.[4] Thus, using knowledge of the generative process, the listener can identify the most likely tree given a melody; this is the reasoning behind Bod's "likelihood" criterion. As for the "simplicity" criterion, it is preferable to build trees out of larger subtrees where possible, since these may capture patterns in the data that are missed by smaller subtrees.

Bod's model can be trained by giving it a corpus of annotated melodies, from which it learns the probabilities of different subtrees; it can then be tested by giving it new melodies for which it must derive the correct trees. A complication arises here, however. Due to the large number of subtrees in a tree, the model cannot possibly count all possible subtrees in a large corpus of melodies. Nor can it consider all possible combinations of subtrees in analyzing a melody. To solve this problem, Bod adopts a "Monte Carlo" approach. In training—where the model is building up a library of different subtrees with their frequency of occurrence—the model only counts certain randomly chosen subtrees, ignoring all others. In testing, also, only a random subset of subtrees in the library are considered in searching for the best tree.

Using this method, Bod tested his model on the Essen Folksong Collection. As described in section 3.3, this is a large corpus of melodies encoded with pitch and rhythm; it is also annotated with phrase structure information. The model was trained on the complete collection (6,217 songs) except for a 1000-song random subset, which was then used for testing. The model identified 87.3% of boundaries correctly.[5] This is an impressive level of performance; by comparison, in another test using the Essen corpus, the phrase analysis model of Temperley (2001a) labeled only 75.5% of boundaries correctly.

While the performance of Bod's model is admirable, one might question its very "data-driven" approach. That is to say, the model "learns" about phrase structure from examples, but does not appear to generalize. Most other models of phrase structure, such as those of Tenney and Polansky (1980), Lerdahl and Jackendoff (1983), and Temperley (2001a), have operated using general rules. One rule which is reflected in virtually all models is that there is a preference for phrase boundaries after long notes. Bod's model does not incorporate this rule in any explicit way. No doubt it is incorporated indirectly; for example, the model may assign high probability to a phrase subtree like figure 8.3B, which ends with a long note. But this is a very specific rule, only applying to phrases which have exactly 5 notes and end with a scale-degree $\hat{1}$ which is 3 units in duration. Bod's model seems to have no way of capturing the "long-note" rule in a more general fashion. Earlier models have also put forth other general principles about phrase structure: that phrase boundaries tend to occur at changes of register, at parallel points in the metrical structure, and in alignment with repeated patterns. Again, Bod's model only seems able to capture such generalizations in a very laborious and inefficient way, if at all. Admittedly, it is presently an open question to what extent human perception of phrase structure operates by general rules (like most other models), or by data-driven pattern-matching (like Bod's model). In any case, Bod's model sets a high standard in its level of performance; it remains to be seen whether "rule-based" models of grouping will be able to match it in this respect.

## 8.3 Raphael and Stoddard: Harmonic Analysis

Much of Western music—including common-practice music and most popular and folk music—could be described as "harmonic" in character. By this I mean that it is organized into short segments governed by harmonies (chords), such that each pitch is a member of the harmony or is ornamental to it in some way. Harmony is of course an important branch of music theory, and has been widely studied in music psychology as well. The usual computational question then arises: How can the harmonies of a piece be identified from the notes? Once again, we will not attempt to survey the considerable body of work that has addressed this issue (see Temperley 2001a for a review), but will focus on one study that has taken a probabilistic approach to it.

Bayesian Models of Other Aspects of Music

The model of Raphael and Stoddard (2004) takes a piece represented as pitches in time, and derives a harmonic analysis for it. The piece is divided into short segments of constant rhythmic length, such as a half-measure. The model's task is to assign each segment a key label, comprising a tonic (C, C♯, etc.) and a mode (major or minor), and a chord label indicating the function of the chord in relation to the key. This representation corresponds to what is usually known as Roman numeral analysis, the standard way of representing chords in tonal music theory. For example, a chord labeled "V/C major" would be the triad on the fifth degree in C major, that is, a G major chord; "IV/D minor" would be the triad on the fourth degree in D minor, or a G minor chord. The authors adopt the approach of hidden Markov models—seen earlier in Raphael's automatic transcription system and also in my own polyphonic key-finding system, presented in chapter 6. In the generative model they assume, the "label" (tonic, mode, and chord) of a segment depends only on the label of the previous segment. Each segment has a pre-ordained number of notes, and the pitches for these are chosen using probabilities conditional on the segment label: depending on whether the note is the root, third, or fifth of the chord, a non-chord note of the scale, or a non-scalar (chromatic) note. (Only pitch-class labels are generated; register is ignored.) This creates a "bag" of pitch-classes for each segment. (A bag—also known as a "multiset"—is like a set, except that multiple copies of an item are allowed.)

It may be seen that this approach is very similar to the approach proposed in chapter 6 for polyphonic key-finding. There, I suggested a generative model in which a piece is divided into segments; a key label is chosen for each segment, dependent only on the key of the previous segment; and a pitch-class set is generated for each segment, dependent only on the current key. The big differences (so far) are that segments in the Raphael-Stoddard model are labeled with chords as well as keys, and that pitch-classes are generated as a "bag" rather than simply as a set. (With regard to pitch generation, the Raphael-Stoddard model is actually more like the monophonic pitch model of chapter 4.) Indeed, one could extend the analogy still further. Just as pitches in our earlier models were generated from key-profiles, one could represent the Raphael-Stoddard pitch generation process with "chord-profiles" (though Raphael and Stoddard do not use this term), indicating the probability of each pitch-class given a chord and a key.

Given this model, one can determine the most probable structure (a series of segment labels) for a surface (a series of pitch-class bags) just as we did in chapter 6. Given key-chord labels for segments $(X_n)$, pitch-class bags $(Y_n)$, and individual probabilities for pitch-classes given the segment label $(d(y_k))$:

$$P(\text{structure} \mid \text{surface}) \propto \prod_n P(X_n \mid X_{n-1})P(Y_n \mid X_n)$$

$$= \prod_n \left(P(X_n \mid X_{n-1}) \prod_k d(y_k)\right) \tag{8.3}$$

This is the approach taken by Raphael and Stoddard. They then use a dynamic-programming approach, similar to that proposed in chapter 6, to recover the optimal structure given the surface.

Raphael and Stoddard propose several further modifications to this basic model. They stipulate that the key label of each segment $K_n$ (comprising both tonic and mode) depends only on the key label of the previous segment. Regarding the chord labels $(C_n)$: if $K_n = K_{n-1}$, $C_n$ is conditional only on $C_{n-1}$. This makes sense, and indicates that the probability of (for example) I going to V does not depend on the key. If $K_n \neq K_{n-1}$, the chord label is chosen independently of the previous chord. The probability of key transitions, $P(K_n \mid K_{n-1})$, is also determined in a relative way, so that, for example, the probability of moving from C major to D minor is the same as moving from F major to G minor; again, this accords well with the relative understanding of key in music theory.[6] Essentially all of these modifications simplify the model, since they mean that fewer parameters are needed; for example, instead of having parameters for every $P(K_n \mid K_{n-1})$, the model only needs parameters for each *relative* key transition (e.g., a shift from a major key to a minor key a whole-step higher).

Given such a model, we might expect that the parameters would be set on a corpus—for example, counting the proportion of major-key segments which are followed by a shift to a minor key a whole-step higher, or the proportion of notes that are the third of the current chord. The authors take an interesting approach to this problem: the model is trained on an *unannotated* corpus, showing pitch and rhythm information but no key or chord labels. This may seem impossible: how could one determine, for example, what proportion of notes are chordal thirds without knowing what the chords are? Raphael and Stoddard's approach is based on the idea that any model (or parameter set) assigns some probability to the data; the best model (parameter set) is then the one that yields the highest probability. (This is essentially the idea of

Bayesian Models of Other Aspects of Music

"cross-entropy," introduced in section 2.3.) The model starts with some arbitrary parameter set; using this set, the most probable structure is found given the data. This structure then provides an empirical count of transitions and states—the proportion of notes that are the third of the chord, and so on—which can be used to adjust the parameters.[7] The process is then repeated over and over again, as long as $P(\text{data} \mid \text{model})$ continues to improve. This technique, known as the Baum-Welch algorithm (or more generally as "expectation maximization"), has been widely used in computational linguistics (Manning and Schütze 2000).

Raphael and Stoddard's approach is the most promising yet proposed for the modeling of harmonic analysis. One could take issue with certain aspects of the model, such as the fact that it takes no account of voice-leading. (In particular, notes followed by stepwise motion are much more likely to be "ornamental" and not part of the current chord.) However, I wish to focus here on one fundamental issue. The Raphael-Stoddard model essentially accomplishes two tasks: it labels segments with chords (roots), and it labels them with keys. (The model may not explicitly identify roots—rather, it uses functional "Roman-numeral" labels. But if the key is known, knowing the Roman numeral for a chord is essentially the same as knowing the root; either can be derived from the other.) Most recent models have treated root-labeling and key identification as separate problems. Models such as Temperley and Sleator's (1999) and Pardo and Birmingham's (2002) generate root labels for segments, in a key-neutral way; other models (such as those discussed in chapter 4) identify key without considering harmony. One might wonder what the justification is for Raphael and Stoddard's approach; in what way do key analysis and root analysis depend on each other? Raphael and Stoddard do not discuss this issue. One possible benefit of this approach is that information about chord transitions can be encoded in functional terms: the model can learn that V–I is a common progression while V–ii is not. The value of this is unclear. One might argue that some of the most basic rules of harmonic progression do *not* depend on functional labels but could be specified in key-neutral terms, such as the preference to continue the previous chord or to descend by fifths. On the other hand, there might be cases where knowledge of key would help in root-labeling. Consider the two-note chord E–G, which can imply either a C major chord or an E minor chord; in a C major key context, the root is surely more likely to be C, whereas in an E minor context, a root of E seems more probable.

Another justification for Raphael and Stoddard's approach is more fundamental. One could have separate key-finding and harmonic models, both of them probabilistic, each one entailing an independent process for generating pitches. And indeed, it is possible that human perception works that way, in terms of the generative models assumed by listeners. But in fact, this generative model really makes no sense; it cannot be that pitches are actually generated by two different, independent processes. Key and harmony must be combined in some way in the process of pitch generation, and Raphael and Stoddard propose one hypothesis about how this might occur.

**8.4 Mavromatis: Modeling Greek Chant Improvisation**

The next study concerns a kind of musical behavior that we have not yet considered: improvisation. Improvisation is defined in the *New Grove Dictionary* as "the creation of a musical work ... as it is being performed" (Sadie 2001: XII, 94). While almost all music performance could be considered creative in some sense (with regard to parameters such as dynamics, expressive timing, and the like), improvisation—as the above definition suggests—usually implies the creation of aspects essential to the work itself, such as pitches and rhythms. Improvisation is an important part of many musical idioms, and is a rich area for psychological study, though it has received little attention in music cognition thus far.

Mavromatis (2005) presents a probabilistic model of chant improvisation in the style of the Greek Orthodox Church. Greek chant is improvised, but is highly constrained by the text being sung, in particular, the stress pattern of the text. The chanter must choose a pitch pattern that matches the pattern of strong and weak syllables; for example, it is considered inappropriate to have an upward leap on an unstressed syllable. (Mavromatis addresses only the pitch dimension of chant, not musical rhythm or meter.) There are certain general constraints on the style as well, concerning opening patterns, cadential formulae and the like. Figure 8.4 shows a set of examples of correct chant melodies. The stress pattern (indicated with x's) would be given to the chanter, who would then improvise an appropriate melody (such as one of the ones shown). Chanting is still widely practiced in the Greek Orthodox Church, though the practice has been passed on largely by oral tradition and imitation, and the rules and conventions for it have never been systematically codified. Mavromatis's goal was to develop a model which could produce

**Figure 8.4**
From Mavromatis 2005. A family of Greek chant phrases, for the chant mode
*Echos 1*. The stress pattern is marked with x's: two x's = stressed syllable, one
x = unstressed syllable, no x = no change of syllable ("melisma"). (Reprinted
by permission of the author.)

stylistically correct improvisations, given an input stress pattern, thus perhaps shedding light on the cognitive mechanisms involved in this behavior.

Mavromatis models the process of chant generation using a kind of *finite-state machine*. A finite-state machine is a network of nodes, representing states, with transitions between them. The machine begins at some opening state and then moves from state to state via transitions. Each state is labeled with an output symbol; this is the output that the machine produces when it goes through that state. (Sometimes, output symbols are attached to transitions rather than states.) In a *probabilistic* finite-state machine, each transition is labeled with a probability, indicating the probability of that transition being taken. (The probabilities of all transitions out of a state must sum to 1.) The simplest kind of finite-state machine, an *acceptor*, simply produces a string of output symbols (along with a probability for that output). In a finite-state *transducer*—the kind of machine used by Mavromatis—the machine also takes a string of input symbols. The model moves through states while "reading" the input; transitions are labeled with input symbols, and the transition taken at any point must match the next symbol in the input string. States are again labeled with output symbols, and the sequence of states in the model's path determines the output string.

Figure 8.5 shows a portion of Mavromatis's model. Ovals are states, labeled with pitches (output symbols); arrows connecting them are transitions, labeled with stress levels (input symbols). Each pitch is associated with the stress level of the transitions going into it. The model reads in a sequence of stress levels and outputs a sequence of pitches, thus simulating the chanter's improvisation. The model is probabilistic, in that every transition has a certain probability of being taken (these probabilities are not shown in the figure). However, the path taken through the model (and thus the output sequence) is also constrained by the series of stress symbols in the input: a transition must be taken whose stress symbol matches the next symbol in the input.[8]

The middle of figure 8.5 (the long horizontal box) corresponds to the first part of the phrases in figure 8.4, up to the first dotted line and including the following G. Assume an input pattern of S1–S1–S2–S1–S2. Starting from the "begin" node, a path must be found through the model that is compatible with this input string. One such path is *begin–703–703–704–705–2*, which allows the entire input string to be "consumed." The resulting pitch sequence, D–D–E–F–G, corresponds to the opening of phrase 3 in figure 8.4. In this case, then, the model successfully

Bayesian Models of Other Aspects of Music

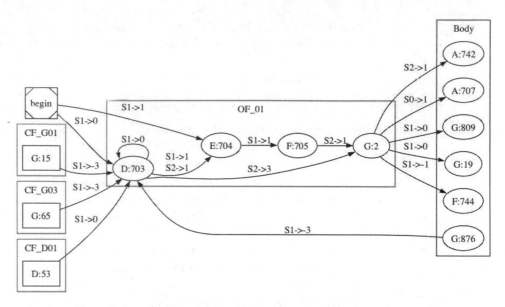

**Figure 8.5**
Part of Mavromatis's final model (2005). Nodes indicate pitches; numbers on nodes are simply for identification purposes. The symbols S0, S1, and S2 indicate the required stress level for each transition: S2 = stressed, S1 = unstressed, S0 = melisma. (Numbers after the stress symbols indicate melodic intervals and can be disregarded here.) (Reprinted by permission of the author.)

generates at least one of the correct melodies for this stress pattern. The model might allow multiple output strings for a given input—just as there might be multiple correct chant melodies for a given stress pattern.

The problem Mavromatis addresses is to arrive at the *optimal* finite-state transducer for the style of Greek Orthodox chant. As we saw in chapter 2, one way to evaluate probabilistic models is by using the cross-entropy approach: the optimal model is the one that assigns highest probability to the data. Given an input string, a finite-state transducer assigns a probability to any output string for that input. This probability is given by the product of the probabilities on all the transitions the machine passes through in generating that output.[9] (Output strings that cannot be generated at all receive a probability of zero.) Thus one could select the best finite-state transducer by finding the one that assigned the highest probability to a corpus of training data (stress patterns with output melodies).

As we saw earlier, choosing between models based on cross-entropy alone is not very satisfactory. In this case, one could make a very simple finite-state machine, simply consisting of a set of nonbranching paths, one for each input–output pair in the training data; such a model would achieve minimal cross-entropy, but would be very complex and would also have no ability to generalize to unseen data. To address this problem, Mavromatis adds another criterion to the evaluation process, which is *simplicity*—defined simply as the number of nodes in the model. Here Mavromatis draws on the theoretical concept of "minimal description length" (Rissanen 1989). Given a body of data and a model, one can create an encoding of the data consisting of (1) a description of the model and (2) a description of the data given the model. We can evaluate a model on the length of the resulting encoding of the data: the shorter the better. The model description will be shorter if the model is simpler; the data description will be shorter if the model assigns the data higher probability. (This draws on a fundamental principle of information theory—that the cross-entropy between a model and data corresponds to the number of binary symbols or "bits" required to encode the data given the model.) There is an intimate connection here, in fact, with our beloved expression $P(\text{surface} \mid \text{structure})\ P(\text{structure})$, indicating the probability of a structure given a surface. $P(\text{data} \mid \text{model})$, the data description length, corresponds directly to $P(\text{surface} \mid \text{structure})$. The simplicity component, the model description length, corresponds to $P(\text{structure})$; one could argue that these two are equivalent as well, if one makes the (not unreasonable) assumption that the probability of a structure is a function of its simplicity. (This is really just the well-known principle of Occam's razor; other things being equal, the simpler theory is more likely to be true.)

Mavromatis developed a procedure in which the model gradually modifies itself to achieve the optimal configuration. It begins as a very simple collection of nonbranching paths, one for each input–output pair (the "cheating" solution described in the previous paragraph). It then evolves, through a process of "state-merging," so as to arrive at the structure that is optimal under the "minimal-description-length" criterion. (Figure 8.5 is a portion of this final model.)

Mavromatis's approach is conceptually elegant, in that the model may be evaluated based solely on its internal structure and its performance on the training data (using the "minimal-description-length" principle), without the need for further testing on unseen data. Such testing would still seem desirable, as a way of further validating the model; this has not yet been done, though Mavromatis identifies it as a project for the future. The model could also be evaluated in other ways. For example, is there independent evidence that the structure of the finite-state machine corresponds to chanters' internal representations? Mavromatis provides anecdotal evidence of this: points that emerge as important "decision points" in the model are sometimes also indicated as such in chanters' annotations of chant text. In any case, Mavromatis's project is certainly an impressive and original application of probabilistic methods to musical problems, and opens the door to many other possibilities.

8.5
Saffran et al.:
Statistical Learning
of Melodic
Patterns

Why do we do Bayesian music research? There seems to be general agreement that the value of such research lies, in large part, in what it can tell us about human cognitive processes. One might wonder, then, whether the role of Bayesian inference in music perception has been studied more directly—for example, in experimental music psychology. In fact, hardly any work of this kind has been done. This is not too surprising, since it is only in the last few years that Bayesian models of music perception have even been proposed; hopefully, this approach will gain more attention among psychologists in the coming years. However, there is one important line of psychological research which—while not exactly Bayesian—deserves mention here.

A group of researchers has investigated the way that listeners extract patterns from musical sequences (Saffran et al. 1999). In one study, subjects were played long sequences of tones, constructed from a small set of three-tone units, but without any explicit marking of those units (by pauses or the like). After this training phase, subjects were played two three-tone units—one that had been used in the sequence just heard and one that had not—and were asked which one was more "familiar." Subjects performed well at this task, indicating that they were able to learn the patterns based on statistical information alone. This phenomenon—known as "statistical learning"—has also been demonstrated with 8-month old infants, and has been found with linguistic patterns as well (Saffran et al. 1996). More recently, further studies (Creel et al. 2004) have explored statistical learning of nonadjacent patterns—for example, a pattern of three notes alternating with three unrelated notes. It appears that listeners have difficulty identifying nonadjacent patterns, but can do so if the patterns are differentiated from the unrelated notes in some way, for example, by pitch register or timbre.

While these authors have not (to my knowledge) proposed a Bayesian explanation for their findings, one could well view them in Bayesian terms. (We will confine our attention here to studies using patterns of

**Figure 8.6**
A random melody. The melody was generated (by me) according to the criteria used by Saffran et al. (1999) in generating their stimuli (they may not have used this exact melody). Two segmentations are shown; letters above segmentation A indicate repeating segments.

adjacents notes, e.g. Saffran et al. 1999.) The "structure" here is a series of underlying musical units, each one containing several notes. In listening to a melody, perhaps, the listener considers different segmentations—that is to say, different groupings of the notes into units. Let us assume that all groups of notes are, *a priori*, equally likely to occur as units, and all sequences of units are also equally likely, except that structures containing repeating units are more probable than others. (This assumes a generative process in which a composer creates a set of units and combines them more or less arbitrarily, but prefers to repeat units already used.) For example, in figure 8.6, segmentation A is more probable than segmentation B because A uses only 4 different units, whereas segmentation B uses 8. (As in section 8.2, there is no real separation of structure from surface here; $P$(structure | surface) is simply proportional to $P$(structure).)

Clearly, there is a fundamental difference between this statistical learning process and the processes explored elsewhere in this book. In key-finding and meter-finding, the listener's probabilistic knowledge is (presumably) acquired from a large sample of music heard over a long period. In statistical learning experiments, by contrast, the learning occurs over a few minutes. However, the short-term learning paradigm employed by Saffran et al. may be appropriate for the kind of musical structure that is involved. What is at issue in these experiments is "motivic structure"—the network of repeated (or similar) melodic patterns in a piece. And structure of this kind is quite idiosyncratic to particular pieces; every piece has its own individual motives. Someone listening to Beethoven's Fifth Symphony or Mozart's Fortieth has to learn the motives of the piece "on the spot," so to speak—just like in a statistical learning experiment—and then immediately apply this knowledge so as to recognize subsequent instances within the piece.

Bayesian Models of Other Aspects of Music

What statistical learning research tells us is that listeners are sensitive to the frequencies of musical elements, even "structural" elements that can only be indirectly inferred from the surface.[10] Certainly, this is essential to anything that could be considered "Bayesian perception." It would be interesting to look for other indicators of Bayesian processes in music perception. Are listeners able to identify structural elements even when the relationship between surface and structure is probabilistic—for example, when the surface realization of a repeating unit in a melody varies slightly on each occurrence? Can listeners learn probabilistic dependencies between the structural units themselves? And can they apply all of this knowledge in perception, to recover an underlying structure from a complex musical surface? Addressing these questions experimentally could tell us much about the psychological plausibility of the Bayesian models presented here.

# 9
# Style and Composition

In previous chapters, we have focused mainly on modeling music perception. We have touched on compositional phenomena here and there—notably in chapter 7, where I suggested that the ambiguity of different pitch-class sets might shed light on some conventions of common-practice harmony—but only in an incidental way. In this chapter, we focus squarely on the empirical modeling of compositional practice: pieces of music and the compositional processes that gave rise to them.[1] I will argue that, given a model which successfully describes a body of music, we can go further and claim the model as a description of cognitive representations involved in the creation of that music. In some cases, this approach simply confirms common assumptions about the cognitive structures involved in composition. However, it may also allow us to test theories whose validity (with regard to the compositional process) is uncertain or controversial. This approach also has applications to issues of musical style. By positing different generative models for different musical styles, we can model the differences between them, in a more quantitative and rigorous way than has been possible before.

Before proceeding any further, we should examine the underlying premise of this chapter—a premise which, to some, may seem highly problematic. How can we make claims about the cognitive processes involved in composition, based only on "musical" evidence—analysis (statistical or otherwise) of the resulting musical objects?[2] I would respond to this concern in two ways. First of all, I would suggest that music theorists and others in fact do this quite routinely—though often only in an indirect way. For example, when we describe one chord as "prolonging" or "elaborating" another, or describe one theme as a "variant" or "transformation" of a previous one, I would argue that there are implicit claims here about the compositional process—claims about how the composer generated and organized musical materials. I would argue, furthermore, that claims of this kind are entirely legitimate—even when, as is often the case, they are based only on musical evidence, without any independent support (from what we know about the composer's education and background, evidence from letters and sketches, etc.). To take an extreme example: Suppose we found a piece by a composer whom we knew nothing about, and found that the pitches of the piece could be grouped—completely and in a musically convincing way—into statements of a twelve-tone row (a pattern in which each of the twelve pitch-classes is used exactly once). Would we not be justified in asserting this row structure as part of the composer's compositional process? Surely we would. Even if we had no other evidence that the composer had used "serial" procedures—indeed, even if external evidence made this seem very unlikely (if it was an eighteenth-century composer, for example)—the use of such procedures would seem to be proven on musical grounds alone. My point, then, is that claims about composition based on purely musical evidence are made all the time, and that this approach is, in principle, completely valid. This is not to say, of course, that *specific* claims of this type are always valid: this must be determined on a case-by-case basis. What I propose here, in effect, is a quantitative and objective way of resolving such questions.

Our approach here relies centrally on the notion of *cross-entropy*. In chapter 2, I introduced cross-entropy as a measure of the "goodness of fit" between a model and a body of data. I suggested that cross-entropy could allow us to choose between different models in a completely empirical fashion, without any other prior assumptions—or rather, with only the assumption that all models were equal in prior probability. Each model assigns some probability to the data; the best model is the one that assigns the highest probability. In this chapter, we will adopt this approach with regard to music. We will begin by considering two rather simple illustrations of this approach, using models proposed in earlier chapters for European folk music. We will then consider the possibility of using probabilistic generative models to characterize differences between styles. Finally, we will consider the prospect of using this approach to test a well-established—but as yet untested—theory of tonal pitch structure, Schenkerian theory.

**Figure 9.1**
"Romani13," from the Essen corpus.

**9.1**

**Some Simple
Cross-Entropy
Experiments**

In chapter 4, we examined a corpus of European folk melodies, treating each melody simply as a sequence of pitches (without rhythmic information), and sought to model the process of key perception. We now consider the same corpus of data—again, focusing only on the pitch dimension—but address a different question: what is the best model of *the data itself*, that is, the one that assigns it the highest probability? Let us consider just one song from the test set—a song identified as "Romani 13," shown in figure 9.1—and two possible models of the song, Model 1 and Model 2. Under Model 1, all pitches within the complete pitch range of the song (a range of 10 semitones, F4 to D5) are equally likely; thus each pitch has a probability of 0.1. Each pitch is generated as an independent event; the probability of a sequence of pitches is therefore the product of their individual probabilities. We will call this simple model the "baseline" model. There are 28 pitches in the song, yielding an overall probability of $(0.1)^{28}$. Let us now express this in terms of cross-entropy. As explained in section 2.3, the cross-entropy between a model and a body of data essentially represents the probability of the data as assigned by the model, but with a few twists: we take the logarithm, add a negative sign, and express the quantity in a "per-symbol" fashion. For a body of data $D$ with $n$ events, and a model $P_m$:

$$H(D, P_m) = -(1/n) \log P_m(D) \tag{9.1}$$

Thus the cross-entropy of Model 1 with "Romani 13" ($R$) is as follows:

$$H(R, P_{m1}) = -(1/28) \log(0.1)^{28} = -\log(0.1) = 2.30 \tag{9.2}$$

In a case like this, where the model assigns the same probability to all events, it can be seen that the cross-entropy is simply the negative log probability of a single event.

Model 2 uses the pitch model proposed in chapter 4. Recall that this model can be used to estimate the probability of a sequence of pitches: this is the joint probability of the pitch sequence with a key and a central pitch, summed over all keys and central pitches (equation 4.5). For "Romani 13," the model yields a log probability of −49.37. The cross-entropy is simply the negative per-symbol version of this:

$$H(R, P_{m2}) = -(1/28)(-49.37) = 1.76 \qquad (9.3)$$

We have, then, two measures of the cross-entropy of "Romani 13": 2.30 from Model 1, 1.76 from Model 2. Since Model 2 yields a lower cross-entropy than Model 1, we can conclude that Model 2 is a better model of the song.

What does it mean, in the current context, to say that Model 2 is a "better" model of the song than Model 1? It means that Model 2 fits, or describes, the data better in a quantitative sense; to put it another way, we could say that Model 2 *reduces the uncertainty* of the data (in relation to the baseline model, Model 1). But this also means, I submit, that Model 2 *explains* the data better than Model 1; that is, it is more likely to describe the generative process that gave rise to the data. Now, in my original presentation of the rhythm and pitch models, I cautioned against viewing them as models of the creative process, stating that they were only models of how *listeners* might model this process for perceptual purposes. But now I wish to qualify this position. Certainly I would not claim that the monophonic pitch model of chapter 4 is a *complete* model of the process of folk-song composition. The model really only knows about three things: key (as represented in key-profiles), range, and pitch proximity. It neglects many other kinds of knowledge that undoubtedly play a role in the creative process—cadential patterns and other conventional gestures; repeated patterns or motives; considerations of phrase structure, large-scale form, and harmonic shape; and so on. I would claim, however, that the model's knowledge is *part* of the human knowledge that goes into the compositional process. Key-profiles (or something like them) act as a probabilistic constraint on composition, in that the composer generally chooses notes from the scale of the chosen key; range and pitch proximity constrain the compositional process in a similar way. (Folk songs may of course have evolved over a long period and may have had many different "composers," but that does not affect the present point.)

In fact, all of this is probably uncontroversial. There is much independent evidence for the psychological reality of scales and the preference for small intervals: for example, evidence from perception experiments (Krumhansl 1990; Schellenberg 1997) and the representation of scales in key signatures.[3] A more tricky question is this: suppose there were no other evidence? Suppose that "Romani 13" came to us from outer space—perhaps with the pitches represented as integers—and nothing was known about the process that gave rise to it? Would we be justified in positing scale structures, range, and pitch proximity as causal factors in its generation? I would argue that the answer is yes. Even without any other evidence, the mere fact that Model 2 lowers the uncertainty of the data gives support to it as an account of the generative process—at least, compared to the alternative ("baseline") model. Of course, if one produced a model (call it Model 3) that generated the data with still higher probability than Model 2, then *that* model would be preferred. But the point is that—other things being equal—we are justified as accepting, as a causal model of the data, whichever model assigns it the highest probability.

In the outer-space story in chapter 2, I argued that it was important for the model to be tested on unseen data. Otherwise, the cross-entropy criterion is open to mischief: in the current case, for example, one could simply define a model that assigned a probability of 1 to the exact sequence of pitches in "Romani 13," yielding a cross-entropy of $-\log(1) = 0$, the best possible score. Besides testing on unseen data, I suggested that another solution to this problem is to consider the criterion of simplicity. In that case, the "$P(\text{data}) = 1$" model would rate poorly, being highly complex. In many cases, it is sufficient to appeal to common sense on this issue; when we are dealing with large bodies of data, such trivial "$P(\text{data}) = 1$" models become absurdly complex and can simply be disregarded. There are also ways of quantifying the simplicity of a model, such as the "minimal description length" approach used by Mavromatis (2005) (see section 8.4).[4]

Let us consider another use of cross-entropy to evaluate models of compositional practice, this time in the rhythmic domain. Once again, we consider two possible models, each of which assigns a probability to a pattern of onsets in time (disregarding pitch). We apply both models to "Romani 13," using the performance in the Essen test set. (Recall that the songs were performed on a MIDI keyboard, and thus reflect "unquantized" timing.) As we did in chapter 3, we simplify the problem by assuming a timeline of pips, spaced 50 msec apart; each note-onset is rounded to the nearest pip. (Again, imagine a rhythmic performance that came to us in this form from outer space.) Model 1 simply treats every pip as independent; each pip has a probability of .12 of generating a note-onset (this is roughly the density of notes in the Essen test set), and a probability of .88 of not generating one. The probability of the onset pattern $T$ is the product of these probabilities for all 275 pips in the song, or $(.12)^{28} + (.88)^{247} = 1.83 \times 10^{-36}$. Thus

$$H(T, P_{m1}) = -(1/275) \times \log(1.83 \times 10^{-36}) = 0.331 \qquad (9.4)$$

Model 2 is the meter-finding model proposed in chapter 3; as described there, this model can be used to estimate the probability of an onset sequence, by calculating the probability of the pattern in combination with a metrical structure and summing this over all metrical structures. The model yields a log probability of $-83.9$ for the song, or a cross-entropy of $-(1/275) \times -83.9 = 0.305$. Here again, the lower cross-entropy score for Model 2 seems to be justification (if any were needed) for arguing that Model 2 is more plausible than Model 1 as a model of the psychological processes that went into generating the onset pattern; in particular, it provides evidence for metrical grids as playing a role in that process. (The difference in score between the two models is small in this case, and one might argue that this test alone is not very decisive.)[5]

This same logic might be applied to other kinds of musical structure. Consider harmony, an aspect of music that has not been explored in depth here but was discussed briefly in chapter 8 with regard to the work of Raphael and Stoddard (2004). Assume a model similar to Raphael and Stoddard's, which derives a harmonic structure from a pattern of notes. The close parallels between Raphael and Stoddard's harmonic model and our probabilistic key-finding models have already been mentioned; without going into detail, the reader can perhaps see how such a model could be used to assess the probability of a musical surface, in much the same way as our key-finding and meter-finding models—by summing over the joint probabilities of all possible structures with the surface. As yet another example, consider motivic analysis—the analysis of pieces into repeating or similar intervallic or rhythmic patterns. One could devise a generative model which generated melodies by concatenating short melodic segments, but which favored repeating segments that had already occurred. (This possibility was mentioned in chapter 8, with regard to the experimental work of Saffran et al. [1999].) Such a model would then give higher probability to pieces using repeated patterns—thus entailing the general claim that "short melodic patterns often tend to repeat themselves." Particularly in a piece that is dominated by a single motive—such as the first movement of Beethoven's Fifth Symphony—it seems clear that this principle reduces the uncertainty of the piece (for example, helping us predict what will happen next), and thus becomes a plausible claim about the compositional process.

To recapitulate the argument so far: Bayesian models of music perception naturally yield judgments of the probabilities of musical surfaces. As such, they offer general predictions about the nature of those surfaces—for example, that pitches tend to remain within a scale or that intervals between notes tend to be small. Testing these surface predictions, through the idea of cross-entropy, can be an indirect way of testing the generative models behind them. If a theory can be shown to reduce the uncertainty of musical surfaces, this provides a kind of validation for the theory with regard to the generative process. Essentially, this is just a very rigorous way of stating something that is perhaps self-evident: certain kinds of musical principles and structures—key, range, pitch proximity, meter, harmony, and motives—yield predictions about the kinds of things that happen, and do not happen, in musical surfaces; if the predictions are borne out, that gives credence to these structures as part of the generative process.

The experiments conducted here are not particularly revelatory. The role of key, pitch proximity, and meter in the composition of folk songs is not really in doubt, so the cross-entropy approach merely confirms what was already assumed. Moreover, in these experiments, our Bayesian pitch and rhythm models were only compared to very primitive alternative models, which I am sure no one would seriously advocate; the fact that the Bayesian models outscored them is not much of a victory. Still, I would argue that this approach has valuable potential for the future. In a case where multiple models of a musical corpus have been proposed, the cross-entropy method could provide an objective way of deciding between them. Again, the criterion of "goodness of fit" might not be the only important one in deciding between models; we might also consider the criterion of simplicity, and other cognitive or historical evidence about the compositional process. But goodness of fit is certainly *one* important criterion, and the cross-entropy approach provides a useful way of quantifying it.

One area where cross-entropy might be very valuable is in evaluating principles of melodic structure. As discussed in chapter 5, a number of theories of melodic expectation have been proposed (Schmuckler 1989; Narmour 1990; Cuddy and Lunney 1995; Krumhansl 1995; Bharucha 1996; Schellenberg 1996, 1997; Lerdahl 2001; Larson 2004; Margulis 2005). These theories, and the musical principles they entail, might also be construed as claims about melodic construction—given the reasonable assumption that listeners' melodic expectations are shaped by the nature of actual melodies. If these theories could be formulated in a probabilistic manner, they could be tested on data such as the Essen corpus using the cross-entropy technique. As one example, consider the principle of inertia—the tendency for melodies to continue in the direction they are going (Larson 2004). To test the inertia idea, one could incorporate it into our pitch model, by assigning higher probability to melodies that follow inertia. (We could do this, for example, by conditioning the pitch probabilities of each event on the previous *two* events—so that scale-degree $\hat{3}$ might have a higher probability after $\hat{1}$–$\hat{2}$ than after $\hat{3}$–$\hat{2}$.) If the inertial model assigned higher probability to the data than the non-inertial model, this would provide compelling support for the role of inertia in the creation of folk melodies.

In short, the cross-entropy idea has the potential to be of great value in evaluating and comparing theories of musical structure and compositional processes. This idea also has relevance to the problem of characterizing differences between styles, as we explore in the next section.

## 9.2 Modeling Stylistic Differences

In chapter 3, I proposed a simple model of rhythmic organization in traditional European music. Under this view, each piece has a hierarchical metrical structure, with beats at each level roughly equally spaced (though not *exactly* equally spaced in human performance), and with note-onsets more likely to occur at stronger beats. It is interesting to consider this framework with respect to another musical style in which rhythm has been particularly well studied: traditional sub-Saharan African music. In many ways, the rhythmic character of traditional sub-Saharan African (hereafter just "African") music is fundamentally similar to that of traditional European (hereafter just "European") music. African music features metrical grids of several levels, with duple or triple relationships between levels. There are also significant differences, however. Much more than European music, African music is characterized by frequent metrical conflicts—patterns of accentuation that go against the underlying meter (see Jones 1959; Chernoff 1979; and Agawu 1995, as well as Temperley 2001a and citations therein). For example, one often finds a note on a weak beat with no note on the following strong beat; the traditional African melody in figure 9.2 (from Nketia 1974) shows numerous examples of this. Such conflicts, known as *syncopations*, are not unheard of in common-practice music but are much less common. It has

**Figure 9.2**
A Bwali (Manyema) melody, from Nketia 1974, p. 143. Notes on weak eighth-note beats with no note on the following beat are marked "*"; notes of this type just before a downbeat are marked "*!".

also been observed—though less widely—that traditional African music features a strictness of pulse far beyond that of European music (Jones 1959: 38; Chernoff 1979: 97). European music features deliberate, noticeable fluctuations of pulse—known as *rubato*—used for expressive purposes. (Here I have in mind particularly European art music of the common-practice period, where fluctuation in tempo is an important expressive device.) Such fluctuations are virtually absent in traditional African music.

Another interesting style to consider is rock. Like traditional African music, rock features a great deal of syncopation; accented events on weak beats are commonplace (Temperley 1999; Stephenson 2002). (I define "rock" quite broadly here—as the term is often used—to include a wide range of late-twentieth-century Anglo-American popular music: soul, heavy metal, disco, 1980s synth-pop, and so on.) Rock also features an extremely strict tempo with little expressive fluctuation. Indeed, in much recent popular music, human musicians have been replaced by drum machines and other electronic music sources capable of superhuman rhythmic regularity, without much noticeable loss of expressivity (at least as far as most listeners are concerned)—further evidence that fluctuation in tempo is not a very important source of expression in rock. A contrast emerges, then, between traditional European music on the one hand (with high tempo flexibility and low syncopation), and traditional African music and rock on the other (with low tempo flexibility and high syncopation).

These differences between styles can be characterized quite well using our probabilistic framework. Syncopation relates to the alignment of events with beats: a more syncopated style is one in which the probability of events on weaker beats is relatively high. In our model of

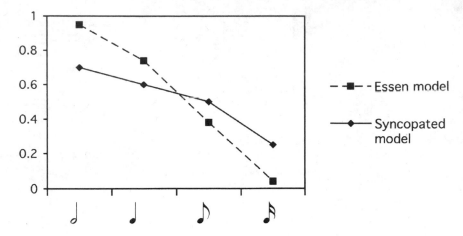

**Figure 9.3**
"Note-beat profiles" for two models—one derived from the Essen collection and one for a (hypothetical) more syncopated style. Values indicate probabilities of a note-onset at a beat of the corresponding metrical level.

traditional European rhythm, we derived information from the Essen corpus regarding the probability of event-onsets at beats of different levels; this information, which we could call a "note-beat profile," is shown in figure 9.3 (the "Essen" model). (Our earlier model had no value for 16th-note beats; I calculated this value from the corpus as roughly .04.) Unfortunately, no encoded database of African or rock melodies is available. However, we can imagine what the note-beat profile for a more syncopated style might look like; a hypothetical example is shown in figure 9.3 (the "syncopated" model). The probability of notes at higher levels is lower (in relation to the Essen model); at lower levels, it is higher. Figure 9.4 shows rhythms generated with the two profiles; it can be seen that the number of syncopations (notes on weak beats, not followed by a note on the next strong beat) is a good deal higher in the "syncopated" rhythm than in the Essen rhythm.[6]

We now consider the difference relating to strictness of tempo. I suggested that traditional European music allows much more flexibility in tempo—rubato—than African music or rock does. Let us consider just the tactus level. In our metrical model, the amount of fluctuation in the tactus is controlled by the function relating each tactus interval to the previous one. As shown in figure 3.6, given a tactus interval $T_{n-1}$ of a certain length, the following interval $T_n$ is likely to be close to it but perhaps slightly longer or shorter. (A complete metrical model needs to have

A.

B.

**Figure 9.4**
Rhythms generated stochastically, using the note-beat profiles in figure 9.3: (A) the Essen note-beat profile and (B) the syncopated note-beat profile.

such curves for each possible tactus length; taken together, these curves constitute what we will call the "tempo function" of the model.) The degree of tempo flexibility in a generative model can be controlled by the "width" of these curves. A fairly wide curve (such as that labeled as the "rubato" model in figure 9.5) will allow great tempo flexibility; a narrow curve (the "strict" model) will imply a stricter tempo. These curves are purely hypothetical, but they illustrate in a schematic way how we might model the difference between a "strict-tempo" style like traditional African music or rock, and a "flexible tempo" style like traditional European music.

This suggests a way that the observed differences between different rhythmic idioms might be quantitatively described—leading to distinct generative models for the different styles. As usual, we could test our models on their ability to assign high probability to the data they are intended to describe. It should be the case that the "European" model will assign higher probability to European data (e.g., European folk songs or classical music), while the "African" model assigns higher probability to African data. Thus, the probabilistic approach yields both a way of quantitatively modeling the differences between styles, and a way of empirically testing these models. (It might be observed, also, that there is something *complementary* about these differences. Both rubato and

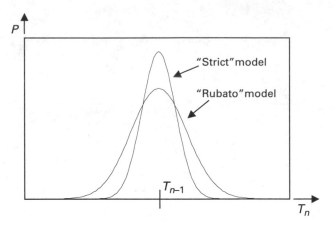

**Figure 9.5**
Distributions for a tactus interval $T_n^-$ (as a function of $T_{n-1}$) for two hypothetical styles: a "strict" style and a "rubato" style.

syncopation increase complexity or ambiguity, and it seems natural that a style which had more syncopation would feature a stricter tempo to compensate for it. We will investigate this possibility in the next chapter.)

We have been focusing in this section on generative musical processes —composition and performance—but of course, one of the premises of this study is that generative models are also involved in perception. If we assume that listeners tune their perceptual models to the musical environment, we might expect that African and European listeners would possess different metrical models, reflecting the different degrees of syncopation and rubato in the corresponding styles. It is important to note that—if the current view is correct—the difference between these models is, in a way, rather small. The same basic principles are involved in both cases; all that differs, really, is the numerical parameters—the precise shape of the tempo functions and note-beat profiles in the two styles.

The idea that listeners of different backgrounds possess different models has interesting implications. In some cases, this might lead to differences in the structures that were inferred; for example, two listeners might perceive different metrical structures in the same piece. Another question concerns listeners who are familiar with multiple styles; for example, many listeners today have great familiarity with both common-practice music and rock. Do such listeners have multiple models, which they can activate for different musical styles as the situation demands? It is also possible that such listeners could use their "style models" to *iden-*

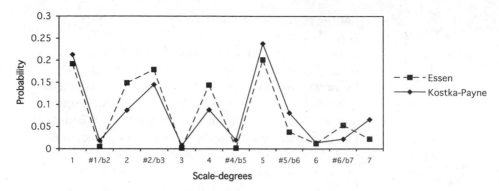

**Figure 9.6**
Scale-degree distributions (counting every event) for minor-key sections, in the Essen corpus and Kostka-Payne corpus.

*tify* the style of music they hear—for example, by trying out two models and seeing which one assigned higher probability to the data. These would seem to be interesting questions for experimental study.

These ideas are suggestive, also, with regard to pitch organization and key. As noted earlier, we can think of scale-degree distributions as representing basic cognitive constraints that guide the compositional process—so that, for example, composers tend to favor notes in the tonic triad and to avoid chromatic notes. Consider scale-degree distributions in two different corpora we have studied, the Kostka-Payne corpus (which we will take to represent common-practice European art music) and the Essen corpus (representing European folk music). As was observed earlier, these distributions are very similar. There is one difference which seems significant, however, namely that $\flat\hat{7}$ is higher than $\hat{7}$ in minor keys in the folk song corpus, but lower in the common-practice corpus (figure 9.6 shows the minor-key profiles for these two corpora).[7] If the current reasoning is correct, we would expect listeners to internalize these differences, so that people exposed mainly to common-practice music would have different key-profiles from those familiar mainly with folk music. Such listeners might have different intuitions about the stability and tension of events, and also different expectations for future events. For a listener who is familiar with both styles, the profiles could be used to determine the style of a melody, according to which model assigned it higher probability: if a minor-key melody used $\flat\hat{7}$ much more than $\hat{7}$, we might be inclined to hear it as "folkish." The idea that we might identify a style of music by the scale it uses is, perhaps, not particularly novel;

but the probabilistic approach provides a rigorous way of modeling this process.

This raises a further question: What are the limits, if any, on the kinds of models listeners can learn? With regard to pitch, for example, one might wonder about the ability of listeners to learn a new pitch-class distribution. If listeners are flexible in this regard, it opens up wide possibilities for composition: it means that a composer could set up a particular pitch-class distribution at the beginning of a piece and thus condition listeners' perceptions accordingly (with regard to expectations, judgments of tension and appropriateness, and so on). On the other hand, it might be that our perception is much less malleable: in hearing a piece with an unconventional pitch-class distribution, we simply impose our tonal key-profiles on it, yielding a highly ambiguous key judgment and a (probably unsatisfactory) experience in which many events are judged as tense, unexpected, and inappropriate. There is some evidence that listeners have considerable flexibility in this regard. Oram and Cuddy (1995) did experiments in which listeners were played melodies generated from unconventional pitch-class profiles, specifically designed to thwart any sense of conventional tonality; they were then given probe-tones and asked to judge the "goodness of fit" of the tones given the context. It was found that listeners did, indeed, show sensitivity to the context melodies, giving high ratings to the tones that were often used in the context. In a similar study, Castellano, Bharucha, and Krumhansl (1984) performed probe-tone experiments on Western listeners using classical Indian music and found that they were sensitive to the unfamiliar pitch-class distributions used in that music. Such experiments suggest that, to some extent at least, listeners are able to attune themselves to novel and unfamiliar kinds of pitch organization.

## 9.3 Testing Schenkerian Theory

Earlier in this chapter, I argued that the cross-entropy approach could provide a valuable means of testing the validity of music theories. In this section, we will consider how this approach might be used to test one well-known theoretical paradigm, Schenkerian theory. Developed by the Austrian music theorist Heinrich Schenker (1868–1935), this is an influential and important theory of pitch organization in common-practice tonal music. Schenkerian theory has been construed in different ways—as a theory of composition, as a theory of perception, or simply as an interesting way of hearing music (see Temperley 2001b for discussion of these goals and their roles in Schenkerian scholarship); here I wish to examine Schenkerian theory as it relates to composition. I argued earlier that a theory of musical structure could be evaluated on its ability to assign high probability to musical pieces; if it succeeded, that alone would give it credence as a model of the compositional process. My aim here is not to actually undertake this formidable project with Schenkerian theory, but simply to explore, in a very preliminary way, some of the issues that might arise in such a project.

While presentations of Schenkerian theory differ on certain matters of interpretation and emphasis, there is broad agreement on a number of basic points; see, for example, Schenker 1935/1979, Jonas 1934/1982, Schachter 1981, Forte and Gilbert 1982, and Cadwallader and Gagne 1998. We will limit our attention to monophonic music (as we did in section 9.1); while most of the common-practice repertoire is polyphonic, monophonic works also exist (such as Bach's violin and cello suites) and it is generally accepted that Schenkerian theory applies to such music.

The central idea of Schenkerian theory is pitch elaboration—also called "prolongation" or "diminution." Notes elaborate one another in a recursive fashion; note X may be elaborated by note Y, which in turn is elaborated by note Z. To test the theory using the cross-entropy approach, we need to formulate it as a probabilistic generative model. A fairly simple solution suggests itself as to how this might work. We begin with a single pitch, and generate one or more new pitches as elaborations: The newly generated pitches may themselves be elaborated by further pitches. At each note, we must decide how many notes are to elaborate it, the pitches of those notes, and their temporal ordering in relation to the "head" note. All of these decisions could be controlled, as usual, by probabilities. (We consider only pitch here, not rhythm; Schenkerian structures are generally assumed to be unspecified with regard to rhythm, at least at higher levels.) Using these probabilities, the model generates a tree structure; the probability of the tree is the product of the probabilities on the decisions that generated it. The surface, as usual, is a pattern of pitches; a structure, defined as a complete tree, *entails* a surface, so that $P(\text{surface} \mid \text{structure}) = 1$ for that surface. The probability of a surface is thus equal to $\sum P(\text{structure})$, summed over all structures that entail it.

Schenkerian analysis allows a variety of different kinds of elaborations. A note can be elaborated melodically by a single other note: either at an interval of a half-step or whole-step (an "incomplete neighbor"), or a skip of a major or minor third, perfect fourth or fifth, or major or minor sixth (a "consonant skip"). These elaborations may be applied to any note, and may occur either before or after the generating note, in either registral direction. (Notes may also be elaborated in a vertical manner—"consonant support"—but we will not consider that possibility here.) Elaborations may also arise by filling in the interval between two notes ("passing-tone" or "linear progression"). The theory also allows alteration of notes in certain ways after they are generated—by octave transfer, deletion, displacement, or substitution. For the moment, we will assume that only single-note elaborations are allowed, and we will not allow any alterations of notes. Schenker also stipulated that a complete piece must have, as its top-level structure, a fundamental line or *Urlinie* featuring descending stepwise diatonic motion from $\hat{5}$ to $\hat{1}$, $\hat{3}$ to $\hat{1}$, or $\hat{8}$ to $\hat{1}$; we will include this requirement here. (The *Urlinie* is assumed to have an associated I–V–I harmonic structure; we return to this below.) Notice, then, that we are assuming a very restrictive form of the theory, which only allows some of the elaborations and transformations that are actually used. Thus our model may exclude some structures that should be allowed, but hopefully will not include any that should be disallowed.

Two major problems arise here. One is the role of harmony. Some entities in Schenkerian analyses are essentially harmonic rather than melodic—so-called *Stufen*. *Stufen* play an essential role in Schenker's theory; in particular, a tonal piece must have a "top-level" I–V–I harmonic pattern. It is not clear, however, how *Stufen* constrain musical surfaces. *Stufen* do not need to be present as literal chords—the notes can be presented sequentially rather than simultaneously, and in some cases they are not even present at all; for example, many Bach suite movements end with incomplete V or I chords. (This is the case for many folk melodies as well, some of which surely qualify as tonal pieces—figure 9.1, for example.) It is also not clear how the generation of *Stufen* should be integrated with the generation of notes. One possibility is that *Stufen* could be viewed simply as emergent features of the note-generation process. For example, the bass note of a chord could be generated first as a linear elaboration, and the upper notes of the chord generated from the bass note. This is the approach used in earlier attempts to formalize Schenker, notably those of Kassler (1977) and Smoliar (1980).[8] In that case, no explicit recognition of *Stufen* would be needed in the generative process. Clearly, this is a major issue in the formalization of Schenkerian theory, but we will not attempt to resolve it here.

A second, related, problem concerns the role of counterpoint. Schenker and his followers maintain that strict counterpoint—for example, as codified by Fux (1725/1971)—has a profound connection to common-practice composition. However, the exact nature of this relationship is quite unclear. Some, such as Peel and Slawson (1985), have gone so far as to claim that the higher levels of a Schenkerian analysis are strictly governed by traditional contrapuntal rules. Most other authors have argued for a more indirect relationship between counterpoint and "free composition"—observing, for example, that both idioms are constructed from fluent, largely stepwise lines, and that they share certain basic patterns such as passing-tones (Forte and Gilbert 1980; Cadwallader and Gagne 1998). Again, the role of counterpoint would seem to arise mainly in connection with polyphonic music (though a single melody can, in some cases, imply multiple contrapuntal lines). We will therefore evade this issue and press on—acknowledging that the issues of harmony and counterpoint will have to be resolved before anything like a complete formalization of Schenkerian theory can be achieved.

The proposal, then, is that our generative model will be a recursive process in which notes are generated as elaborations of other notes. One might wonder, at this point, why it is necessary to make the model probabilistic. We could consider a model which simply generated a set of structures in an all-or-nothing fashion. The hope is that some melodies would be generated, and others would not; in effect, the model would then be assigning high probability to some melodies and zero to others. This would be analogous to a grammar in the tradition of theoretical ("generative") linguistics, in which word sequences are judged as "grammatical" or "ungrammatical" by the grammar according to whether they can be generated (Chomsky 1965). Earlier attempts to implement Schenkerian analysis computationally have taken this approach (Kassler 1977; Smoliar 1980). If such a model succeeded in generating actual tonal melodies and not generating many others, it could, indeed, claim success on these grounds alone. This hope seems unrealistic in the case of Schenkerian theory, however. Essentially, the rules for single-note elaborations proposed above (and remember that this is only a subset of the actual elaborations and transformations allowed by the theory) allow any note to be elaborated by a note at any interval within the range of a major sixth (except tritones). This means that virtually any sequence of random notes—within, say, a one-octave range—can be generated in some way: that is, there will be some way of connecting the notes in an acceptable Schenkerian "tree." Indeed, a note sequence of substantial length—even a random sequence—will probably be generable in an astronomically huge number of different ways. My own computational experiments—

**Figure 9.7**
A random 15-note melody (generated from an even distribution over the notes C4–B4). The analysis shown is one of 324,977 analyses generated by a Schenkerian "parser" which finds all analyses using just one-note elaborations (incomplete neighbors and consonant skips). The elaborations are indicated by slurs, as is customary. The beamed notes indicate the highest-level line or *Urlinie*; elaborations can then be traced recursively from these notes (for example, the first B♭ is elaborated by the C♯ two notes earlier, which is in turn elaborated by the E's on either side).

using a simple Schenkerian "parser" which finds all possible analyses of a melody, using the rules outlined above—confirm this. Figure 9.7 shows a randomly generated 15-note melody (generated from an even distribution over a one-octave range, C4 to B4), and one of the 324,977 analyses found.[9] (The parser *does* require that the analysis contain an *Urlinie*—in this case it is B♭–A–G.)

Thus, a version of Schenkerian analysis which simply judges melodies as "generable" and "nongenerable" is unlikely to have much power in reducing the uncertainty of common-practice music. However, this is not necessarily cause for despair. It is clear that Schenkerian analysis, as it is usually practiced, does not involve such an "all-or-nothing" model. When we are doing a Schenkerian analysis of a tonal piece, we do not find ourselves torn between millions of different possible analyses. Rather, we quickly "zero in" on one or perhaps a few different analyses. No doubt this is because our internal models assign higher probabilities to some configurations rather than others. Again, a parallel with linguistics is appropriate. Traditionally, syntax in language has been modeled using hierarchical tree structures, similar in some ways to those used in Schenkerian analysis.[10] Early attempts to parse language using tree-based grammars ran into problems of massive ambiguity; it was found that an ordinary English sentence might have thousands of different parses. But clearly, speakers of English are able to overcome this ambiguity problem and comprehend sentences successfully. It was found that by building probabilistic knowledge into grammars, the ambiguity problem could be greatly reduced (Manning and Schütze 2000). From this point of view, our Schenkerian experiment is just another example of how probabilistic knowledge is useful—perhaps necessary—for modeling musical processes of generation and perception.

Adding probabilities to our Schenkerian grammar might greatly alleviate the ambiguity problem, and might have the added effect of distinguishing better between stylistically "good" and "bad" melodies—assigning high probabilities to the former and low probabilities to the latter. This could be done in many ways. We could, for example, assign higher probabilities to some kinds of elaborations than others; perhaps consonant skips are more common than incomplete neighbors, or preceding elaborations are more likely than following ones. We could probabilistically limit the number of elaborations of a single note. Or we could control the way elaborations are combined—regarding the temporal ordering of different elaborations in relation to the "head" note, for example, or the way elaborations are combined hierarchically. But which of these options should we pursue? Here, the massive literature on Schenkerian analysis is of little help to us; this literature offers little discussion—even of an informal nature—pertaining to the relative probability of these different configurations. This is not exactly a criticism; developing a probabilistic model of Schenkerian theory has simply not been a concern for most Schenkerians. One might argue, also, that pedagogical treatises on Schenkerian theory provide information about this implicitly and informally, by giving certain elaborations earlier and more prominent discussion. One could also glean this information directly from Schenkerian analyses, by examining the frequency of different elaborations.[11]

I will offer just two examples of how probabilistic information might give Schenkerian analysis predictive power with regard to tonal music. One important and common transformation in Schenkerian analysis is the *Zug* or "linear progression"—a stepwise diatonic line connecting two notes of a triad. The interval spanned is most often a third, fourth, fifth, sixth, or octave. Given the importance of these elaborations, a probabilistic Schenkerian model should probably assign much higher probability to them than to the "unary" elaborations discussed above. This, in itself, might help somewhat in raising the probability of tonal pieces. My main point, however, concerns the specific way that linear progressions are used. Linear progressions not only affect surface melodic patterns, but also have more large-scale implications; in particular, they can affect harmony. In the passage in figure 9.8, for example, the harmonic progression I–V6–IV6–I6/4–ii6–I6 seems odd and improbable in conventional harmonic terms; it features strange root motions like V–IV and ii–I. The harmony makes more sense if we view it as generated by a descending linear progression in the bass, Bb–A–G–F–Eb–D, which then dictates (or at least constrains) the choice of harmonies above. By

**Figure 9.8**
Mozart, Symphony No. 40, I, mm. 28–33.

**Figure 9.9**
Bach, Suite for Violoncello No. 1, Gigue, mm. 13–16. The passage contains two "third-progressions" (according to my analysis), A–G–F♯ and B–A–G; these are shown with upward-pointing stems.

assigning higher probability to harmonic patterns that are built on bass-line linear progressions, a harmonic model could accommodate such passages better than one based on traditional harmonic logic alone. This, then, might be the basis for an "uncertainty-reducing" prediction about tonal music.

Another example concerns the alignment of pitches with meter. Some Schenkerian theorists have observed that, in general (though certainly not always), higher-level notes tend to be accented in certain ways, specifically occurring at metrically strong beats (Schachter 1976: 320; Cadwallader and Gagne 1998: 13). Often, with a higher-level linear progression, one finds that its notes are all placed on strong beats. (Figure 9.9, from the Gigue to Bach's Suite No. 1 for Violoncello, shows an example; notice that the notes of both "third-progressions" are all metrically strong.) Notice that this observation does not concern pitch patterns or rhythm patterns in themselves, but rather, the alignment of the two: it says that, of all the possible rhythmic realizations of a Schenkerian tree that one might find, the more likely ones are those in which high-level events are metrically strong.[12] Here again, there appears to be the basis for a testable prediction about tonal music, although there are many issues to be resolved in terms of how exactly it would be expressed.

I end this chapter with a challenge. It seems to me to be incumbent on those who believe in Schenkerian theory as a model of the compositional process to show how it reduces the uncertainty of tonal music. Again, this is just a precise way of saying something that is really common sense. If a theory is put forth about the structure of a particular musical idiom, then we expect that theory to make substantive predictions about the kinds of things that happen, and do not happen, in the music. Other aspects of music theory—principles of key, harmony, meter, and motivic structure—certainly pass this test. I have suggested two ways that Schenkerian theory might be construed to make predictions about musical surfaces; no doubt there are others. For those who argue for Schenkerian theory as an account of cognitive processes involved in composition, showing that the theory can reduce the uncertainty of common-practice music would lend powerful support to their claims.

# 10
## Communicative Pressure

Our explorations in previous chapters have assumed a certain view of musical communication. Under this view, music functions to convey certain structures from the mind of the producer (or producers) to the mind of the perceiver, via a surface representation. A musical style is characterized by probabilistic constraints on the nature of structures, and on the relationship between structures and surfaces. For musical communication to occur successfully, there must be agreement on these constraints between producers and perceivers. For example, if someone judged the key of a tonal melody using very different key-profiles from those proposed in chapter 4 (such as profiles which gave higher probability to chromatic notes than scalar notes), they might well infer a different key from that intended by the composer. Thus successful musical communication depends on shared knowledge about the style. I will argue here, however, that it depends also on the nature of the style itself. We can imagine styles in which musical communication was difficult or impossible, in that even a listener with a complete knowledge of the style would not be able to recover the intended structures from surfaces. In order for musical communication to occur successfully, such situations must be avoided. I will argue that this principle, which I call *communicative pressure* (Temperley 2004c), has been a powerful force in the shaping of musical styles.

Later in the chapter, we will consider communicative pressure with regard to meter, key, and other kinds of musical structure that we have been concerned with in this book. However, we will begin with an illustration of communicative pressure from a rather different domain:

traditional rules of voice-leading and their relationship to auditory perception.

**10.1
Communicative
Pressure in Rules
of Voice-Leading**

For centuries, an important part of compositional theory and pedagogy has concerned *voice-leading*: the construction and combination of melodic lines. In his 2001 article "Tone and Voice," David Huron attempts to relate the conventional rules of voice-leading to principles of auditory perception. He argues that many of these rules—as well as other regularities not captured by traditional rules but reflected in musical practice—can be attributed to a fundamental compositional goal: "The goal of voice-leading is to create two or more concurrent yet perceptually distinct 'parts' or 'voices.' Good voice-leading optimizes the auditory streaming" (2001: 32).

An example of Huron's approach is his explanation of the rule forbidding parallel perfect consonances (perfect fifths and octaves) (2001: 31; see figure 10.1A). Perfect consonances naturally tend to fuse into a single perceived pitch; pitches that comodulate (move by the same interval) also tend to fuse. Thus the danger of fusion should be especially strong with two voices which form a perfect interval and then comodulate; and this is exactly the situation forbidden by traditional voice-leading rules. A second example is the general avoidance of small harmonic intervals (close chord spacing) in low registers (figure 10.1B)—a well-known compositional principle that has also been empirically confirmed in studies of musical corpora (2001: 14–18; see also Huron and Sellmer 1992). This is compositionally advantageous, Huron argues, because small harmonic intervals in a low register tend to produce auditory masking (due to the interference between partials of the two tones that are within the same critical band).[1]

Consider these findings in light of the idea of communicative pressure. The composer conceives of certain patterns or configurations of notes, and wants those notes to be correctly identified by the listener. From the listener's point of view, the goal is to identify the intended notes from the

A.          B.

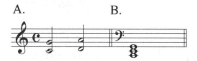

**Figure 10.1**
(A) Parallel perfect fifths. (B) Close chord spacing in a low register.

auditory signal—what I described in section 8.1 as the "transcription" problem. I suggested there that our usual "surface-structure" model could be applied to the transcription process, but in a rather different way: in this case the pattern of notes is the *structure*, and the surface is the auditory signal itself. What Huron's work suggests is that there are certain things the composer can do to make this process easier. The composer can facilitate note identification by avoiding parallel perfect intervals; if two notes are fusing into one, that presumably means that one of the notes is not being correctly identified. Similarly, avoidance of small harmonic intervals in low registers reduces auditory masking, which might hinder the identification of notes in another way. Thus some important aspects of compositional practice seem to be attributable to composers' desire to facilitate pitch identification.[2]

Another illustration of communicative pressure from Huron's work concerns the avoidance of part-crossing (2001: 24, 35). It has been shown experimentally that listeners are reluctant to hear crossing voices; two lines crossing over one another in an X pattern are more likely to be heard as a "V" containing the upper notes and an upside-down "V" containing the lower ones (Deutsch 1975; see figure 10.2). Thus, if composers wish for their intended structures of polyphonic lines to be perceived, they would be well advised to avoid crossing voices. Here again, this is reflected in compositional teaching, where voice-crossing is generally discouraged.[3]

The focus of Huron's study is on common-practice Western music. He does find support for some of his claims from other musical styles; however, he makes no claim that the phenomena he discusses are universal. As he points out, we would only expect composers to facilitate pitch identification (or the grouping of pitches into lines) if the communication of this information was one of their goals; and in some music, it may not

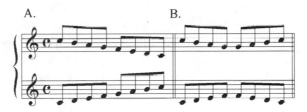

**Figure 10.2**
A pattern of crossing scales (A) will tend to be heard as a V-shaped line containing the upper notes and an "inverted V" containing the lower ones (B).

be a goal. A composer might, by contrast, deliberately create ambiguity and obscurity as to the pitches of the piece; or the entire dimension of pitch might be irrelevant to the composer's communicative aims.

Huron's work on voice-leading provides a compelling demonstration of the explanatory power of communicative pressure. In what follows I will consider some other applications of this idea, broadening its scope in two fundamental ways. First, while Huron is primarily concerned with the identification of notes themselves, or the grouping of notes into lines, I will focus on other kinds of structures that are inferred from note information: meter, harmony, and key. Secondly, while Huron's focus is primarily on common-practice music, I will suggest that communicative pressure provides a powerful tool for explaining differences between styles. In particular, the communicative-pressure idea suggests that certain theoretically independent aspects of styles may be correlated, in ways that seem to agree remarkably well with the empirical facts.

## 10.2
## The Syncopation-
## Rubato Trade-Off

In this section we explore the idea of communicative pressure as it relates to the meter-finding model presented in chapter 3. This model was based on two well-accepted principles of meter perception. First, beats tend to be regularly spaced; given a series of beats 600 msec apart, we expect the next beat to occur roughly 600 msec after the last one. Second, notes (specifically onsets of notes) tend to coincide with beats, especially strong beats. I also introduced the notion of "phenomenal accent"—meaning anything that gives emphasis to an event, such as a long note, a loud note, or a change of harmony (though this was not incorporated into our computational model). In general, accented events are more likely to coincide with strong beats than unaccented ones.

In chapter 9, we compared the nature of meter in several musical styles, focusing on two phenomena: syncopation and rubato. I showed how the amount of syncopation and rubato in a style can be expressed in terms of the parameters of a generative model. A style with a high degree of syncopation will have a relatively flat "note-beat profile"—the probability of a note on a weak beat will be relatively high (figure 9.3). A style with a high degree of rubato will have a relatively flat "tempo function"—a tactus interval of a certain length will allow a wide range for the following interval (figure 9.5). I then suggested that a comparison of styles with regard to syncopation and rubato reveals an interesting pattern. Some styles, such as common-practice music, allow quite a high degree of rubato, but feature very little syncopation; other styles, notably traditional African music and rock, allow much less flexibility in tempo but have a high degree of syncopation. We might call this complementary relationship the "syncopation-rubato trade-off." The set of data we have considered (three styles) is admittedly very small, and hardly a basis for strong cross-cultural generalizations. Still, it seems to deserve further investigation. It seems intuitively clear that both syncopation and rubato add complexity to the perceptual task, and thus we might expect that a style which had more of one would have less of the other. Can our probabilistic approach help us explain, in a more rigorous way, the apparent trade-off between syncopation and rubato?

It is not difficult to find specific situations in which the combination of syncopation and rubato would cause perceptual difficulties. Consider a simple pattern with syncopation, figure 10.3A, and a simple pattern with rubato, figure 10.3B. It seems plausible that listeners could recover the correct metrical structure in such cases. But now consider a pattern that involved both syncopation and rubato, such as figure 10.3C; the last beat is delayed, but the last event is slightly before the beat. In this case, the actual pattern of events is the same as in figure 10.3D (the last event maintains the regular pattern of 600 msec onset intervals), and the perfectly regular metrical structure of 10.3D is surely what would be inferred, rather than the intended structure shown in 10.3C. The intended rhythm would therefore be misconstrued.

Examples such as figure 10.3 seem to indicate some kind of complementary relationship between syncopation and rubato. But this is not yet an explanation for the syncopation-rubato trade-off. In what follows, I will explore a more general explanation for why styles with high syncopation tend to have low rubato, and vice versa. My goal is to show that syncopation and rubato contribute to perceptual difficulty in an additive way, such that the combination of the two should make perception more difficult than either one alone.

Consider the complete set of possible metrical structures. For the sake of argument, we retain the assumptions of chapter 3 that possible beat locations are confined to "pips" spaced 50 msec apart, that structures consist of three beat levels in duple or triple relationships, and that tactus intervals must be between 450 and 1100 msec; still, the number of possible metrical structures for (say) a one-minute time-span is mind-bogglingly huge. Imagine that we give each of these possible structures a numerical label (1, 2, 3, etc.), and arrange these labels on a line. We can

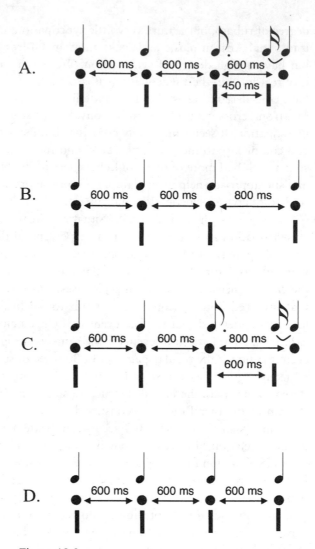

**Figure 10.3**
Four simple rhythmic patterns. Music notation indicates the intended rhythm; dots indicate tactus-beat locations in time; vertical bars indicate event-onsets in time. (A) A syncopated pattern. (B) A pattern with rubato. (C) A pattern with syncopation and rubato. (D) A perfectly "straight" pattern.

generate a distribution which represents the probability of each of these structures occurring. Now consider the effect of rubato on this distribution. Recall that increasing rubato is equivalent to flattening the "tempo function," relating each tactus interval to the previous one. It seems clear—though I will not try to prove this rigorously—that adding rubato will also flatten the overall distribution of metrical structures. If there is *no* rubato, only structures with a completely regular tempo will ever occur; the overall distribution of structures will therefore be very uneven or "spiky," with only a small number of structures having non-zero probability. If extreme rubato is allowed, so that each tactus interval is basically independent of the previous one, then all kinds of very irregular tactus levels will be allowed, and the distribution will be much more even. In this way, we can think of the functions in figure 9.5 as representing the distribution of complete metrical structures for a "rubato" style and a "strict" style. Recall from chapter 2, also, that the evenness or "flatness" of a distribution can be described in terms of entropy: flatter distributions have higher entropy. Thus we could state the following principle: *In styles with more rubato, the distribution of metrical structures will have higher entropy.*

Now consider the set of possible complete musical surfaces (where a surface is defined simply as any monophonic pattern of onsets on the "pip" timeline), and imagine enumerating them as we did with structures. For each metrical structure, we can create a distribution over all surfaces which is the probability of each surface given that structure. I suggested earlier that the amount of syncopation in a style can be represented by the probability of notes on beats of different levels: a style with a flatter (more uniform) note-beat profile will have more syncopation (figure 9.3). We can generalize this to the relationship between complete metrical structures and musical surfaces. If a note-beat profile was very uneven—so that, for example, level 3 beats had an onset probability of .9 and all other beats had an onset probability of 0—then the entire probability mass (for surfaces given a structure) would be devoted to a small set of possible surfaces. By contrast, if (for example) level 3 beats, level 2 beats, level 1 beats and non-beat pips all had onset probabilities of .1, then the distribution of surfaces given a structure would be much flatter. Thus more syncopation leads to a flatter distribution of surfaces given a structure. Again, we can express this in terms of entropy: *In styles with more syncopation, the distribution of surfaces given structures will have higher entropy.*

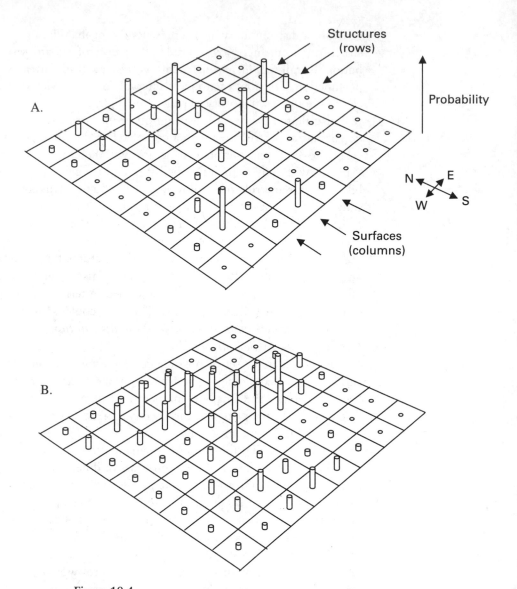

**Figure 10.4**
(A) A "rhythm function" for a style. (B) A rhythm function for a more syncopated style.

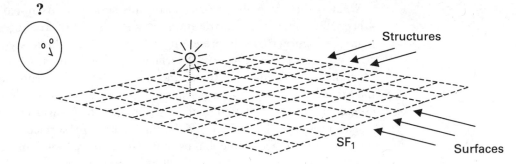

**Figure 10.5**
A visual analogue of meter perception. The listener sees a light in a column (surface) and must identify the correct row (structure).

Now imagine all metrical structures and surfaces arrayed in a plane (figure 10.4A; values represented are purely hypothetical). Each structure is a "row," lying along the east–west axis; surfaces are "columns" lying along the north–south axis. We now create a probability distribution over this 2-D grid (so that the total probability mass distributed over the grid is 1). The probability mass in a row indicates the overall (prior) probability of a structure; the mass in a column indicates the probability of a surface; the probability in a certain cell of the grid (represented by a vertical bar) indicates $P(\text{structure} \cap \text{surface})$. The values for the cells in a column are proportional to $P(\text{structure} \mid \text{surface})$, and the values for the cells in a row are proportional to $P(\text{surface} \mid \text{structure})$.

This offers a way of thinking about the process of rhythmic communication. Let us assume that both producers and perceivers have the complete 3-D probability function shown in figure 10.4A—we will call this a "rhythm function." The producer chooses a structure, and then generates a surface from it. A light goes on above the cell corresponding to this surface-structure pair (figure 10.5). Imagine the perceiver located to the north of the grid, as shown on the figure. The perceiver sees a light go on in the column of a certain surface—call it $SF_1$—but does not know which structure (row) the light is in. How does the perceiver guess the correct row? The perceiver has access to the complete probabilities in figure 10.4A; thus the rational thing to do is simply to choose the structure for which $P(\text{structure} \mid SF_1)$ is highest—corresponding to the cell in the $SF_1$ column with the highest probability. This strategy may not *always* produce the correct answer, but it is the best the perceiver can do.

What is the effect of syncopation on this situation? As noted above, syncopation causes the distribution of surfaces given structures to be flatter. In figure 10.4A (representing a "straight" rhythmic style), each structure has a very uneven $P(\text{surface} \mid \text{structure})$ function; in figure 10.4B (a syncopated style), these functions are flatter. It seems clear that the perceiver's job will be harder in the case of the syncopated style. The essential point is that flattening the distributions for $P(\text{surface} \mid \text{structure})$ will also result in flatter distributions for $P(\text{structure} \mid \text{surface})$: flattening the rows also flattens the columns (compare figures 10.4A and B). And this means the perceiver's guesses will be correct less often. (If we assume the perceiver always guesses the most probable structure for a surface, the correct rate will simply equal $P(\text{structure} \mid \text{surface})$ for this most probable structure, and flattening the distribution will lower this value.)

Now consider the effect of rubato. Increasing the amount of rubato in a style means flattening the distribution of the structures themselves, so that the probability mass is more evenly distributed across rows. What effect will this have on the perceptual process? This is not so obvious. More rubato will mean that the rows are more equal in their total probability mass. But will this mean a flattening of the distributions in individual columns? Under certain assumptions, it seems that it might. If the shape of all the $P(\text{surface} \mid \text{structure})$ functions was the same (or similar), then flattening across these functions would cause the $P(\text{structure} \mid \text{surface})$ functions to flatten, also. On the other hand, if the $P(\text{surface} \mid \text{structure})$ functions all had peaks for different surfaces, then flattening the $P(\text{structure})$ function might not have much effect. In short, it seems that a flattening of the $P(\text{structure})$ distribution might increase the difficulty of meter perception under some conditions, but not necessarily always.

Let us summarize this rather speculative discussion. To explain the syncopation-rubato trade-off in mathematical terms, we need to show that syncopation and rubato contribute to perceptual difficulty in some kind of additive way so that the combination of the two makes accurate perception more difficult. It seems clear that flattening the conditional probabilities of surfaces—as syncopation does—will make accurate perception harder. Whether flattening the distribution of structures—as rubato does—will make perception harder is less obvious; but it seems that this would occur at least under some conditions. What I have offered here, then, is a partial explanation for the syncopation–rubato trade-off; perhaps further work in this direction will yield a more complete explanation.

**10.3**
**Other Examples of**
**Communicative**
**Pressure in**
**Rhythm**

The syncopation–rubato trade-off points to a more general prediction: The latitude for expressive variation in tempo will be greater in idioms where the meter is more strongly reinforced by the notes. In Bayesian terms, when $P(\text{surface} \mid \text{structure})$ functions are highly uneven—so that particular surfaces strongly indicate particular structures—the $P(\text{structure})$ function may be flatter, and vice versa. This principle is interesting to consider with regard to stylistic variations within common-practice music—generally defined as Western art music from about 1600 to 1900, and embracing the Baroque (c. 1600–1750), classical (1750–1830), and Romantic (1830–1900) periods.

It is generally accepted that the use of rubato varies considerably from one period to another. In particular, it is used much more extensively in Romantic-period music than in the music of earlier periods. This is true historically, in that the use of rubato among performers seems to have increased as the classical period gave way to the Romantic; Czerny, writing in 1847, lamented the (as he regarded it) excessive use of rubato "in recent time" (Rosenblum 1991: 383). With regard to modern performance practice, the greater use of rubato with Romantic-period music as opposed to that of earlier periods is readily apparent in modern piano performances, and is generally affirmed and approved in pedagogical treatises on performance expression (Barra 1983: 119–121; Lampl 1996: 56). (I will limit this discussion to piano music; this is the largest and most important solo repertoire, and solo performance provides the most scope for expressive timing, unhindered by considerations of ensemble coordination.) Two authors suggest that Chopin's music is especially appropriate for rubato (Stein 1962/1989: 39; Matthay 1913: 64–65); Matthay mentions Chopin Nocturnes in particular.

Does the current approach shed any light on why Chopin Nocturnes, and other similar pieces, might be especially well suited to the use of rubato? Figure 10.6 shows two fairly typical openings of Chopin Nocturnes. Communicative pressure suggests that the opportunity for rubato would be greatest in cases where the meter is very strongly established and reinforced, so that the probability of the metrical structure given the notes is high. Certainly, there is very little syncopation in these passages—accented events (e.g. long notes in the melody) generally occur on strong beats—but this is generally true of common-practice music of all periods. I wish to draw attention to another aspect of these passages: they feature strong repeated patterns in the left hand. The patterns do not always repeat exactly, but they are at least repeated in terms of their general shape or "contour"; in both cases, the pattern continues

Communicative Pressure

A.

**Figure 10.6**
Two openings of Chopin Nocturnes: (A) Op. 27 No. 2; (B) Op. 9 No. 2.

**Figure 10.7**
Mozart, Sonata K. 309, I, mm. 1–9.

throughout the entire piece with only slight variations. Theorists have generally agreed that repeated patterns are an important cue to meter (Steedman 1977; Temperley and Bartlette 2002); once we have identified a certain position in the pattern as metrically strong, we expect subsequent strong beats to be similarly placed. This—as well as the very consistent alignment of accented events with strong beats—means that the meter of each passage is very strongly reinforced. Repeated patterns such as these are found pervasively throughout the piano music of Chopin as well as other Romantic composers (Schumann and Mendelssohn, for example); they are less prevalent in classical-period music. Consider figure 10.7, the opening of a Mozart sonata. We do find some repeated patterns (such as the left-hand pattern in mm. 3–5), but they are relatively fleeting; the short passage shown in figure 10.7 arguably contains three quite different textures.[4] In this important respect, one could say that the meter is asserted and maintained more strongly in the Chopin passages than in the Mozart.

Because of the extreme rhythmic clarity of the Chopin pieces, one can see how they could be played with considerable freedom without obscuring the beat; in the Mozart, by contrast, while perception of the beat in a fairly strict performance would be unproblematic, a substantial degree of rubato might cause confusion. (An analogy could be drawn here with the simple patterns in figure 10.3.) Thus, the construction of the Chopin

EXCERPT 1

(Joplin)

(Morton)

**Figure 10.8**
Two excerpts from "Maple Leaf Rag," as performed by Scott Joplin (1918) and Jelly Roll Morton (1938). From *The Smithsonian Collection of Classic Jazz* (AS 11892), transcribed by the author. Continued on opposite page.

passages seems to inherently allow for more liberties in tempo than the Mozart. This reasoning may explain why Romantic piano music—and especially a particular type of Romantic piano music, involving repeated patterns in the left hand—seems more well suited to rubato than much other (e.g., classical period) music.[5]

Another case of interaction between compositional practice and expressive timing is seen in the transition from ragtime to jazz. Figure 10.8 shows two performances of excerpts from the "Maple Leaf Rag"—the first by Scott Joplin, recorded in 1918; the second by Jelly Roll Morton, recorded in 1938.[6] It can be seen that both performances feature a good deal of syncopation—long (and hence accented) notes on weak eighth-note beats, such as the octave E♭ on the fourth eighth-note of the right hand in the second measure of Joplin's performance of Excerpt 1. But the Morton performance is notably more syncopated than the Joplin, particularly with regard to the left hand. In the Joplin, left-hand events are perfectly aligned with beats (all notes longer than an eighth-note occur on strong eighth-note beats), while in the Morton, several long left-hand events in both excerpts occur on weak eighth-note beats, with

EXCERPT 2

(Joplin)

(Morton)

**Figure 10.8**
(continued)

Communicative Pressure

no event on the following strong beat. Thus the Morton performance creates a certain degree of metrical instability. Another significant difference between these performances—not shown in the transcriptions in figure 10.8, but readily apparent from hearing them—is that the Morton performance features a "swing" tempo while the Joplin does not. "Swing" refers to a mode of performance in which the first half of each quarter-note beat is longer than the second half; or, to put it another way, events on strong eighth-note beats are longer than those on weak eighth-note beats.[7] (Swing can be approximated by a 2:1 ratio, though a true swing feel is more variable than this.) The Morton performance is decidedly swung, while the Joplin features a perfectly "straight" tempo.

Is there a complementary relationship between these differences? If we think of swing as a kind of expressive timing, analogous to rubato, this might seem to be a counterexample to the current argument, as the Morton performance features both more swing and more syncopation. However, I suggest we view swing in a different way. Notice that one effect of swing tempo is to provide a constant reminder to the listener of where the strong eighth-note beats are (since the strong eighth-note beats are longer than the weak ones). But this is exactly the information that is somewhat obscured by the left-hand syncopations (long notes on weak eighth-note beats) in Morton's performance. Thus Morton counterbalances the destabilizing effect of his syncopations by reinforcing the meter in another way. These two performances in themselves may prove little, but they reflect well-documented broader developments in the transition from ragtime to jazz. The shift from the "even-note" rhythms of ragtime to the swing feel of jazz is well attested (Schuller 1968: 67, 217), as is the increase in the degree and complexity of syncopation over the same period (Waterman 1974: 47; Sales 1984: 28–29). The "communicative pressure" idea may offer an explanation for the roughly contemporaneous occurrence of these changes.

The preceding discussion reminds us that performers as well as composers play an essential role in the communicative process. In many styles, of course, the division between performers and composers assumed in common-practice music is problematic in any case. In traditional African music and in jazz, the extensive use of improvisation blurs this distinction. In rock, too, the composer-performer distinction is often questionable; many performers write their own songs, and the members of a band (the drummer, for example) may well have composed their own parts. In any event, the important point is that the final musical object results from the activities of one or more creators—composers, performers, improvisers—and the behavior of all of these may be affected by communicative pressure.

<table>
<tr>
<td>

**10.4**
**"Trading**
**Relationships"**

</td>
<td>

The syncopation–rubato trade-off, and related phenomena discussed in the previous section, are examples of "trading relationships"—a term due to Joseph Swain (1997: 141–167), who introduces it in a discussion of historical change in music and language. In the evolution of languages, Swain notes, changes sometimes seem to arise as a way of restoring information lost due to other changes. For example, in Middle English, the case of nouns (subject or object) was indicated by word endings, but word order was relatively free; as the word endings began to drop out, word order became more fixed (with the subject preceding the verb and the object following it), thus indicating case in a different way. (The role of communicative pressure in language is discussed further below.) Swain suggests an analogous case in music, relating to cadences. In the Renaissance, the standard authentic cadence was defined as a complex of rhythmic and contrapuntal features; a typical example is shown in figure 10.9. As the common-practice tonal system took shape, these rhythmic-contrapuntal features became less rigid and were replaced by the more general V–I harmonic pattern, which takes a wide variety of rhythmic and contrapuntal forms in tonal music.

</td>
</tr>
</table>

It must be said that Swain's cadence example is not entirely convincing, or at least is not fully explained.[8] Still, the general idea of trading relationships is an extremely suggestive one, and relates very directly to the idea of communicative pressure. The function of any communication system, linguistic or musical, is to convey certain types of information: for example, syntactic relations in the case of language. If the source of this information is lost (e.g., case endings in Middle English), some other means must be found of conveying it (fixed word order). Another causal pattern may occur as well: if a kind of information, already present in

**Figure 10.9**
A typical Renaissance cadence.

the language in one form, is introduced in another form as well, the initial form of the information becomes redundant and may drop out. (That is to say, case endings in Middle English may have dropped out *after* the rise of fixed word order because they were no longer needed.) But this second mechanism, too, may be explained as a consequence of communicative pressure; if we assume that the need to convey information may motivate the rise of certain features in the system, it follows naturally that such features may drop out when they become informationally redundant. In short, one may reasonably invoke the idea of communicative pressure without being certain of the exact cause-effect relationships involved. Consider the earlier argument regarding the shifts in compositional practice and performance practice between the classical and Romantic periods. Did an increase in expressive timing among performers exert pressure on composers to increase their reinforcement of the meter (e.g., by writing repeated left-hand patterns), or did the use of metrically obvious and uniform textures by Romantic composers allow greater leeway for expressive timing by performers? I will not attempt an answer to this question; it could perhaps be answered through close study of the chronological relationship between the two phenomena (the rise of repeated left-hand patterns and the rise of rubato), and perhaps through consideration of other causal factors. For example, if there is reason to believe that the rise of rubato resulted from extramusical forces—perhaps from the Romantic era's fondness for spontaneous personal expression—then it may seem more probable that the change in performance triggered the change in composition rather than the other way around.

Swain restricts "trading relationships" to cases of historical change within a style, where the loss of information in one form is compensated for by its emergence in another form. The complementary changes in composition and performance between the classical and Romantic periods would be one example of this; the increase in syncopation and rise of swing tempo in early jazz would be another. However, the term might also be applied in any case where the same information is conveyed in different ways in different styles. This is essentially the case with the syncopation–rubato trade-off observed between common-practice music and traditional African music. Let us consider two other examples of trading relationships between styles.

In both common-practice music and jazz, an important kind of information conveyed is harmonic structure; pitches are grouped into short segments, each one associated with a harmony. The perception of harmony is a complex process, which has been the subject of several computational models (the probabilistic model of Raphael and Stoddard [2004] was discussed in chapter 8; see also Temperley 2001a). By all accounts, this process requires a method of choosing a root for a given set of pitches: generally, a root is preferred such that all of the pitches, or as many as possible, are chord-tones of the root. (Some notes may be regarded as non-chord-tones—not part of the chord—but the use of these is highly constrained.) For example, the pitches G–B–D are all legal chord-tones of the root G (G is $\hat{1}$ of G, B is $\hat{3}$ of G, and D is $\hat{5}$ of G); therefore G is a possible root. In common-practice music, the set of possible chord-tones is very limited: for the most part, only $\hat{1}$, $\hat{3}$, $\hat{5}$, $\flat\hat{3}$, and $\flat\hat{7}$ are used, though certain others (like $\flat\hat{5}$ and $\flat\hat{9}$) may be found under limited circumstances. (The numbers here indicate "chord-degrees"—pitches in relation to a root.) In jazz, by contrast, a wide variety of chord-tones is used beyond those allowed in common-practice music, sometimes known as "extensions": $\hat{9}$ (or A above a root of G), $\flat\hat{9}$ (A♭), $\sharp\hat{9}$ (B♭), $\widehat{11}$ (C), $\sharp\widehat{11}$ (C♯), $\flat\widehat{13}$ (E♭), $\widehat{13}$ or $\hat{6}$ (E), and the major seventh (F♯) are all commonly found in jazz. (Not all combinations of these chord-tones are usable, and there are naturally many other constraints on how they may be used appropriately [Grigson 1988; Dobbins 1994]; but that does not affect the present point.)

There is another very significant difference between jazz and common-practice harmony as well. In common-practice music, roughly speaking, any registral ordering (or "inversion") of the pitches in a chord is allowed; a C dominant seventh may be spaced with any of its notes—C, E, G, or B♭—in the bass. (There are, again, constraints on the use of inversions; second-inversion triads are particularly restricted in their use.) In jazz, however, such chordal inversions are quite rare; the vast majority of chords are in "root position," with the root in the bass. Thus while common-practice music has a more limited set of chord-tones, it is less restricted in terms of which chord-tone may occur in the bass. It can be seen, once again, that these differences are complementary. Suppose a style allowed both a wide variety of chord-tones and considerable freedom of inversion—so that any note of a chord could be placed in the bass. This might lead to severe problems of ambiguity, because chords might have multiple possible roots. Consider the pairs of chords in figures 10.10A, B, C, and D, all of which are common chords in jazz; within each pair, it can be seen that the two chords contain the same pitch-classes. If inversion were freely allowed, the second chord could be interpreted as an inversion of the first (or the first an inversion of the

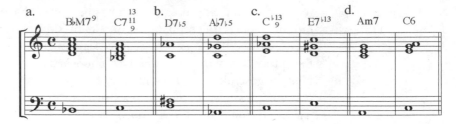

**Figure 10.10**
Four pairs of chords, all common chords in jazz, shown with their jazz notations. Within each pair, both chords contain the same pitch-classes.

second). For example, in the first pair, C7(9/11/13) could be interpreted as an "inverted" B♭M7(9). The last pair—A minor seventh and C major with an "added sixth"—is of particular interest, because (unlike the first three pairs) both of these chords are widely used in common-practice music; there, however, they are both interpreted as A minor seventh chords (the second one in first inversion). Again, if a style allowed both first inversions and added sixths, these chords would be ambiguous: is the second chord C6 or Am6/5? In short, it seems to be no coincidence that jazz, which allows a greater variety of chord-tones than common-practice music, also has less tolerance for chordal inversion.

The claims put forth above—that chordal inversions are more frequent in common-practice music than in jazz, and that chordal extensions are less frequent—will, I hope, seem intuitively correct to those familiar with both styles. However, it seemed prudent to subject these assumptions to an empirical test. For common-practice music, the Kostka-Payne corpus was used—a set of 46 harmonically analyzed excerpts from the common-practice repertoire (see section 6.2). The jazz corpus was taken from *The New Real Book* (Sher 1988)—a collection of lead sheets (showing melodies and chord symbols), spanning a range of jazz styles, created primarily from the composers' original lead sheets and from transcriptions of jazz performances. The first 50 songs in *The New Real Book* constituted the jazz corpus used in this test (the songs are arranged alphabetically). In each corpus, I counted the total number of chords, the number of chords in inversion (i.e. not in root position), and the number of chords using extensions—defined as any chord-tone other than $\hat{1}$, $\flat\hat{3}$, $\hat{3}$, $\hat{5}$, or $\flat\hat{7}$.[9] Table 10.1 shows the results. It can be seen that, indeed, the proportion of inverted chords in common-practice music (36.9%) is much higher than in jazz (13.8%), while the proportion of

**Table 10.1**
Inverted and extended chords in two corpora.

| Corpus | Number of chords | Number of chords in inversion | Number of "extended" chords (using chord-tones other than 1, ♭3, 3, 5, and ♭7) |
|---|---|---|---|
| Kostka-Payne corpus (46 excerpts) | 866 | 320 (36.9%) | 94 (10.8%) |
| New Real Book (first 50 songs) | 2521 | 347 (13.8%) | 1228 (48.7%) |

extended chords is much lower (10.8% in common-practice music versus 48.7% in jazz). Thus the trading relationship hypothesized above seems to be borne out.

In some cases, the value of the trading-relationship idea may be in posing new questions, rather than in explaining already observed facts. My final example is a case in point, and concerns the communication of key or tonal center. It was argued in chapter 6 that the primary cue to key perception in common-practice music is the distribution of pitch-classes in use—and particularly the scale collection (since the strongest distinction in key-profiles tends to be between scalar and nonscalar pitches). In common-practice music, each major or minor key has its own scale (if we assume the harmonic minor scale in minor). However, this raises a question for so-called "modal" styles of music. The term "modal" generally refers to styles in which the diatonic (major) scale is used, but where the "tonic" position of the scale assumed in common-practice music is not necessarily the tonal center. Styles commonly characterized as modal in this sense include Gregorian chant and some types of European and Anglo-American folk music; another example is rock music, whose modal character has been attested by several authors (Moore 1993; Temperley 2001a; Stephenson 2002). For example, a rock song using the C major scale might have a tonal center of C (Ionian mode), but the tonal center might also be G (Mixolydian), D (Dorian), or A (Aeolian). Clearly, then, the tonal center of songs in rock and other modal styles cannot be conveyed by scale collection, since any diatonic scale is ambiguous between several tonal centers. How, then, are tonal centers conveyed in modal styles? We should remember that scale-degree distributions in common-practice music also reflect a distinction between tonic-triad and non-tonic-triad notes; it may be that in modal styles, these distinctions are especially pronounced, so that the tonic can still be identified distributionally by the greater frequency of tonic-triad notes. On the other hand, it may be that the tonal center is conveyed by quite different means in modal styles. In modal melodies in the Essen corpus, for example, the tonal center sometimes seems to be indicated by its placement at the beginning and ending of phrases. In rock, it has been suggested by both Stephenson (2002) and myself (2001a) that the metrical placement of harmonies may be an important cue: in particular, the tonic harmony tends to occur at hypermetrically strong points. All of this is quite speculative and requires further study. The point is that, in modal styles, we would expect to find other cues to the tonal center besides scale collection; what those cues are is an interesting and unresolved question.

## 10.5 Low-Probability Events in Constrained Contexts

In this section we consider a rather different application of communicative pressure. I will introduce the idea using a simple nonmusical example. Assume that you take a commuter train every day; every day the conductor makes a series of announcements, including either "The cafe car is open" or "The cafe car is closed," but 99% of the time the cafe car is declared to be closed. We assume, also, that there is some probability of the message being mistransmitted (due to noise on the PA system, for example), so that the intended word "closed" might be misheard as "open" or vice versa. In this situation, it might be difficult for the message "The cafe car is open" to ever be communicated. From the perceiver's point of view, if the word "open" is perceived, it may seem more likely that it is really a distorted version of the word "closed," given the very low prior probability of "open." From the communicator's point of view, the problem may be solved by adding extra information: by saying, for example, "And here's something very unusual: the cafe car is open." The extra information (assuming it is provided every time the rare message is read) provides a context that is associated with the rare message; the context increases the prior probability of the rare message from the perceiver's perspective, making it more likely to be perceived as intended. More generally, the communication of a low-probability event can be facilitated if the event is consistently accompanied by some kind of context that is associated with the event and increases its prior probability.

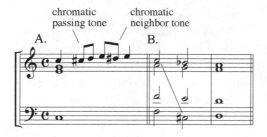

**Figure 10.11**
(A) Chromatic non-chord tones. (B) A "cross-relation." (From Aldwell and Schachter 2003, p. 424.)

How might this principle apply to music? Let us return to the domain explored by Huron: the conventional rules of common-practice composition and their relationship to auditory perception. At the level of notes, the most obvious kind of "rare event" is chromatic notes, or notes outside the scale of the current key. As shown in chapter 6, the vast majority of notes in common-practice music are diatonic (within the scale); each chromatic scale-degree constitutes only about 2% of events.[10] The principle put forth above predicts that chromatic notes would occur only in highly constrained contexts; and this is indeed true. For the most part, chromatic notes occur as non-chord-tones, resolved by a half-step and usually prepared by half-step motion as well—so-called chromatic neighbor tones and passing tones (figure 10.11A). (Chromatic tones may also occur as part of chromatic harmonies—such as augmented sixth chords—but even then they are almost invariably resolved by half-step.) Also of interest here is the idea of the "cross-relation": a juxtaposition of a scale-degree and a chromatically altered version of that same degree in different voices, such as C and C♯ (see figure 10.11B). In their textbook *Harmony and Voice Leading* (2003), Aldwell and Schachter give a complex treatment of this phenomenon. While suggesting that cross-relations are generally best avoided, they suggest five cases where they are tolerable; four out of five of these usages depend on stepwise resolution of at least one of the notes in the cross-relation.[11] This fits in well with the "constrained context" idea. Notice that, in cross-relations, one of the tones must be chromatic, no matter what the tonal context is; no scale contains both C and C♯. (Indeed, it is sometimes uncertain which tone is chromatic; in figure 10.11B, the C♯ is scalar in the local context of D minor, but might be chromatic in relation to a larger context of C major.)

By the current logic, the rarity of chromatic notes combined with the imperfect process of note transmission (notes may be misheard, masked, played slightly out of tune, and so on) means that chromatic notes run the risk of being misidentified. The requirement of stepwise resolution of such tones restricts their contexts, and therefore increases their prior probability: if we hear a $\sharp\hat{1}$ scale-degree (like the C# in figure 10.11A), we may not be sure we heard it correctly, but if scale-degree $\hat{2}$ follows, the probability is greatly increased. Thus, the stepwise resolution of chromatic tones can be seen as a way of constraining the context of rare events. A similar argument could be made for "secondary dominants"— chords, normally outside the current key, which function as dominants for a chord within the key. Again, these chords are presumably low-probability harmonic events (and also involve low-probability pitches, i.e. pitches outside the scale); but they also occur in highly constrained contexts, as they are almost invariably followed by their corresponding tonic chords.

This explanation may seem somewhat counterintuitive, as it goes against the traditional thinking about chromatic tones and secondary dominants. It suggests that the stepwise resolution of chromatic tones arose as a way of facilitating their perception. Traditionally, however, chromatic tones have been regarded as a way of elaborating the following diatonic tone, or filling in the space between two diatonic tones (see, for example, Aldwell and Schachter 2003: 13). By this conventional reasoning, it is the diatonic tone that motivates the chromatic one rather than the other way around. (A similar point could be made about secondary dominant chords.) Still, these two explanations may not be mutually exclusive. Even if we allow that chromatic tones arose as, and function as, elaborations, there are many conceivable ways that one tone might elaborate another. The communicative pressure idea predicts that patterns of elaboration will be favored in which the context of the chromatic tone is highly constrained.

In the case of both chromatic tones and secondary dominants, the essential context of the rare event follows the event rather than preceding it. (Chromatic tones are usually preceded by stepwise motion as well, but this is not as consistent as their stepwise resolution.) This is not a fatal problem for the current argument. Consider the commuter train example: The conductor might say "The cafe car is open, yes, you heard me right," but this subsequent contextual reinforcement could function to increase the probability of the previous rare message as well. Still, this seems less desirable from a communicative point of view; if the subsequent context of an event is crucial to its identification, this means one can only be certain of the event after it has occurred. In the case of secondary dominants, for example, recognition of the chord would presumably be easier if the resolution chord (the corresponding tonic) preceded the dominant rather than following it; in this case, the probability of the secondary dominant occurring would be raised by the event before it, thus facilitating its identification when it occurred. (Presumably, the tonic of a secondary dominant chord is generally a fairly probable event— even when not preceded by its own dominant—because it is usually a diatonic chord within the key of the larger context.) The fact that the supportive contexts of rare events in common-practice music usually seem to follow the events is a challenge for the communicative-pressure theory that requires further consideration.[12]

**10.6
Conclusions**

I have suggested that a number of phenomena in musical styles can be explained by the idea of communicative pressure. The idea is reflected in the work of Huron, showing that a number of rules and regularities in common-practice composition can be seen as strategies to facilitate the identification and grouping of pitches. Communicative pressure also accounts for a number of complementary differences between styles (what Swain calls "trading relationships"): the greater degree of syncopation and lower degree of rubato in traditional African music and rock versus common-practice music; the particular appropriateness of rubato in pieces with consistent repeated patterns (e.g., much Romantic piano music); the rise of swing tempo and the higher degree of syncopation in jazz as opposed to ragtime; and the greater variety of chord-tones and lower tolerance for chordal inversion in jazz as opposed to common-practice music. Finally, the idea that low-probability events occur in constrained contexts may account for certain rules of common-practice harmony, such as the highly constrained treatment of chromatic tones and secondary dominant chords.

As noted earlier, Huron's claims regarding the facilitation of pitch and voice perception are not put forth as universals; rather, they depend on the goals of the composer. In some cases a composer might wish to discourage the perception of clear pitches and lines; in such cases, the masking effect of dense low-register harmonies might be considered desirable. The same applies to the claims made here. It has been suggested that the need to communicate metrical structure can exert pressure on composition and performance—as reflected, for example, in the trade-off between syncopation and rubato. But this only applies in cases where the communication of meter is among the composer's and performer's aims. Some music, at least according to conventional wisdom, simply does not have meter, in the sense of an underlying hierarchical structure of regular pulses. Examples include Gregorian chant, recitative in opera, some kinds of traditional African music, and much twentieth-century art music. In such cases, the communicative-pressure argument (at least with regard to meter) simply does not apply.[13]

One might suppose that the communicative-pressure idea would be applicable to communication generally, not just music. In general, communication functions to convey information from a sender to a receiver via some kind of "surface"; if the information is not recoverable from the surface, the communicative process fails. It is natural to wonder if this principle applies in revealing ways to the other primary system of human communication, language. As noted above, Swain points out several interesting examples of "trading relationships" in language, such as the contemporaneous loss of case endings and rise of fixed word order in Middle English. He also discusses examples from phonology: for example, the loss of final stop consonants in Chinese coincided roughly with the rise of tone distinctions in vowels, suggesting that some kind of informational trade-off may have been involved (1997: 143, 153). However, exploration of the large literature on language change and evolution reveals surprisingly little discussion of trading relationships and communicative pressure generally. Trading relationships of the kind discussed by Swain are for the most part mentioned only briefly, and communicative pressure is usually put forth only cautiously, and often skeptically, as an explanation (Pyles 1971; Kiparsky 1982; Danchev 1991; Labov 1994). A few studies have investigated the role of communicative pressure more directly. One active area is the study of syntactic choices—where there is more than one way of expressing something: for example, in an embedded clause, people can either include the complementizer *that* or not ("I said I would go"/"I said that I would go"). In such cases, we might wonder if communicative pressure is involved; do people include the complementizer in cases that would otherwise be ambiguous? While some studies have found evidence for the role of communicative pressure in syntactic choice (Elsness 1984; Temperley 2003), other research has cast doubt on this idea (Ferreira and Dell 2000; Wasow and Arnold 2003). At present, then, the whole idea of communicative pressure holds a rather marginal status in the study of language—as evidenced by the fact that there is no widely accepted term for it (the term "communicative pressure" is, again, my own invention).

In a sense, the idea of communicative pressure brings us full circle. We began our musical investigations by addressing problems of perception—meter-finding and key-finding. I suggested that these perceptual processes were guided by assumptions about the process whereby music was generated. I argued, further, that listeners' generative models are tuned to reflect the statistical properties of the music that they encounter; thus, in an important way, perception is shaped by production. But now we see that the influence also flows the other way. Composers (and performers and improvisers) wish for their intended structures to be perceived by listeners; but not every possible style is equally conducive to this. The desire to communicate exerts pressure on productive musical behaviors, and thus, on the evolution of musical styles. Many questions remain unanswered here, and many avenues await further investigation. But I hope I have shown that the Bayesian approach provides a powerful set of tools for investigating music perception, production, and the complex ways in which they interact.

# Notes

1. More extensive treatments can be found elsewhere. Coverage of basic probability and Bayes' rule can be found in probability texts such as Ross 2000. Regarding other concepts used in the book, such as cross-entropy and hidden Markov models, an excellent source is Manning and Schutze 2000.

2. Throughout this book, we will be assuming probability functions that take only discrete values as input, not continuous values. Strictly speaking, probability functions taking discrete values should be called *probability mass functions*.

3. The length of the signal does matter in one sense: A signal with 1,000,000 symbols provides a much more reliable test than one with (say) 10 symbols, because it more reliably represents the behavior of the source. But my point here is that, simply from the point of view of judging the "fit" of each model to the signal, the length of the signal does not matter.

4. Normally, cross-entropy and entropy are expressed using log base 2 rather than log base $e$ (the natural logarithm). However, one log base can be converted to another simply by multiplying by a constant.

5. The use of the term "entropy" is complex and sometimes confusing. Mathematically, it is usually defined as shown in equation 2.26—as a simple function of the distribution of symbols in a body of data. Entropy in this sense can be measured quite straightforwardly and objectively; for example, we could measure the entropy of the English language, treating letters as events, as a function of the distribution of letters in the language. However, the term is also sometimes used to mean the amount of information in a body of data *from the point of view of a particular perceiver or model*—one might call this "subjective" entropy. For example, Claude Shannon (1951)—who first proposed the definition of entropy in equation 2.26—went on to propose a measure of the entropy of English which is essentially the amount of information that each letter in a passage of English text conveys to a English speaker. This is much lower than the "objective" entropy;

following a "q," the next letter is almost always "u" and an English speaker knows this, so it conveys very little information. Many other authors have also used entropy in the subjective sense, such as Meyer (1957/1967) and Manning and Schütze (2000). But subjective entropy can also be viewed as *the cross-entropy between a model (or perceiver) and the data*; this terminology seems clearer, and I will adopt it here. (One could defend Shannon's "subjective" use of the term by saying that English is not a single random variable, but rather a process which goes through a series of states, each one of which is a variable with its own distribution; Shannon's measure of the entropy of English represents the average entropy across all of these states. But there is no objective way to define these states and their distributions; it can only be done from the point of view of a particular model. For example, in a first-order Markov model—see section 2.5 below—the current state is defined by the previous symbol. Thus it seems preferable to acknowledge the role of the model by describing this as cross-entropy rather than entropy.)

As noted above, entropy in the objective sense is sometimes construed as a measure of the information or uncertainty in a body of data. This characterization, too, makes more sense when applied to cross-entropy rather than entropy, since the amount of information conveyed depends on the model or perceiver that is receiving the data. Objective entropy could only be regarded as a measure of information or uncertainty if we assume a model which "knows" nothing more than the distribution of symbols in the data.

6. More precisely, what Youngblood (and most of the authors discussed here) measured was *redundancy*: $1 - H/\log n$, where $H$ is entropy and $n$ is the size of the "alphabet" of symbols in use. Higher redundancy means lower entropy; 0 is the minimum redundancy possible with an alphabet of size $n$, while 1 is the maximum.

Youngblood also considered another measure of entropy, in which the probability of each pitch was conditioned on the previous pitch; this is actually better regarded as the cross-entropy between the data and a first-order Markov model of the data. (See note 5.)

7. The idea of cross-entropy would be relevant here (although Cohen does not discuss this). One could define a listener's model of (for example) scale-degree distribution, based on a study of their musical experience or perhaps by other means (for example, through psychological experiments). One could then measure the cross-entropy of this model with a particular corpus, in order to determine the complexity or uncertainty of the corpus for that listener. This is somewhat similar to what I undertake in section 7.2—though what I propose there is presented as a measure of "tonalness" rather than complexity.

An interesting empirical approach to measuring listeners' uncertainty is a study by Witten et al. (1994), using a so-called "gambling paradigm." In this paradigm, subjects are given money (or pseudo-money); then, in listening to music, they indicate their expectations for future notes by betting on the notes. The amount of money they accrue is then an indicator of their uncertainty, or the information conveyed to them by the music.

## Chapter 3

1. See for example Drake et al. 2000; Toiviainen and Snyder 2003. Such studies indicate a high level of agreement in the perception of meter across different levels of musical training.

2. Hidden Markov models (see sections 2.3 and 6.1) could be considered a simple kind of graphical model; but graphical models also include more complex kinds of probabilistic networks such as this one.

3. The term "generative" is used here in a specific sense, to refer to a model which generates musical surfaces from structures. This is not to be confused with "generative" in the sense of Lerdahl and Jackendoff's (1983) theory, which has more in common with the understanding of the term in theoretical ("generative") linguistics.

4. The Essen Folksong Collection will be used quite extensively in this study. Unfortunately, very little is known about how the corpus was created: the method of gathering the data, when and where it was gathered, criteria for inclusion, and so on. The project was supervised by Helmut Schaffrath, who provided very little public information about this before his death in 1994. (Schaffrath [1991] and Selfridge-Field [1995] give information about the computational encoding of the data, but not about its sources.) It is believed that much of the data comes from published collections of folk songs (Eleanor Selfridge-Field, personal communication). The corpus also includes a large number of non-European songs, but these were not used in the current study.

5. Regarding the $T_1$ distribution, a difficult problem was encountered. As noted earlier, experimental research has shown that the most likely tactus interval is around 700 msec. One might suppose that the $T_1$ distribution should have a peak somewhere around this value, sloping off in either direction. However, on initial tests, it was found that such a distribution tended to make the tactus level too slow in a large number of cases. Upon reflection, we can understand why this occurs. Every tactus beat involves a stochastic decision, to determine exactly where the beat should be located; the more decisions are made, the lower the probability of the beat sequence. Thus, other things being equal, a tactus level with longer intervals (say in the 1000-msec range) will be higher in probability than one with shorter intervals (say 500 msec). (The *total* probability mass of tactus levels in the 500-msec range and the 1000-msec range is roughly the same; but in the 500-msec case, the probability mass is divided among far more different tactus levels, so the probability of each one is lower.) To alleviate this problem, it was necessary to skew the probability values for the initial tactus interval very strongly, making smaller tactus intervals more likely.

6. We cannot assume that the first note-onset of the piece is necessarily on a tactus beat; the song might begin with an upbeat or "anacrusis." Thus we consider a range of possible positions for the first tactus, before (and including) the first note-onset.

7. A parallel arises here with standard techniques used with hidden Markov models. Maximizing $P(\text{surface} \mid \text{structure})$ corresponds to finding the most probable path through a hidden Markov model given an observation sequence; $P(\text{surface})$ corresponds to the overall probability of the observation sequence.

For both of these problems, dynamic programming is typically used, just as it is here (Manning and Schütze 2000).

8. The test set was created by Paul von Hippel, and was "stratified" so as to include songs from all ethnic categories represented in the Essen corpus. The original test set contained 80 songs, but 15 contained irregular meters and were therefore excluded.

9. The most comparable test that could be found is one performed by Desain and Honing (1999), using a corpus of national anthem melodies. In this case, however, the melodies were "quantized"—represented with perfectly regular timing—and the models being tested were only judged on whether they identified the correct period and phase of the tactus level. Regarding the Bayesian models described earlier, Cemgil's (2000a) model was tested only on very simple, four-onset patterns; Cemgil et al.'s (2000b) model was tested on polyphonic piano performances, but only with regard to the tactus level. Raphael's (2002a) model was tested on two pieces, one polyphonic and one monophonic, with regard to its ability to identify the correct score-times for events, although the model was restricted to score positions that actually occurred in the piece.

10. The Melisma model is more powerful than the probabilistic model in other ways as well. It can handle polyphonic input; it generates five metrical levels; it considers such factors as harmony and parallelism; and it is capable of changing time signatures in the middle of a piece (none of the songs in the Essen test set do change time signatures, but the model did not assume this).

11. In polyphonic music, this might not be the case. But even there, an intelligent model would know that polyphonic music generally consists of several mono-phonic "lines"—streams of non-overlapping notes, proximate in pitch—rather than a texture of independent notes overlapping haphazardly.

**Chapter 4**

1. Very recently, key-finding from audio data has become an active area; see, for example, the submissions to the MIREX 2005 audio key-finding competition, http://www.music-ir.org/evaluation/mirex-results/audio-key/.

2. Butler (1989) also argues that tritone intervals play a special role in key-finding regardless of their ordering, as each tritone occurs in only two major scales (this is sometimes known as the "rare-interval" theory). As I have argued elsewhere, however (2001a: 183), this phenomenon is also compatible with a distributional view of key-finding: tritones fit only two scales in distributional terms and therefore strongly imply the two corresponding keys.

3. Strictly speaking, a normal distribution takes a continuous variable $x$ and indicates the probability of $x$ being within a certain range. However, it can also be used with discrete values, by normalizing so that the outputs of the function for all possible values of $x$ sum to 1.

4. We assume that $c$ is an integer, for reasons that will become clear below (see note 5). In estimating $c$ from a given melody, the observed mean pitch is rounded to the nearest integer.

5. Estimating the variance of the range profile $(\sigma_r^2)$ and the variance of the proximity profile $(\sigma_p^2)$ is more difficult than it might first appear. We could observe the

sheer variance of pitches around the mean pitch of each melody, but this is not the same as $\sigma_r^2$; rather, it is affected by both $\sigma_r^2$ and $\sigma_p^2$. (Similarly, the sheer variance of melodic intervals, as shown in figure 4.6, is not the same as $\sigma_p^2$.) So another method must be used. It is a known fact that the product of two normal distributions is another normal distribution, $N(\mu_t, \sigma_t^2)$, whose mean is in between the means of the distributions being multiplied (Petersen and Petersen 2005):

$$N(c, \sigma_r^2)N(p_{n-1}, \sigma_p^2) \propto N(\mu_t, \sigma_t^2) \qquad (4.8a)$$

where $\sigma_t^2 = 1/(1/\sigma_r^2 + 1/\sigma_p^2) = \sigma_r^2\sigma_p^2/(\sigma_r^2 + \sigma_p^2)$ $\qquad (4.8b)$

and $\mu_t = \sigma_t^2 \times (c/\sigma_r^2 + p_{n-1}/\sigma_p^2) = \dfrac{\sigma_r^2\sigma_p^2}{\sigma_r^2 + \sigma_p^2} \times \dfrac{c\sigma_p^2 + p_{n-1}\sigma_r^2}{\sigma_r^2\sigma_p^2} = \dfrac{c\sigma_p^2 + p_{n-1}\sigma_r^2}{\sigma_r^2 + \sigma_p^2}$ .

$$(4.8c)$$

We assume (as explained below) that the first note of each melody is affected only by the range profile, not the proximity profile. Thus the variance of the range profile can be estimated as the variance of the first note of each melody around its mean pitch; in the Essen corpus, this yields $\sigma_r^2 = 29.0$. Now consider the case of non-initial notes of a melody where the previous pitch is equal to the mean pitch ($p_{n-1} = c$); call this pitch $p_x$. (It is because of this step that we need to assume that $c$ is an integer.) At such points, we know from equation 4.8c above that the mean of the product of the two profiles is also at this pitch:

$$\mu_t = \frac{p_x\sigma_p^2 + p_x\sigma_r^2}{\sigma_r^2 + \sigma_p^2} = p_x \qquad (4.9)$$

Thus we can estimate $\sigma_t^2$ as the observed variance of pitches around $p_{n-1}$, considering only points where $p_{n-1} = c$. The Essen corpus yields a value of $\sigma_t^2 = 5.8$. Now, from equation 4.8b above, we can calculate $\sigma_p^2$ as 7.2.

6. Recall that the RPK profile values are calculated as the product of proximity-profile, range-profile, and key-profile values, and only the key-profile values depend on the key. Thus, one might wonder if key probabilities could be determined from the key-profile values alone (everything else being constant across keys): that is, $P(k \mid \text{pitch sequence}) \propto P(k) \prod K_n$, where $K_n$ are the key-profile values for all pitches in the melody. The problem is that the RPK values are not simply the product of the three profiles, but are normalized to sum to 1; this was found to have a small effect on the model's key-finding behavior in some cases.

7. The models of Vos and Van Geenen (1996) and Temperley (2001a) are capable of identifying changes of key; for these models, the figures indicate the number of cases in which the models identified the correct initial key of the subject. The results for Longuet-Higgins and Steedman and for Vos and Van Geenen are as reported in their publications. Regarding the Krumhansl-Schmuckler model, the test reported here (using my own implementation) simply involved giving each entire fugue subject to the model. Krumhansl (1990) also tested the Krumhansl-Schmuckler model on the Bach fugue subjects in a different way: in her test, the model was run on successively longer portions of the fugue subjects (first one note, then two notes, then three notes, etc.) until it got the right answer and then stopped. My testing method is of more relevance here, since it is the way other key-finding models have been tested and thus allows comparison.

8. One might wonder if the $\hat{7}$ vs. $\flat\hat{7}$ difference also accounts for the poor performance of the Longuet-Higgins/Steedman model on the Essen corpus. To test this, the Longuet-Higgins/Steedman model was run again on the Essen corpus, except with $\flat\hat{7}$ rather than $\hat{7}$ assumed as scalar for minor keys. Surprisingly, the model performed even less well than before, guessing the correct key on only 39 out of 65 melodies (60.0%).

**Chapter 5**

1. No doubt pitch and rhythm are in fact *not* independent. But to specify exactly how they are related is by no means an easy task. We discuss this issue briefly in section 5.5.

2. Two groups of subjects were used in the experiment, a musically trained group and an untrained group. The test reported here uses the average ratings for the two groups, as was done by Cuddy and Lunney (1995) and Schellenberg (1997).

3. In Cuddy and Lunney's data, the second tone was always either C4 or F♯4, but they do not make clear which trials had C4 and which ones had F♯4. In the current test, the second note was set to C4 in all cases. After optimizing the parameters, the same test was run with the second note as F♯4 in all patterns (with the optimized parameters described above), yielding a correlation of .851 (compared to .870 with C4 as the second tone). Re-optimizing the parameters to the F♯4 data could perhaps improve this value.

4. This particular error is really a matter of harmonic structure—the horn phrase conflicts with the surrounding harmony—and thus outside the scope of the current models; but I mention it as it is an especially well-known example.

**Chapter 6**

1. In cases where the correct analyses indicated two keys within a single segment (e.g., a pivot chord), half a point was given to the model if its judgment corresponded with either "correct" key.

2. One feature of the profiles worth mentioning is the ranking of tonic-triad notes. Theoretically, the tonic would surely be given higher status than the third and fifth; and both the major and minor K-K profiles reflect this. In the minor-key Kostka-Payne profile, however, $\hat{5}$ exceeds $\hat{1}$, as it does in the major Temperley profile and both the major and minor Essen profiles. This curious departure between theory and perception, on the one hand, and compositional practice, on the other, is mysterious and deserves further attention.

3. To a large extent, the errors made by the model were the same as those made by the CBMS model, and the following discussion echoes some of the same points made in Temperley 2001a.

4. Several models have been proposed for how pitch spellings might be identified; see Temperley 2001a; Cambouropoulos 2003; and Meredith 2003.

5. In figure 6.9, one might point to the F major triad in the bass line in mm. 1–2 as a harmonic cue. However, to explain the sense of modulation to C major in these terms is much more difficult. One finds a C major triad outlined in m. 6; but E minor, G major, and F major triads are also present in mm. 5–7 and at

least as prominent. The top voice in m. 9 also outlines a C major triad, but the sense of C major is established well before this.

## Chapter 7

1. This chapter builds on ideas put forth in Temperley 2001a concerning the use of preference-rule systems to characterize musical tonalness and ambiguity. However, the Bayesian framework makes possible a more rational and effective solution to these problems than what was proposed there.

2. Another principle sometimes cited is that the closely related keys are those whose key signature differs by one sharp or flat from that of the home key. (Clearly, this is related to the idea of overlapping scale collections.) In Baroque music, in particular, the use of secondary keys is described extremely well by this principle. In C major, the closely related keys by this rule would be G, F, Dm, Am, and Em. It can be seen from figure 7.2 that these five keys, plus the parallel minor, constitute the six most closely related keys to C major according to the K-P profiles. (The K-K profiles do not quite yield this result, as Gm is slightly closer than Dm.) Similarly, the closely related keys to A minor by this criterion— Dm, Em, C, G, and F—constitute (along with the parallel major) the six keys with the highest correlations to A minor.

3. It is difficult to see how the difference in "remoteness" between major and minor keys could be captured in a symmetrical spatial representation such as the Chart of Regions or the 4-dimensional space of keys proposed by Krumhansl and Kessler (1982).

4. The Kostka-Payne key-profiles do not actually represent probability distributions, but rather joint distributions of twelve variables (one for each pitch-class). If $P_a(pc)$ and $P_b(pc)$ are the probabilities for a pitch-class given by two profiles, the cross-entropy for that variable is given by $P_a(pc) \log(P_b(pc)) + (1 - P_a(pc)) \log(1 - P_b(pc))$; the total cross-entropy between the two profiles is given by the sum of the cross-entropies for all the variables. (We cannot use the cross-entropy method with the Krumhansl-Kessler profiles, since these are not interpretable as probabilities; many of the values are not between 0 and 1.)

It can be seen from table 7.1 that the cross-entropy measure is slightly asymmetrical: The distance from C major to A minor is not the same as from A minor to C major. It was noted earlier that, in a way, key relations *are* asymmetrical: for example, the dominant seems closer than the subdominant. But the asymmetries in the cross-entropy scores are so small that it would seem questionable to make too much of this.

5. This approach to measuring tonalness brings to mind an earlier experiment of Krumhansl (1990), using the Krumhansl-Schmuckler (K-S) key-finding algorithm. Recall that the K-S algorithm outputs scores (correlation values) for each key. One might suppose we could use these scores to judge tonalness; a tonal passage will yield a good "fit"—a high correlation score—with at least one key, while a nontonal passage will not yield a high score for any key. Krumhansl applied this method to two pieces, one tonal and one nontonal. In the case of Schubert's *Moment Musical* No. 1, she found that the input vector yielded a very high correlation with G major (though she notes that this is not generally considered

the main key of the piece); in the case of Schoenberg's *Farben*, she found that no key yielded a statistically significant correlation. Thus it seems that this correlation method might be a good way of predicting tonalness. However, there is a problem here. The standard correlation formula used by the K-S model normalizes the values of both vectors to have a variance of 1 and a mean of 0. What is problematic is the normalization of the variance of the input vector values (representing the duration of each pitch-class in a passage). Consider a hypothetical passage, passage A, in which all pitch-classes of the C major scale are used equally often, and no others are used at all; consider also passage B, in which all twelve pitch-classes are used, but pitch-classes within the C major scale are used very slightly (say 1%) more often than others. After normalization, the two passages would be treated as equivalent by the K-S model. But they are surely not equivalent in tonalness; passage A should be judged as much more tonal than passage B. It may well be that the K-S model will often yield lower maximum correlation values for less tonal pieces (as was the case in Krumhansl's experiment). But the case described above suggests that the correlation method will, in some cases, yield highly counterintuitive results.

6. The results here depend on the setting of the "change penalty"—the probability of not modulating. On both the Schumann and Chopin examples, I set this probability at .99. In Temperley 2004b, I presented the same Schumann example, but with a change penalty of .998; this caused the model to stay in D major throughout.

7. Lerdahl (2001) makes a useful distinction between "sequential tension," the tension of each event relative to the previous one, and "hierarchical tension," the tension of an event in relation to the larger context. In those terms, the current model could be faulted for essentially only considering sequential tension, not hierarchical tension. On the other hand, recent psychological research (Cook 1987; Bigand and Parncutt 1999) has called into question the extent to which listeners comprehend large-scale tonal structure and key relations.

8. For comparing key probabilities in proportional terms, as we do here, it is in fact unnecessary to consider either $P(\text{key})$ and $P(\text{pcset})$; for a given segment, these are the same for all keys. One could calculate ambiguity simply as the ratio between the top two values of $P(\text{pcset}|\text{key})$. But the meaning of $P(\text{key}|\text{pcset})$—the probability of a key given the pitch-class set—seems more relevant in the current context.

9. I have also found this to be true in another corpus. In a study of the first eight measures of all Mozart and Haydn string quartet movements, it was found that $\hat{7}$ was more than three times as common as $\flat\hat{7}$ in minor-key movements.

10. Such explanations go back to Zarlino himself (1558/1968: 21–22), and are echoed also in the writings of later theorists; see Crowder 1985 for discussion.

11. Here we are assuming the K-P profiles. This result emerges under both the correlation method (column B of table 7.1) and the cross-entropy method (column C). The cross-entropy measure of distance actually has a rather intuitive meaning here. Recall that this measure indicates the probability that a piece generated stochastically using the key-profile of one key will actually reflect the key-

profile distribution of another key. In effect, this indicates the "danger" that a piece intended to be in one key will be misinterpreted. But the data in table 7.1 suggests that this danger is in fact *lower* for minor keys than for major keys.

12. One could also consider the prior probability of major and minor keys here. We have been assuming that all keys are equal in prior probability; but if—as seems likely—minor keys are actually less commonly used than major keys, then the relative probability (tonalness) of the harmonic minor scale and subsets of it will be even lower. The problem is that, if one asks why composers might have used minor less often than major, the answer surely relates in part to its expressive meaning; so there is a danger of circularity. Thus it seems best to leave prior probabilities out of the argument.

13. Another way to proceed would be to calculate the probability of all nonmodulating analyses of the passage (treating segments as measures as before), dividing the analysis scores by the number of measures, and then finding the top-two ratio between them. This would produce similar results to treating the entire passage as a single segment. In fact, if each measure contained the same pitch-class set, the results would be identical.

14. See for example the second theme of Schubert's C major String Quintet, fourth movement (mm. 48 ff.). In the Schubert, the scale collection in use strongly favors a IV–I6 interpretation; note the use of F♯. But the point here is simply that this progression is not inherently incompatible with the IV–I6 interpretation. Admittedly, nontonic openings of a theme like this one are uncharacteristic, perhaps nonexistent, in Bach's music.

15. See Haydn's String Quartet Op. 64 No. 2, 1, for a similar use of this set at the beginning of a piece.

16. It is also common for the V7 to be used without scale-degree $\hat{2}$ (D), creating the sets C–E–F–G–B for V7–I and C–E♭–F–G–B for V7–i. But even with this change, both the V7–I set and the V7–i set have very high clarity values (9.65 for V7–I, 15.60 for V7–i).

**Chapter 8**

1. This does not of course mean that listeners identify *all* of the notes of a polyphonic piece, such as the inner voices and the bass line. Most listeners would be unable to sing back the inner voices of a piece; but this does not mean they are not being identified at an unconscious level. This remains an open issue.

2. The term "automatic transcription" is problematic. To literally transcribe sound into music notation requires not only identification of the notes, but also other information, such as meter, key signature, pitch-spellings, rhythmic values, and voice separation. Sometimes "automatic transcription" is defined to include these kinds of musical information, but it is also used simply to refer to identification of notes in terms of timepoints and (enharmonic) pitch categories, and we will use it that way here.

3. Three other Bayesian transcription studies came to my attention too late to be included in this discussion: Cemgil, Kappen, and Barber 2003; Davy and Godsill 2003; and Abdallah and Plumbley 2004.

4. This is not quite true, since a tree might be generated by different combinations of subtrees. Strictly speaking, we should say that the probability of a complete *derivation* of a tree is given by the product of all the subtree probabilities involved.

5. Actually, the model was evaluated in a slightly more complex way, using the concepts of *precision* and *recall*. Recall indicates the proportion of correct items (phrase boundary locations in this case) that the model identified; precision indicates the proportion of the model's identified items that are correct. These two measures are combined in a measure known as $F$, where $F = 2 \times (\text{Precision} \times \text{Recall})/(\text{Precision} + \text{Recall})$. The model achieved an $F$ score of 87.3%.

6. A further complication is the addition of rhythmic information: the probability of a certain type of note—root, third, scalar nonchordal, and so on—is conditioned on the note's metric position, the intuition being that chordal notes are more likely to be metrically strong.

7. Actually, in doing the empirical count, the procedure considers *all* possible structures, weighted according to their probability given the data.

8. Transitions may also generate input symbols in a probabilistic fashion; it can be seen that one transition in figure 8.5 (between states 703 and 704) generates two different input symbols. Again, these probabilities are not shown.

9. To be precise, the probability for the output string will be given by the sum of the probabilities for *all* the paths through the model yielding that output string. (Strictly speaking, this yields the joint probability of the input and the output; but for a given input string, this is proportional to the probability of the output given the input.)

10. Some "probe-tone" experiments have also explored listeners' sensitivity to novel distributions—e.g. Oram and Cuddy 1995—but only with surface elements (notes).

**Chapter 9**

1. The term "compositional practice" is problematic. Some might use it to refer simply to the objects resulting from composition; in that case, the claim "every 17th note in this piece is middle C" might be considered a claim about compositional practice even if it entailed no claim about the compositional process. However, I will use "compositional practice" in a stronger sense, to imply both the processes of composition and the resulting musical objects.

2. This is a controversial issue in music theory; for a penetrating discussion, see Haimo 1996. Haimo's concern is to establish what kind of evidence is required—musical or otherwise—to draw conclusions about a composer's intentions. However, Haimo draws a distinction between "intentional" and "intuitive or unconscious" behavior on the part of the composer; his concern is the former, not the latter. My concern, rather, is to distinguish mental representations that were part of the composer's creative processes at all (either consciously or unconsciously) from those that were not. This is in keeping with the usual approach of cognitive science, which seeks to establish the nature of mental processes and representations, and is generally less concerned with whether they are conscious

or unconscious. (It seems likely that much knowledge involved in composition is unconscious. For example, a child could surely use the diatonic scale in creating a melody without having any conscious knowledge of that construct.)

3. It is not so obvious, however, that the cognition of modern listeners (as represented by experimental evidence) and composers of art music (as represented in key signatures of notated scores) can be taken to represent the cognition of folk-song composers and performers of earlier times.

Another issue arises as well: How accurately do the pitches and rhythms of the Essen transcriptions represent the folk songs as originally performed? Did the transcribers perhaps correct notes that seemed "wrong" but were actually intended—or perhaps even force notes into a system of pitch and rhythm categories that was not in fact in the producer's mind? Unfortunately, as noted earlier (chapter 3, note 4), very little is known about how the Essen corpus was created.

4. As well as testing a model on its ability to assign high probability to data generated from the source of interest, we could also test its ability to assign low probability to data *not* from the source. That is to say: If we give Models 1 and 2 a completely "ungrammatical" pitch sequence, something that we know intuitively could never occur in a folk song, we would expect Model 2 to assign it lower probability than Model 1. In fact, a model that performs better on positive tests is likely to do so on negative tests as well, for simple mathematical reasons. For every (well-defined) probabilistic model, the probabilities of all possible data sets must sum to 1. Thus, if Model 2 generally assigns higher probability to "good" melodies than Model 1 does, it must also assign lower probability to other ("bad") melodies.

5. Again, this case is complicated by the fact that the musical object is the product of at least two individuals, the composer and the performer; but that does not affect the main point.

Even more than in the pitch case, the conclusion here—that metrical grids play a role in the generative process—may seem foregone; for one thing, I performed the song from conventional Western notation, which is based on metrical grids. In the case of a folk song created and transmitted without any use of music notation, however, the role of metrical grids in composition and performance would not be so obvious.

6. The generative model used here treats each beat independently, without considering (for example) whether a note on a weak beat is followed by a note on a strong beat (though the possibility of such a model was considered in section 3.7). But even when beats are considered independently, the syncopated model generates more weak-beat notes in proportion to strong-beat notes and thus naturally leads to more "syncopated" notes.

7. In this case, I counted each event in the Kostka-Payne corpus, rather than just counting pitch-classes as present or absent in each segment (as I did in figure 6.4). This allows proper comparison with the Essen counts, which were also done this way (the Essen data here is the same as in figure 4.7).

8. Kassler (1977) and Smoliar (1980) propose computer systems for performing Schenkerian analysis. Like the model sketched here, their models generate pieces

using recursive pitch elaborations. In Smoliar's system, the choice of elaborations to use is entirely up to the user; as Smoliar states, his system is not intended to achieve "the automation of musical analysis" but is (as his article title suggests) simply a "computer aid." Kassler's system appears to operate autonomously, though this is not entirely clear. Kassler shows that his model is capable of generating some tonal pieces; however, he does not say how many analyses it generates for each piece, nor does he discuss whether the model fails to generate nontonal pieces.

Brown et al. (1995) offer an interesting discussion of *Stufen*, and propose a possible constraint on their generation. It is not clear, however, how they would integrate the generation of *Stufen* with the generation of notes.

9. This Schenkerian parser was built using the publicly available Link Grammar Parser (Sleator and Temperley 1993; http://www.cs.link.cmu.edu/link/).

10. Linguistic trees are of a rather different kind from Schenkerian trees, in that a distinction is made between terminal "surface" entities (words) and nonterminal ones (things like noun phrase or verb phrase); the elaborations in a tree expand a nonterminal entity into a word or other nonterminals. (See Cohn and Dempster 1992 for discussion of linguistic, Schenkerian, and other kinds of hierarchical structures.)

11. Of interest in this regard is a study by Larson (1997–98). Larson examines published Schenkerian analyses and tallies the different kinds of elaboration patterns that are used. Larson's aim is to examine whether these choices are explained by his theory of "musical forces." This is a nice illustration of how probabilistic constraints on Schenkerian analysis could be studied empirically.

12. To formalize this, we could assume a generative process whereby a metrical structure is generated, a Schenkerian tree structure of pitches is generated independently, and then principles such as the one just stated are used to place the events of the Schenkerian tree in the metrical grid. Of course, our metrical model already tells us that note-onsets are more likely at certain points in the grid (i.e. strong beats), but our current rule would say specifically that higher-level events in the tree are especially likely at strong beats, and perhaps also that events within a single elaboration are likely to be similarly placed in relation to the meter.

**Chapter 10**

1. As Huron points out, the avoidance of small intervals in low registers might also be attributed to the avoidance of sensory dissonance.

2. The clarification of pitch structure may also account for other phenomena not addressed by Huron; one example is "melodic lead." In studies of performance timing, it has been found that performers tend to play melody notes slightly earlier (20–50 msec) than other nominally simultaneous notes. Palmer (1996) has suggested that this tendency may have evolved to facilitate identification of notes, as slightly asynchronous notes tend to be identified more easily than perfectly synchronous ones. (This raises the possibility that performers, as well as composers, may be affected by communicative pressure—a point that will be important in following sections.)

3. See for example Gauldin 1988: 35. Huron (1991) has also found evidence for the avoidance of voice-crossing in compositional practice.

Huron makes a similar argument regarding the preference for small melodic intervals (2001: 22–26). He cites a variety of evidence that composers tend to favor small intervals, and suggests that this may be a response to perceptual expectations. This may be true; however, we must be careful that our reasoning does not become circular. Our general assumption in this study has been that perceptual expectations are shaped by compositional practice; in chapter 4, for example, our perceptual model of pitch proximity was based on the distribution of melodic intervals in the Essen corpus. So which is it—composition influencing perception, or perception influencing composition? Quite possibly, both of these causal forces are in operation—and have operated for centuries, in a complex interactive process. This does mean, however, that one must be cautious about attributing the mere *correlation* between the perceptual tendency and the compositional tendency to either causal force.

4. Ratner (1980: 26–27) cites frequent shifts of texture and mood as a hallmark of the classical style. (Ratner actually refers to "topics" rather than to textures per se, but it is clear that topics are often associated with contrasting textures.) In Romantic-period music, by contrast, uniformity of texture has been cited as a characteristic feature: speaking of Romantic music generally, Grout (1980: 559) notes that "long sections, even entire movements ... may continue in one unbroken rhythmic pattern."

5. There are, of course, exceptions to these generalities. Some classical-period pieces feature a left-hand pattern repeated throughout an entire section or movement—this is not uncommon in slow movements, such as that of Mozart's Piano Sonata K. 545. Conversely, Schumann and Brahms are known for sometimes using quite extreme syncopations (see Krebs 1999 for a thorough study of this aspect of Schumann's style).

6. In Morton's performance, excerpt 2 actually begins the piece, and is followed by excerpt 1, but the correspondence between the excerpts in Morton's and Joplin's performances seems indisputable.

7. The word "swing" is defined in many different ways in jazz, and is often simply characterized as some kind of undefinable "feel" (Ulanov 1952: 5). But the sense assumed here—referring to an uneven long-short division of the beat—is one widespread use of the term (Megill and Demory 1983: 230–231).

8. Perhaps Swain's example can be strengthened with some more attention to the details. In both Renaissance and common-practice styles, cadences are vitally important, partly as cues to segmentation (indicating the ends of phrases and sections) but also indicating the establishment of a tonal center. (We can speak of "tonal centers" in Renaissance music, even though the idea of key is not yet really applicable.) Thus it would not be surprising if the need to communicate cadences significantly affected the evolution of Western music. What needs to be explained, however, is the apparent fact that the common-practice style allows more freedom in the construction of cadences than the Renaissance style. Is there

some way in which cadences were more clearly—less ambiguously—identifiable in common-practice music, thus allowing more flexibility in their contrapuntal features? One possible answer lies in the emerging tonal system. In Renaissance music, an entire piece generally uses a single pitch collection (usually the C major scale); there is no modulation from one scale to another, except for the chromatic alterations at cadences. For this reason, the only thing really indicating a tonal center is often the cadence itself. This also means that numerous different cadences on different tonal centers might possibly occur at any time. In common-practice music, by contrast, a cadence is generally prepared by a shift to the key of the cadence (indicated by a shift to the corresponding scale) in the preceding measures; a cadence can only occur in the key of the preceding context. Other things being equal, then, if the Renaissance style allowed greater freedom in the construction of cadences, the proportion of possible pitch patterns interpretable as cadences would be much higher in Renaissance music—perhaps unacceptably high, so that cadences would often be perceived where they were not intended. The stricter definition of cadences in the Renaissance style avoids this problem, or (conversely) the contextual constraints on cadences in common-practice music allow them to be more loosely defined in their intrinsic features.

9. One might question my definition of "extensions." By my rule, the $\flat\hat{5}$ degree is counted as an extension; thus diminished triads (and diminished or half-diminished sevenths) are counted as "extended chords." This is contrary to the usual understanding in common-practice theory, where the $\flat\hat{5}$ of a diminished triad is regarded as an essential part of the chord, substituing for the perfect fifth (and altering the function of the chord). On the other hand, the $\flat\hat{5}$ chord-degree in jazz often *is* used as a true extension (sometimes spelled as $\sharp\hat{11}$)—an elaborating tone added above a dominant seventh chord (see figure 10.10B, for example). So there was really no way of classifying this tone that would be true to its usage in both styles. (The vast majority of "extended" chords found in the common-practice corpus were, in fact, diminished triads or seventh chords built on them.) One might also question the labeling of the major seventh as an extension. But in any case, the current argument does not depend on whether a particular tone is considered an extension or not. The point is that, in any style where a large number of chord-tones above the root are allowed (whether they are extensions or essential tones), the widespread use of inversion as well may result in frequent ambiguities; so we would not expect to find these two conditions in combination.

10. Recall that the key-profiles in figure 6.4 indicate the proportion of segments in which scale-degrees occur, rather than the sheer frequency of scale-degrees. The 2% figure given here was calculated from the actual frequency of scale-degrees.

11. See Aldwell and Schachter (2003: 424–425), figures 25-3, 25-4, 25-5, 25-6, and 25-7, each of which illustrates a point about an acceptable usage of cross-relations. Figures 25-3, 25-5, and 25-6 clearly involve stepwise motion; in figure 25-7, illustrating "chromaticized voice exchange," the authors say that the "harshness" of this device can be softened by the use of stepwise motion (a "passing chord"). (See also their pp. 232 and 400.)

12. This phenomenon relates to the "anchoring principle," posited by Bharucha (1984), which states that unstable events tend to be followed by more stable and referential events. But no explanation has been given for why events should tend to precede, rather than follow, their anchors.

13. This actually raises a problem for the whole communicative-pressure idea. The theory predicts that, in music where the communication of meter is a goal, we should not find both a high degree of syncopation and a high degree of rubato. But if we were confronted with such music, we might simply assume that it did not have any intended meter—because we did not perceive one—and thus that the prediction did not apply; there is, then, a danger of circularity. While this is a problem, it is not a fatal one. There are often external cues as to whether a metrical structure is intended in a kind of music: notation, for example. One reason for thinking that no metrical structure is involved in Gregorian chant or recitative is because none is included in the way the music is notated. Still, the possibility of circular reasoning is a real danger that we should bear in mind when applying the communicative-pressure theory.

# References

Abdallah, S. A., and M. D. Plumbley. 2004. Polyphonic transcription by non-negative sparse coding of power spectra. In *Proceedings of the 5th International Conference on Music Information Retrieval*. Http://www.elec.qmul.ac.uk/department/staff/research/samer.htm/.

Agawu, V. K. 1995. *African Rhythm*. Cambridge: Cambridge University Press.

Aldwell, E., and C. Schachter. 2003. *Harmony and Voice Leading*. Belmont, Calif.: Wadsworth Group/Thomson Learning.

Barra, D. 1983. *The Dynamic Performance: A Performer's Guide to Musical Expression and Interpretation*. Englewood Cliffs, N.J.: Prentice-Hall.

Bello, J. P., G. Monti, and M. Sandler. 2000. Techniques for automatic music transcription. *Proceedings of the First International Symposium on Music Information Retrieval*. Http://www.elec.qmul.ac.uk/people/juan/publications.htm/.

Bharucha, J. J. 1984. Anchoring effects in music: The resolution of dissonance. *Cognitive Psychology*, 16, 485–518.

Bharucha, J. J. 1987. Music cognition and perceptual facilitation: A connectionist framework. *Music Perception*, 5, 1–30.

Bharucha, J. J. 1996. Melodic anchoring. *Music Perception*, 13, 383–400.

Bigand, E., and R. Parncutt. 1999. Perceiving musical tension in long chord sequences. *Psychological Research*, 62, 237–254.

Bod, R. 2002. A unified model of structural organization in language and music. *Journal of Artificial Intelligence Research*, 17, 289–308.

Brawley, J. G. 1959. Application of information theory to musical rhythm. Unpublished master's dissertation, Indiana University.

Brooks, F. P., A. L. Hopkins, P. G. Neumann, and W. V. Wright. 1957. An experiment in musical composition. *IRE Transactions on Computers*, EC-6, 175–182.

Brown, H., D. Butler, and M. R. Jones. 1994. Musical and temporal influences on key discovery. *Music Perception*, 11, 371–407.

Brown, M., D. Dempster, and D. Headlam. 1997. The #IV(♭V) hypothesis: Testing the limits of Schenker's theory of tonality. *Music Theory Spectrum*, 19, 155–183.

Butler, D. 1989. Describing the perception of tonality in music: A critique of the tonal hierarchy theory and a proposal for a theory of intervallic rivalry. *Music Perception*, 6, 219–242.

Cadwallader, A., and D. Gagné. 1998. *Analysis of Tonal Music: A Schenkerian Approach*. New York: Oxford University Press.

Cambouropoulos, E. 2003. Pitch spelling: A computational model. *Music Perception*, 20, 411–430.

Carlsen, J. C. 1981. Some factors which influence melodic expectancy. *Psychomusicology*, 1, 12–29.

Castellano, M. A., J. J. Bharucha, and C. L. Krumhansl. 1984. Tonal hierarchies in the music of North India. *Journal of Experimental Psychology: General*, 113, 394–412.

Cemgil, A. T., P. Desain, and B. Kappen. 2000. Rhythm quantization for transcription. *Computer Music Journal*, 24/2, 60–76.

Cemgil, A. T., H. J. Kappen, and D. Barber. 2003. Generative model based polyphonic music transcription. *Proceedings of IEEE Workshop on Applications of Signal Processing to Audio and Acoustics*. Http://www-sigproc.eng.cam.ac.uk/~atc27/papers.html/.

Cemgil, A. T., B. Kappen, P. Desain, and H. Honing. 2000. On tempo tracking: Tempogram representation and Kalman filtering. *Journal of New Music Research*, 29, 259–273.

Chernoff, J. M. 1979. *African Rhythm and African Sensibility*. Chicago: Chicago University Press.

Chew, E. 2002. The spiral array: An algorithm for determining key boundaries. In C. Anagnostopoulou, M. Ferrand, and A. Smaill (eds.), *Music and Artificial Intelligence*, pp. 18–31. Berlin: Springer.

Chomsky, N. 1965. *Aspects of the Theory of Syntax*. Cambridge, Mass.: MIT Press.

Cohen, J. E. 1962. Information theory and music. *Behavioral Science*, 7, 137–163.

Cohn, R., and D. Dempster. 1992. Hierarchical unity, plural unities: Toward a reconciliation. In K. Bergeron and P. V. Bohlman (eds.), *Disciplining Music*, pp. 156–181. Chicago: University of Chicago Press.

Conklin, D., and I. Witten. 1995. Multiple viewpoint systems for music prediction. *Journal of New Music Research*, 24, 51–73.

Cook, N. 1987. The perception of large-scale tonal closure. *Music Perception*, 5, 197–206.

Creel, S. C., E. L. Newport, and R. N. Aslin. 2004. Distant melodies: Statistical learning of non-adjacent dependencies in tone sequences. *Journal of Experimental Psychology: Learning, Memory, and Cognition*, 30, 1119–1130.

Crowder, R. G. 1985. Perception of the major/minor distinction: Historical and theoretical foundations. *Psychomusicology*, 4, 3–12.

Cuddy, L. L. 1997. Tonal relations. In I. Deliege and J. Sloboda (eds.), *Perception and Cognition of Music*, pp. 329–352. London: Taylor and Francis.

Cuddy, L. L., and B. Badertscher. 1987. Recovery of the tonal hierarchy: some comparisons across age and levels of musical experience. *Perception & Psychophysics*, 41, 609–620.

Cuddy, L. L., A. J. Cohen, and D. J. K. Mewhort. 1981. Perception of structure in short melodic sequences. *Journal of Experimental Psychology: Human Perception and Performance*, 7, 869–883.

Cuddy, L. L., A. J. Cohen, and J. Miller. 1979. Melody recognition: The experimental application of rules. *Canadian Journal of Psychology*, 33, 148–157.

Cuddy, L. L., and C. A. Lunney. 1995. Expectancies generated by melodic intervals: Perceptual judgments of melodic continuity. *Perception & Psychophysics*, 57, 451–462.

Danchev, A. 1991. Language change typology and some aspects of the SVO development in English. In D. Kastovsky (ed.), *Historical English Syntax*, pp. 103–124. Berlin: Mouton de Gruyter.

Danielou, A. 1968. *The Ragas of Northern Indian Music*. London: Barrie and Rockliff.

Davy, M., and S. J. Godsill. 2003. Bayesian harmonic models for musical signal analysis (with discussion). In J. M. Bernardo, J. O. Berger, A. P. Dawid, and A. F. M. Smith (eds.), *Bayesian Statistics VII*. Oxford: Oxford University Press.

Deliege, I. 1987. Grouping conditions in listening to music: An approach to Lerdahl and Jackendoff's grouping preference rules. *Music Perception*, 4, 325–360.

Desain, P., and H. Honing. 1992. *Music, Mind, and Machine*. Amsterdam: Thesis Publications.

Desain, P., and H. Honing. 1999. Computational models of beat induction: The rule-based approach. *Journal of New Music Research*, 28, 29–42.

Deutsch, D. 1975. Two-channel listening to musical scales. *Journal of the Acoustical Society of America*, 57, 1156–1160.

Deutsch, D. 1999. Grouping mechanisms in music. In D. Deutsch (ed.), *The Psychology of Music*, 2nd edition, pp. 349–411. San Diego, Calif.: Academic Press.

Dixon, S. 2001. Automatic extraction of tempo and beat from expressive performances. *Journal of New Music Research*, 30, 39–58.

Dobbins, B. 1994. *A Creative Approach to Jazz Piano Harmony*. Rottenburg, Germany: Advance Music.

Drake, C., and C. Palmer. 1993. Accent structures in music performance. *Music Perception*, 10, 343–378.

Drake, C., A. Penel, and E. Bigand. 2000. Tapping in time with mechanically and expressively performed music. *Music Perception*, 18, 1–23.

Elsness, J. 1984. That or zero? A look at the choice of object clause connective in a corpus of American English. *English Studies*, 65, 519–533.

Ferreira, V. S., and G. S. Dell. 2000. Effect of ambiguity and lexical availability on syntactic and lexical production. *Cognitive Psychology*, 40, 296–340.

Forte, A., and S. E. Gilbert. 1982. *Introduction to Schenkerian Analysis*. New York: Norton.

Fux, J. J. 1725/1971. *Gradus ad Parnassum*. Trans. and ed. A. Mann. New York: Norton.

Gabrielsson, A. 1973. Studies in rhythm. *Acta Universitatis Upsaliensis*, 7, 3–19.

Gauldin, R. 1988. *A Practical Approach to Eighteenth-Century Counterpoint*. Prospect Heights, Ill.: Waveland Press.

Gazzaniga, M. S. (ed.). 1999. *The New Cognitive Neurosciences*. Cambrige, Mass.: MIT Press.

Goto, M. 2001. An audio-based real-time beat tracking system for music with or without drum-sounds. *Journal of New Music Research*, 30, 159–171.

Grigson, L. 1988. *Practical Jazz: A Step-by-Step Guide to Harmony and Improvisation*. London: Stainer & Bell.

Grout, D. J. 1980. *A History of Western Music* (3rd edition). New York: W. W. Norton.

Haimo, E. 1996. Atonality, analysis, and the intentional fallacy. *Music Theory Spectrum*, 18, 167–199.

Hepokoski, J., and W. Darcy. 1997. The medial caesura and its role in the eighteenth-century sonata exposition. *Music Theory Spectrum*, 19, 115–154.

Hiller, L. A., and R. Fuller. 1967. Structure and information in Webern's Symphonie, Opus 21. *Journal of Music Theory*, 11, 60–115.

Hiller, L. A., and L. M. Isaacson. 1959. *Experimental Music*. New York: McGraw-Hill.

Huron, D. 1991. The avoidance of part-crossing in polyphonic music: Perceptual evidence and musical practice. *Music Perception*, 9, 93–104.

Huron, D. 1999. *Music Research Using Humdrum: A User's Guide*. Stanford, Calif.: Center for Computer Assisted Research in the Humanities. Http://dactyl.som.ohio-state.edu/Humdrum/guide.toc.html/.

Huron, D. 2001. Tone and voice: A derivation of the rules of voice-leading from perceptual principles. *Music Perception*, 19, 1–64.

Huron, D., and R. Parncutt. 1993. An improved model of tonality perception incorporating pitch salience and echoic memory. *Psychomusicology*, 12, 154–171.

Huron, D., and P. Sellmer. 1992. Critical bands and the spelling of vertical sonorities. *Music Perception*, 10, 129–149.

Jonas, O. 1934/1982. *Introduction to the Theory of Heinrich Schenker*. Trans. and ed. J. Rothgeb. New York: Schirmer.

Jones, A. M. 1959. *Studies in African Music*. London: Oxford University Press.

Jones, M. R., H. Moynihan, N. MacKenzie, and J. Puente. 2002. Temporal aspects of stimulus-driven attending in dynamic arrays. *Psychological Science*, 13, 313–319.

Jurafsky, D., and J. H. Martin. 2000. *Speech and Language Processing*. Upper Saddle River, N.J.: Prentice Hall.

Kashino, K., K. Nakadai, T. Kinoshita, and H. Tanaka. 1998. Application of Bayesian probability networks to musical scene analysis. In D. F. Rosenthal and H. G. Okuno (eds.), *Computational Auditory Scene Analysis*, pp. 115–137. Mahwah, N.J.: Lawrence Erlbaum.

Kassler, M. 1977. Explication of the middleground of Schenker's theory of tonality. *Miscellanea Musicologica*, 9, 72–81.

Kastner, M. P., and R. G. Crowder. 1990. Perception of the major/minor distinction: IV. Emotional connotations in young children. *Music Perception*, 8, 189–202.

Kersten, D. 1999. High-level vision as statistical inference. In M. S. Gazzaniga (ed.), *The New Cognitive Neurosciences*, pp. 353–363. Cambridge, Mass.: MIT Press.

Kiparsky, P. 1982. *Explanation in Phonology*. Dordrecht: Foris.

Klapuri, A. P. 2004. Automatic music transcription as we know it today. *Journal of New Music Research*, 33, 269–282.

Knill, D. C., D. Kersten, and A. Yuille. 1996. Introduction: A Bayesian formulation of visual perception. In D. C. Knill and W. Richards (eds.), *Perception as Bayesian Inference*, pp. 1–21. Cambridge: Cambridge University Press.

Knopoff, L., and W. Hutchinson. 1983. Entropy as a measure of style: The influence of sample length. *Journal of Music Theory*, 27, 75–97.

Kostka, S. 1990. *Materials and Techniques of Twentieth-Century Music*. Englewood Cliffs, N.J.: Prentice-Hall.

Kostka, S. 1995. *Instructor's Manual to Accompany Tonal Harmony*. New York: McGraw-Hill.

Kostka, S., and D. Payne. 1995a. *Tonal Harmony*. New York: McGraw-Hill.

Kostka, S., and D. Payne. 1995b. *Workbook for Tonal Harmony*. New York: McGraw-Hill.

Krebs, H. 1999. *Fantasy Pieces: Metrical Dissonance in the Music of Robert Schumann*. Oxford: Oxford University Press.

Krumhansl, C. L. 1990. *Cognitive Foundations of Musical Pitch*. New York: Oxford University Press.

Krumhansl, C. L. 1995. Music psychology and music theory: Problems and prospects. *Music Theory Spectrum*, 17, 53–80.

Krumhansl, C. L., and E. J. Kessler. 1982. Tracing the dynamic changes in perceived tonal organization in a spatial representation of musical keys. *Psychological Review*, 89, 334–368.

Krumhansl, C. L., J. Louhivuori, P. Toiviainen, T. Järvinen, and T. Eerola. 1999. Expectation in Finnish spiritual folk hymns: Convergence of statistical, behavioral, and computational approaches. *Music Perception*, 17, 151–195.

Labov, W. 1994. *Principles of Linguistic Change: Internal Factors*. Oxford: Blackwell.

Lake, W. 1987. Melodic perception and cognition: The influence of tonality. Unpublished Ph.D. dissertation, University of Michigan.

Lampl, H. 1996. *Turning Notes into Music: An Introduction to Musical Interpretation*. Lanham, Md.: Scarecrow.

Large, E. W., and M. R. Jones. 1999. The dynamics of attending: How people track time varying events. *Psychological Review*, 106, 119–159.

Large, E. W., and J. F. Kolen. 1994. Resonance and the perception of musical meter. *Connection Science*, 6, 177–208.

Larson, S. 1997–98. Musical forces and melodic patterns. *Theory and Practice*, 22–23, 55–71.

Larson, S. 2004. Musical forces and melodic expectations: Comparing computer models and experimental results. *Music Perception*, 21, 457–498.

Lee, C. 1991. The perception of metrical structure: Experimental evidence and a model. In P. Howell, R. West, and I. Cross (eds.), *Representing Musical Structure*, pp. 59–127. London: Academic Press.

Leman, M. 1995. *Music and Schema Theory*. Berlin: Springer.

Lerdahl, F. 2001. *Tonal Pitch Space*. Oxford: Oxford University Press.

Lerdahl, F., and R. Jackendoff. 1983. *A Generative Theory of Tonal Music*. Cambridge, Mass.: MIT Press.

Lester, J. 1992. *Compositional Theory in the Eighteenth Century*. Cambridge, Mass.: Harvard University Press.

Longuet-Higgins, H. C., and M. J. Steedman. 1971. On interpreting Bach. *Machine Intelligence*, 6, 221–241.

Manning, C. D., and H. Schütze. 2000. *Foundations of Statistical Natural Language Processing*. Cambridge, Mass.: MIT Press.

Margulis, E. H. 2005. A model of melodic expectation. *Music Perception*, 4, 663–714.

Martin, K. 1996. A blackboard system for automatic transcription of simple polyphonic music. M.I.T. Media Laboratory Perceptual Computing Section Technical Report No. 385.

Matthay, T. 1913. *Musical Interpretation*. London: Joseph Williams.

Mavromatis, P. 2005. The *Echoi* of modern Greek church chant in written and oral transmission: A computational model and its cognitive implications. Unpublished Ph.D. dissertation, University of Rochester.

Megill, D. D., and R. S. Demory. 1983. *Introduction to Jazz History*. Englewood Cliffs, N.J.: Prentice Hall.

Meredith, D. 2003. Pitch spelling algorithms. *Proceedings of the Fifth Triennial ESCOM Conference*. Http://www.titanmusic.com/papers.html/.

Meyer, L. B. 1956. *Emotion and Meaning in Music*. Chicago: University of Chicago Press.

Meyer, L. B. 1957/1967. Meaning in music and information theory. In *Music, the Arts, and Ideas*, pp. 5–21. Chicago: University of Chicago Press.

Meyer, L. B. 1973. *Explaining Music*. Berkeley: University of California Press.

Miller, G. A., and G. A. Heise. 1950. The trill threshold. *Journal of the Acoustical Society of America*, 22, 637–638.

Moore, A. 1993. *Rock: The Primary Text*. Buckingham: Open University Press.

Narmour, E. 1990. *The Analysis and Cognition of Basic Melodic Structures: The Implication-Realization Model*. Chicago: University of Chicago Press.

Nketia, J. H. K. 1974. *The Music of Africa*. New York: Norton.

Oram, N., and L. L. Cuddy. 1995. Responsiveness of Western adults to pitch distributional information in melodic sequences. *Psychological Research*, 57, 103–118.

Osherson, D. 1990. Judgment. In D. Osherson and E. Smith (eds.), *An Invitation to Cognitive Science*, vol. 3: *Thinking*, pp. 55–87. Cambridge, Mass.: MIT Press.

Palmer, C. 1996. Anatomy of a performance: Sources of musical expression. *Music Perception*, 13, 433–454.

Palmer, C., and C. Krumhansl. 1987. Pitch and temporal contributions to musical phrase perception: Effects of harmony, performance timing, and familiarity. *Perception and Psychophysics*, 41, 505–518.

Palmer, C., and C. Krumhansl. 1990. Mental representations for musical meter. *Journal of Experimental Psychology: Human Perception and Performance*, 16, 728–741.

Palmer, C., and P. Q. Pfordresher. 2003. Incremental planning in sequence production. *Psychological Review*, 110, 683–712.

Pardo, B., and W. P. Birmingham. 2002. Algorithms for chordal analysis. *Computer Music Journal*, 26/2, 27–49.

Parncutt, R. 1994. A perceptual model of pulse salience and metrical accent in musical rhythms. *Music Perception*, 11, 409–464.

Pearl, J. 1986. Fusion, propagation, and structuring in belief networks. *Artificial Intelligence*, 29, 241–288.

Peel, J., and W. Slawson. 1984. Review of *A Generative Theory of Tonal Music*. *Journal of Music Theory*, 28, 271–294.

Petersen, K. B., and M. S. Petersen. 2005. *The Matrix Cookbook*. Lyngby, Denmark: Technical University of Denmark. Http://www2.imm.dtu.dk/pubdb/p.php?3274/.

Pinkerton, R. C. 1956. Information theory and melody. *Scientific American*, 194, 77–86.

Piston, W. 1978. *Harmony*. New York: Norton.

Ponsford, D., G. Wiggins, and C. Mellish. 1999. Statistical learning of harmonic movement. *Journal of New Music Research*, 28, 150–177.

Povel, D.-J. 1996. Exploring the fundamental harmonic forces in the tonal system. *Psychological Research*, 58, 274–283.

Povel, D.-J., and P. Essens. 1985. Perception of temporal patterns. *Music Perception*, 2, 411–440.

Pyles, T. 1971. *The Origins and Development of the English Language*. New York: Harcourt Brace Jovanovich.

Rahn, J. 1980. *Basic Atonal Theory*. New York: Schirmer.

Raphael, C. 2002a. A hybrid graphical model for rhythmic parsing. *Artificial Intelligence*, 137, 217–238.

Raphael, C. 2002b. Automatic transcription of piano music. *Proceedings of the 3rd Annual International Symposium on Music Information Retrieval*. Http://xavier.informatics.indiana.edu/~craphael/papers/index.html/.

Raphael, C., and J. Stoddard. 2004. Functional harmonic analysis using probabilistic models. *Computer Music Journal*, 28/3, 45–52.

Ratner, L. G. 1980. *Classic Music: Expression, Form, and Style*. New York: Schirmer Books.

Rissanen, J. 1989. *Stochastic Complexity in Statistical Inquiry*. Series in Computer Science, vol. 15. Singapore: World Scientific.

Rosenblum, S. P. 1991. *Performance Practices in Classic Piano Music*. Bloomington: Indiana University Press.

Ross, S. 2000. *Introduction to Probability Models*. San Diego: Academic Press.

Sadie, S. (ed.). 2001. *The New Grove Dictionary of Music and Musicians*, 2nd edition. New York: Grove.

Saffran, J. R., R. N. Aslin, and E. L. Newport. 1996. Statistical learning by 8-month-old infants. *Science*, 274, 1926–1928.

Saffran, J. R., E. K. Johnson, R. N. Aslin, and E. L. Newport. 1999. Statistical learning of tone sequences by human infants and adults. *Cognition*, 70, 27–52.

Sales, G. 1984. *Jazz: America's Classical Music*. Englewood Cliffs, N.J.: Prentice-Hall.

Schachter, C. E. 1976. Rhythm and linear analysis: A preliminary study. *Music Forum*, 4, 281–334.

Schachter, C. E. 1981. A commentary on Schenker's *Free Composition*. *Journal of Music Theory*, 25, 115–142.

Schaffrath, H. 1991. *Computer in der Musik: Über den Einsatz in Wissenschaft, Komposition und Pädagogik*. Stuttgart: J. B. Metzler.

Schaffrath, H. 1995. *The Essen Folksong Collection*. Ed. D. Huron. Stanford, Calif.: Center for Computer-Assisted Research in the Humanities.

Scheirer, E. D. 1998. Tempo and beat analysis of acoustic musical signals. *Journal of the Acoustical Society of America*, 103, 588–601.

Schellenberg, E. G. 1996. Expectancy in melody: Tests of the implication-realization model. *Cognition*, 58, 75–125.

Schellenberg, E. G. 1997. Simplifying the implication-realization model of melodic expectancy. *Music Perception*, 14, 295–318.

Schellenberg, E. G., M. Adachi, K. T. Purdy, and M. C. McKinnon. 2002. Expectancy in melody: Tests of children and adults. *Journal of Experimental Psychology: General*, 131, 511–537.

Schenker, H. 1935/1979. *Free Composition*. Trans. and ed. E. Oster. New York: Longman.

Schmuckler, M. 1989. Expectation and music: Investigation of melodic and harmonic processes. *Music Perception*, 7, 109–150.

Schoenberg, A. 1954/1969. *Structural Functions of Harmony*. New York: Norton.

Schuller, G. 1968. *Early Jazz*. New York: Oxford University Press.

Selfridge-Field, E. 1995. The Essen musical data package. Technical report. Menlo Park, Calif.: Center for Computer-Assisted Research in the Humanities.

Shaffer, L. H. 1984. Timing in solo and duet piano performances. *Quarterly Journal of Experimental Psychology*, 36A, 577–595.

Shannon, C. E. 1948. A mathematical theory of communication. *Bell System Technical Journal*, 27, 379–423.

Shannon, C. E. 1951. Prediction and entropy of printed English. *Bell Systems Technical Journal*, 30, 50–64.

Sher, C. 1988. *The New Real Book*. Petaluma, Calif.: Sher Music.

Shmulevich, I., and O. Yli-Harja. 2000. Localized key-finding: Algorithms and applications. *Music Perception*, 17, 65–100.

Sleator, D., and D. Temperley. 1993. Parsing English with a link grammar. *Third Annual Workshop on Parsing Technologies*. Http://www.link.cs.cmu.edu/link/papers/index.html/.

Sloboda, J. A. 1976. The effect of item position on the likelihood of identification by inference in prose reading and music reading. *Canadian Journal of Psychology*, 30, 228–236.

Sloboda, J. A. 1983. The communication of musical metre in piano performance. *Quarterly Journal of Experimental Psychology*, 35, 377–396.

Sloboda, J. A. 1985. *The Musical Mind*. Oxford: Clarendon Press.

Smoliar, S. 1980. A computer aid for Schenkerian analysis. *Computer Music Journal*, 4/2, 41–59.

Snyder, J. L. 1990. Entropy as a measure of musical style: The influence of a priori assumptions. *Music Theory Spectrum*, 12, 121–160.

Steedman, M. 1977. The perception of musical rhythm and meter. *Perception*, 6, 555–570.

Stein, E. 1962/1989. *Form and Performance*. New York: Limelight Editions.

Stephenson, K. 2002. *What to Listen for in Rock*. New Haven: Yale University Press.

Swain, J. 1997. *Musical Languages*. New York: W. W. Norton.

Swinney, D. 1979. Lexical access during sentence comprehension: Reconstruction of context effects. *Journal of Verbal Learning and Verbal Behavior*, 18, 645–660.

Temperley, D. 2001a. *The Cognition of Basic Musical Structures*. Cambridge, Mass.: MIT Press.

Temperley, D. 2001b. The question of purpose in music theory: Description, suggestion, and explanation. *Current Musicology*, 66, 66–85.

Temperley, D. 2002. A Bayesian approach to key-finding. In C. Anagnostopoulou, M. Ferrand, and A. Smaill (eds.), *Music and Artificial Intelligence*, pp. 195–206. Berlin: Springer.

Temperley, D. 2003. Ambiguity avoidance in English relative clauses. *Language*, 79, 464–484.

Temperley, D. 2004a. An evaluation system for metrical models. *Computer Music Journal*, 28/3, 28–44.

Temperley, D. 2004b. Bayesian models of musical structure and cognition. *Musicae Scientiae*, 8, 175–205.

Temperley, D. 2004c. Communicative pressure and the evolution of musical styles. *Music Perception*, 21, 313–337.

Temperley, D., and C. Bartlette. 2002. Parallelism as a factor in metrical analysis. *Music Perception*, 20, 117–149.

Temperley, D., and D. Sleator. 1999. Modeling meter and harmony: A preference-rule approach. *Computer Music Journal*, 23/1, 10–27.

Tenenbaum, J. B. 1999. Bayesian modeling of human concept learning. In M. S. Kearns, S. A. Solla, and D. A. Cohn (eds.), *Advances in Neural Information Processing Systems*, vol. 11, pp. 59–65. Cambridge, Mass.: MIT Press.

Tenney, J., and L. Polansky. 1980. Temporal Gestalt perception in music. *Journal of Music Theory*, 24, 205–241.

Thompson, W. F., and L. L. Cuddy. 1992. Perceived key movement in four-voice harmony and single voices. *Music Perception*, 9, 427–438.

Thompson, W. F., L. L. Cuddy, and C. Plaus. 1997. Expectancies generated by melodic intervals: Evaluation of principles of melodic implication in a melody-completion task. *Perception & Psychophysics*, 59, 1069–1076.

Toivianen, P., and C. Krumhansl. 2003. Measuring and modeling real-time responses to music: The dynamics of tonality induction. *Perception*, 32, 741–766.

Toiviainen, P., and J. S. Snyder. 2003. Tapping to Bach: Resonance-based modeling of pulse. *Music Perception*, 21, 43–80.

Ulanov, B. 1952. *A History of Jazz in America*. New York: Viking Press.

Unyk, A. M., and J. C. Carlsen. 1987. The influence of expectancy on melodic perception. *Psychomusicology*, 7, 3–23.

von Hippel, P. 2000. Redefining pitch proximity: Tessitura and mobility as constraints on melodic intervals. *Music Perception*, 17, 315–327.

von Hippel, P., and D. Huron. 2000. Why do skips precede reversals? The effect of tessitura on melodic structure. *Music Perception*, 18, 59–85.

Vos, P. G. 1999. Key implications of ascending fourth and descending fifth openings. *Psychology of Music*, 27, 4–17.

Vos, P. G., and E. W. Van Geenen. 1996. A parallel-processing key-finding model. *Music Perception*, 14, 185–224.

Wasow, T., and J. Arnold. 2003. Post-verbal constituent ordering in English. In G. Rohdenburg and B. Mondorf (eds.), *Determinants of Grammatical Variation in English*, pp. 119–154. Berlin: Mouton.

Waterman, G. 1974. Ragtime. In N. Hentoff and A. J. McCarthy (eds.), *Jazz: New Perspectives on the History of Jazz by Twelve of the World's Foremost Jazz Critics and Scholars*, pp. 43–57. New York: Da Capo Press.

Witten, I., L. C. Manzara, and D. Conklin. 1994. Comparing human and computational models of music prediction. *Computer Music Journal*, 18/1, 70–80.

Youngblood, J. E. 1958. Style as information. *Journal of Music Theory*, 2, 24–35.

Zarlino, G. 1558/1968. *The Art of Counterpoint*. Trans. G. A. Marco and C. V. Palisca. New York: Norton.

# Author Index

Fuller, R., 20
Fux, J. J., 174–175

Gabrielsson, A., 25
Gagne, D., 173, 175, 178
Gauldin, R., 221n3
Gilbert, S. E., 121, 173, 175
Godsill, S. J., 217n3
Goto, M., 27
Grigson, L. 199
Grout, D. J., 221n4

Haimo, E., 218n2
Headlam, D., 140
Heise, G. A., 58
Hepokoski, J., 132
Hiller, L. A., 20, 22
Honing, H., 27, 212n9
Huron, D., 33, 54, 58, 69, 182–184,
    203, 205, 220n1, 220n2, 221n3
Hutchinson, W., 20, 84

Isaacson, L. M., 22

Jackendoff, R., 33, 36, 45, 144, 147,
    211n3
Jonas, O., 173
Jones, A. M., 166, 167
Jones, M. R., 26, 71–72, 76
Jurafsky, D., 12

Kashino, K., 141–142
Kassler, M., 174, 175, 219n8
Kastner, M. P., 123
Kersten, D., 12, 13, 14
Kessler, E. J., 50, 51–54, 67, 68, 76,
    84, 86, 89, 91, 100–105, 215n3,
    215n4
Kiparsky, P., 206
Klapuri, A. P., 139–140
Knill, D. C., 13
Knopoff, L., 20, 84
Kolen, J. F., 27, 33
Kostka, S., 84, 85, 86, 89–91, 94, 99,
    100–108, 109, 119, 121, 124, 171,
    215n4, 219n7
Krebs, H., 221n5

Krumhansl, C. L., 36, 50, 51–54, 63–
    64, 66, 67–68, 76, 84, 86, 89–90,
    91, 100–105, 162, 165, 172, 213n7,
    215n3, 215n4, 215n5

Labov, W., 206
Lake, W., 66
Lampl, H., 191
Large, E. W., 27, 33, 71–72, 76
Larson, S., 66, 67, 77, 165, 166,
    220n11
Lee, C., 27, 45
Leman, M., 55
Lerdahl, F., 33, 36, 45, 67, 92, 95–96,
    100, 106, 144, 147, 165, 211n3,
    216n7
Lester, J., 134
Longuet-Higgins, H. C., 27, 50–51,
    55, 63–64, 213n7, 214n8
Lunney, C. A., 66–67, 68–71, 76, 77,
    78, 165, 214n2, 214n3

Manning, C. D., 12, 150, 176, 209n1,
    209n5, 211n7
Margulis, E. H., 67, 165
Martin, J. H., 12
Martin, K., 143
Matthay, T., 191
Mavromatis, P., 151–156
Megill, D. D., 221n7
Meredith, D., 214n4
Mewhort, D. J. K., 50
Meyer, L. B., 1, 19–20, 66, 67, 116,
    123–124, 209n5
Miller, G. A., 58
Miller, J., 50
Moore, A., 201

Narmour, E., 66, 67–68, 69, 77, 165
Nketia, J. H. K., 166, 167

Oram, N., 172, 218n10
Osherson, D., 12

Palmer, C., 26, 36, 50, 220n2
Pardo, B., 150
Parncutt, R., 33, 54, 216n7

Payne, D., 84, 85, 86, 89–91, 94, 99, 100–108, 109, 121, 124, 171, 215n4, 219n7
Pearl, J., 142
Peel, J., 175
Petersen, K. B., 212n5
Petersen, M. S., 212n5
Pfordresher, P. Q., 26
Pinkerton, R. C., 20, 21
Piston, W., 104, 121, 132
Plumbley, M. D., 217n3
Polansky, L., 144, 147
Ponsford, D., 22
Povel, D.-J., 25, 27, 66
Pyles, T., 206

Rahn, J., 81, 110
Raphael, C., 29–30, 45–46, 139, 142, 147–151, 164, 199, 212n9
Ratner, L. G., 221n4
Rissanen, J., 155
Rosenblum, S. P., 191
Ross, S., 209n1

Sadie, S., 151
Saffran, J. R., 156–157, 164
Sales, G., 196
Schachter, C., 108, 119, 121, 173, 178, 203, 222n11
Schaffrath, H., 33, 211n4
Scheirer, E. D., 27
Schellenberg, E. G., 58, 66, 67–68, 69, 77, 162, 165, 214n2
Schenker, H., 81, 135–136, 172–179
Schmuckler, M., 50, 51–54, 63–64, 66, 67, 89–90, 165, 213n7, 215n5
Schoenberg, A., 103, 106
Schuller, G., 196
Schütze, H., 12, 150, 176, 209n1, 209n5, 211n7
Selfridge-Field, E., 211n4
Sellmer, P., 182
Shaffer, L. H., 30, 33
Shannon, C. E., 20, 209n5
Sher, C., 200
Shmulevich, I., 54
Slawson, W., 175

Sleator, D., 27, 43, 46, 150, 220n9
Sloboda, J. A., 25, 26, 74
Smoliar, S., 174, 175, 219n8
Snyder, J. L., 20
Snyder, J. S., 211n1
Steedman, M., 27, 50–51, 55, 63–64, 193, 213n7, 214n8
Stein, E., 191
Stephenson, K., 167, 201, 202
Stoddard, J., 147–151, 164, 199
Swain, J., 197–198, 206, 221n8
Swinney, D., 114

Tenenbaum, J. B., 12
Tenney, J., 144, 147
Thompson, W. F., 66, 100
Toiviainen, P., 54, 211n1

Ulanov, B., 221n7
Unyk, A. M., 66

Van Geenen, E. W., 55, 64, 213n7
von Hippel, P., 58, 69, 212n8
Vos, P. G., 55, 64, 213

Wasow, T., 206
Waterman, G., 196
Witten, I., 21–22, 210n7

Yli-Harja, O., 54
Youngblood, J. E., 20, 21, 84, 210n6
Yuille, A., 13

Zarlino, G., 122–123, 216n10

# Subject Index

Essen folksong collection, 33
  and Bod phrase perception model, 144–147
  creation of, 211n4
  and cross-entropy, 161, 163
  and pitch model, 56–60, 63–64
  and rhythm model, 33, 39–45, 167–168
Expectation, 19, 21, 26, 50, 66–74
Expectation maximization. *See* Baum-Welch algorithm

Finite-state models, 18, 153–156

Generative processes
  for pitch model, 56–62
  for polyphonic key-finding model, 83–85
  for rhythm model, 31–36
Graphical models, 29
Greek chant, 151–156
Gregorian chant, 20, 201, 206

Handel, George Frederic, "Hallelujah Chorus," 95
Harmony
  explaining common strategies of, 131–137
  in jazz vs. common-practice music, 198–201
  as a factor in key-finding, 93
  interaction with meter, 26, 44–45, 77–78
  modeling perception of, 147–151
  in Schenkerian analysis, 174
Haydn, Joseph, 134–135
  String Quartet Op. 74 No. 3, 80
Hidden Markov models, 18–19, 82–83, 142–143, 148

Implication-realization theory, 67–68
Improvisation, 151–156
Independence, probabilistic concept of, 8
Indian music, 123, 172
Inertia, 77, 166
Information theory, 20

Jazz, 194–196, 198–201
Joint probability, 8
Joplin, Scott, "Maple Leaf Rag," 194–196

Kalman filtering, 28
Kern format, 33
Key, 21, 49–64, 79–137
  ambiguity of (*see* Ambiguity, tonal)
  effect on expectation, 71
  and harmony, 150–151
  hierarchical aspect of, 97–98, 116
  key relations, 94–96, 99–108
Key-finding models. *See also* Pitch model; Polyphonic key-finding model
  CBMS, 54–55, 64, 89–90
  Krumhansl-Schmuckler, 51–55, 63–64, 89–90, 100, 215n5
  Longuet-Higgins/Steedman, 51, 63–64
  survey of, 50–56
  Vos–Van Geenen, 55, 64
Key profiles, 51
  CBMS, 54, 86, 91
  Essen, 59–60, 86, 91, 171
  Kostka-Payne, 83–84, 86, 89–92, 99, 100–108, 109, 121, 124, 171
  Krumhansl-Kessler, 51–54, 68, 76, 86, 89–91, 100–105
  Temperley corpus, 86, 90–91
Kostka-Payne corpus, 84, 200. *See also* Key-profiles, Kostka-Payne

Linear progression, 177–178

Major and minor, differences between, 104, 120, 121–125
Markov chain, 18–19, 22
Melodic lead, 220
Mendelssohn, Felix, 20
Meter, 23–47. *See also* Rhythm model
  and Schenkerian analysis, 178
  and stylistic differences, 166–171, 184–197
Meter-finding models. *See also* Rhythm model